Bad Guys

BAD
GUYS

*Women's tales from
the relationship front*

By Brook Hersey

Bishop Books

Copyright © 1994 by Brook Hersey

All rights reserved. No part of this book may be reproduced in any
form or by any electronic or mechanical means, including information storage
and retrieval systems, without permission in writing from the publisher,
except by a reviewer who may quote brief passages in a review.

First Edition

ISBN 0-9638870-0-9

Library of Congress Cataloging-in-Publication information is available

Published by
BISHOP BOOKS
611 Broadway / New York City / 10012

Designed by Barbara Chilenskas
Cover Photograph: Tom Sullivan

PRINTED IN THE UNITED STATES OF AMERICA

✳ Contents

Introduction

First, the bad news. This is not, I'm sorry to say, a book about the fine art of domesticating a bad guy. There are no tips in these pages on "how to kill his wild oats" or "how to get him to see how much he needs you." (One tip on "how to mend a broken heart" did manage to sneak in—see page 9—but it's sort of strange advice and won't work for everyone.)

One of the sad facts about most of the men described in these pages is that there's just plain nothing women can do about them. They are more like acts of nature than diamonds in the rough. No matter how loveable (sexy, understanding, independent, communicative) the women in question are, these men do their trademark damage. Even armed with centuries of cumulative female wisdom, women are unlikely to have any luck "fixing" a bad guy, or "curing" him, or making him "good." (Men do change—but it's been my experience that they have to do it for—and by—themselves.) A woman's only power, in most of these situations, is in deciding when and how to leave.

This book is organized around 49 stories, told by women, of romantic involvement with bad guys. There's the story of the cop who threw watermelon at his girlfriend when she kissed a male friend on the cheek. There's the lawyer who pressed his girlfriend to go to sex clubs with him, but got jealous when she received more attention than he did. There's the businessman who gave his two girlfriends the same watches and the same lingerie—and who planned with both of them to name their first child Elizabeth, after his grandmother. There's the sex-cult veteran, a couple of pathological liars, and the Peruvian drug dealer looking to marry for a green card. There are also many ostensibly more mundane stories, about womanizers, two-timers and the terminally ambivalent "regular" guys who have wreaked painful havoc in women's lives.

What is a "bad guy"? Any man whom a woman has decided, retrospectively, was bad for or to her. Of course, there are many nascent relationships—filled with passion and promise—that don't go anywhere. My aim is not to slap some feminist seal of disapproval on every man who has ever broken up with a woman. The bad guy designation derives from the effect that a man has, rather than from a judgement about his intentions or his character.

In making this decision to label some men "bad guys," I want to be clear about several things. First of all, I'm not making the claim that the women I interviewed are perfect. I *am* fond of most of them—after all, they opened up their hearts to me—but I've made no effort to whitewash them. Some talk openly about their complicity in what happened. Others don't address the issue, but readers who are so inclined will draw their own inferences.

Secondly, this book isn't born out of a wish that our world were populated only with clean-cut commitment-seeking guys with a paycheck in their pockets and a well-thumbed copy of *Backlash* on their night tables at home. All of us have different tastes—in what we like and what we don't. A man one woman might judge to be adventurous in bed might strike another woman as sexually manipulative. A guy one woman might label emotionally deficient might not bother another woman at all.

A related point is that there is a reason why many women get a gleam in their eye and a slightly manic tone in their voice when they talk about some of these so-called bad guys. Many of them are incredibly attractive. Some have great sex appeal. Some are intelligent and articulate. Some take a compelling interest in themselves and their activities, and thus seduce women with the intoxicating sense that the world is an exciting place. The stories that follow are about their allure, as well as about the wreckage they leave in their wake.

The book that follows is organized around different kinds of bad guy. Sorting men according to their behavior is a painfully inexact business. What do you label the guy who lies, cheats, throws violent, jealous tantrums and monitors the length of his girlfriend's skirts? My categories are far from neat and exact.

Because a few of the labels that I'm using will ring familiar, some readers may accuse me of trafficking in stereotypes. This is not my intention at all. If anything, I hope the narratives that follow will serve as a means of examining the validity of stereotypes, and of adding detail and nuance to our understanding of the behaviors that they describe.

I've come up with three overriding categories of bad guy (each category then having several subcategories, which make up the book's chapters, within it). The three categories are: aggressive men, wounded men and hot/cold men. The aggressive men do things to women—like womanize, lie, cheat, bully and take their money—that leave the women hurt and angry when they figure out what's been going on. The wounded men are so deeply enmeshed in their own issues that the women involved with them are cast as caretakers. And the hot/cold men thoroughly confuse and frustrate the women in their lives by barraging them with mixed signals. This behavioral shadowboxing results from the men's fundamental ambivalence about being involved at all.

It seems obvious, but I feel obliged to emphasize that *Bad Guys* is not a blanket putdown of the entire male gender. All men are not "bad." (*Good Guys* would be a longer but, let's be honest, far less compelling book.) Most of the men who appear in these pages are not evil. They're just struggling through life as best they know how. If this book were being told from their point of view, we'd empathize with their loneliness, hear about the incessant clamor of their sexual desires, and share their confusion about having grown up in a culture in which concepts of masculinity are in flux.

But empathy aside, this book is based on the premise that it takes two to have a relationship. It's every bit as much about women as it is about men. The men are seen through women's eyes, described in women's voices. We are taken through these relationships on the women's observational coattails, treated to the details they've chosen to recall, deprived of those details they've forgotten or have decided are too humiliating to tell a stranger with a tape recorder.

And so the collection of narratives offers clues to the place bad guys occupy in the female cosmos. Are there certain kinds of women who are drawn to bad guys? Are bad guys an affliction of youth? What legitimate needs do these men seem to answer? And what causes the epiphanic "clicks" that impel women to cut their losses and bow out?

The concept of victimization is a touchy one in today's gender discourse, and so I want to be clear that what follows is not a catalog of virtuous but hapless women who were "victimized" by men. Many of the women in the stories that follow were victims in the most superficial sense of the word: Bad things happened to them that they didn't ask for (although even that may be debatable in some cases). But these women are most emphatically not victims in the sense of reveling in their pain, or of using their distress as a manipulative tool. These are women who learned from their mistakes, and bear full responsibility for taking care of themselves.

Besides the natural voyeuristic interest of reading about the minute details of other people's relationships, the chapters that follow offer any woman who's ever lost sleep over a bad guy a fellowship of attractive and articulate women who were similarly smitten, and similarly let down. Many of them have subsequently moved on to more satisfying relationships. All have lived to recognize their pain and anger as legitimate, to laugh about the pure ludicrousness of some of these situations, to realize that telling well (and then getting on with their lives) is the best revenge.

I hope that reading these stories will remove some of the shame that sometimes lingers on in the aftermath of a relationship with a bad guy. Many women judge themselves extremely harshly— defeats feed their sense of self so much more than triumphs do. Many of us use two harsh standards to determine how we're doing. One is a vestige from the days predating feminism: that our own value can be measured by the man we've "caught." The second standard is a bizarre but common twist on the healthy premise that we deserve to be loved and respected by the man in our life. The not-necessarily-logical corollary is that if we accept anything less than a man who treats us perfectly, we clearly have problems with masochism, dependency or self-esteem.

In the worst cases, a woman can come out of an affair with a bad

guy condemning herself by both standards: She's (god forbid!) single—and she must be seriously neurotic, because she's upset to have
lost a guy whom she should have seen through and ditched long ago.

Self-blame comes up again and again in these stories. Women
offer up red flags they should have seen, crises when they should
have split for good, unpalatable sides of themselves that arose out
of their pain and confusion. I hope that the stories that follow will
help move readers away from judging themselves.

Bad Guys doesn't purport to be science. At least not in the sense
that I claim to be describing the whole world on the basis of my
comparatively small sample. I talked to 47 women, spending as
much as four hours with each one. Rather than marching them
through a list of set questions, I just turned on my tape recorder
and asked them to start at the beginning. I wanted to hear why
they got involved, as well as why things broke down. My hope is
that the book's authenticity will come from the fact that these
voices ring familiar and true.

After a decade of working in journalism, I will say that I have
never ever had an easier time finding sources. I'd be describing the
book to a near-stranger at a cocktail party, and the next thing I
knew, she'd be slipping me her phone number. Friends suggested
friends, who suggested friends of their own, and the circle
widened outward.

I did make a concerted attempt to break out of the small
bicoastal urban world that I know best. New York and L.A. women
are seasoned raconteurs, so many of their stories came neatly orna-
mented with epiphanies and punchlines. I wanted to include
women who were unpracticed at storytelling, whose experiences
with men had taken place in less liberal environments, where the
pressures and judgements of friends and family might have had a
more substantial effect.

All names and identifying details have been changed—this
despite the fact that a number of women literally begged me to
reveal their bad guys by name. More than one offered to send pictures. There is a sense of anger that some of these men are clearly
repeat offenders, who move on from one cataclysm to do the same
harm to other women. The woman who said "he should have come
with a warning label" was expressing a common sentiment.

But while the names are changed, the women's words are not. I taped interviews and transcribed them. I shortened some slightly, but I never put words in the women's mouths. I believe that how the women tell their stories is as significant as what they say.

Although there are a few grueling stories included, I stopped short of including really pathological (i.e. criminally dangerous) bad guys. Sure, I'm fascinated by the women who love imprisoned serial killers, but "bad guys" has a narrower meaning than that here. I also stopped short of collecting stories about men who are physically, violently abusive. The stories in this book unfolded over months and years, as the women meandered towards self-discovery. I don't want to give the impression that women who are in physical danger have the luxury of this inner probing; it would be a mistake to think there's any point in reading books to "understand" violent men. Those women need to worry about themselves, and are strongly encouraged to enlist professional help.

I read more fiction than nonfiction because I like the fact that novels and short stories leave so much untold. I like being allowed to crack open stories, to make my own judgements about the dependability of a narrator, to build my own sense of character from what he or she notices and chooses to say.

Although the following stories are verbatim transcripts of interviews with real women, I hope that readers will bring some of that attitude to reading them. It's by taking measure of our own inferences, sympathies and visceral reactions that we can take measure of our lives. I have done some generalizing, and some pattern scouting, and I've provided some minimal interpretation. But basically the narratives speak for themselves. I invite readers to make of them whatever they choose.

My Story

When I was in my teens and early twenties, the phrase "bad guy" had an aphrodisiac effect. I thought bad guys glowed with a vivid inner light. They catapulted through life with the speed and recklessness of bicycle messengers. They were mysterious and untameable, the rebels and iconoclasts who added danger and poetry to my well-behaved life. Bad guys took risks I only dreamed about, felt their desires rather than repressing them, and were capable of both boyish pleasure and boyish greed.

I wanted to be like them, but I wasn't. I was a good girl, with all the busy need to keep everyone else happy that that implied.

For a few heady months during my junior year at Harvard, I lusted after a handsome guy with artificially lightened hair and a BMW. I remember an evening when the radio reported that some factory on the periphery of Cambridge had emitted a cloud of toxic gas. I stayed inside. My lust object loaded his video camera into the BMW and sped to the disaster site. What kind of footage was he looking for that would make him rush off into the contaminated night? Some really cool disaster-containment vehicles puttering around in the twilight? I never found out. But this act of rashness was wildly attractive to me. Moving in the orbit of someone who wasn't motivated by safety was the romantic equivalent of adding Tabasco to my mashed potatoes.

This guy was "bad" in the sense that he pursued me in a noisy, confident, no-holds-barred way, while also pursuing many other women. He'd tell me he loved me one day, then the next night, I'd see him dressed in evening clothes, hopping in the BMW with some beautiful woman I'd never laid eyes on before.

Looking back, it's easy to see how this college affair supports one of my theories about bad guys: The qualities we're drawn to are often very closely related to the qualities that leave us crying "bad" in the end. More than this guy's carefully toned body or his sexual proficiency, I was attracted to his selfishness. He did what he wanted, consequences be damned. When he wanted to be with me, he pursued me. When he'd had enough of me, he moved on.

After we broke up, I felt the sting of being left out of some potentially great adventure (which he could create, somehow, but I couldn't?). He wanted to see the new, the different, the unfamiliar. I wanted those things too, but was too locked into a deeply habituated cycle of obedience (I'd love to try sky-diving with you ... but I have to finish my seminar reading). I envied his brashness. He was uncowed, and I wanted to be.

When I tell new acquaintances that I'm working on a book called *Bad Guys*, it's not uncommon for someone to ask me if it's based on my own experiences. The answer that I give reflexively is: no, of course not. The book is structured, I say, entirely around the stories I heard from the women I interviewed. But to say no unequivocally is to deny the obvious: that as interviewer, organizer and writer, I dictated the book's shape and tone.

I am a woman. I've had a number of experiences with men— some happy, some "bad." I gained the trust of the women I interviewed by taking their perceptions seriously, and expressing empathy, support and/or outrage when I felt it to be due. When writing the material that links the various narratives together, my own prejudices obviously determined which of the women's comments I found worthy of emphasis. One reason for this chapter is to allow readers to draw their own conclusions about where I'm coming from, and what biases I might be carrying along for the ride.

The second reason for this chapter is that I can dissect my own life in a way that I can't the lives of my interviewees. In my own life, I can clearly see how my own sense of powerlessness shaped the role that romantic attachments played. I don't mean to imply that other women shared these specific influences—I believe, in fact, that many of the women I interviewed had much healthier senses of entitlement than I, for much of my adult life, did. But I offer up my history as one illustration of the confluence of factors that cause women to be so intrigued by bad guys.

I met my next bad guy in Paris, the year after I graduated from college. I was on assignment for a small magazine, and he—also an American—had come over to apprentice in an artist's studio. The third day I knew him, he showed me a couple of scars on his arm. He'd burned himself after two previous affairs had ended, he told me gravely, to remind himself not to fall for women again. The burns alone established a nearly irresistible challenge: He felt deeply, so deeply that he was attempting to mute his responses, to protect himself from pain by going numb. But he could, I was sure, be moved by sex. After all, he had more than one scar. My seductive skills shifted into overdrive.

We had a passionate ten-day affair, then I had to return to the States. Alone in Paris, with very few people to talk to, the Not-Yet-Bad-Guy bombarded me with letters that were both ardent and thrillingly obscene.

After a few months, he came to New York to visit me. Despite the fact that his parents lived only an hour away, he was adamant that I not tell anyone he was coming. He moved into my apartment, pulled the blinds and stayed.

I was working full-time, so I would get up in the morning while he was still asleep and drag myself into my office. When I got home, his day would just be starting. He would be lying in my bed, smoking cigarettes, drinking scotch and watching TV. He didn't want to talk. He didn't even really seem to notice me, except with a kind of distracted impatience. We'd stay up most of the night. I was waiting for sex. He was staring blankly at the Late Late Movie.

Clearly the brooding emotionalism that I'd been so attracted to was, in fact, brooding depression. Fixated on the memory of the sexual connection we once had, I never once thought: This has turned into a nightmare. It never occurred to me that I'd be better off with this deadbeat out of my house. Instead, I stewed in my own sleep-deprived disappointment and resisted giving up.

After a final ugly rupture, he departed. I've never seen him again. I took to my bed, cried into my cat and reread *Anna Karenina*. (This is the promised heartbreak-recovery tip. The cat's not a requirement, but Tolstoy did it for me. The joy I took in the book was enormous and more than sufficiently distracting. And I remember thinking: Just knowing that I have this book on my shelf will insulate me from future pain. It is sustenance *I can give myself.*)

The next bad guy was tall and pale, with a skittering, caustic wit that turned me on like extra-strength catnip. Despite the fact that he had a girlfriend, I loved to stand in a corner with him at a bar or gallery opening, deconstructing the pretensions of overdressed downtown Manhattan types. This guy's bearing was self-conscious—he couldn't risk a misstep, after all, because he was dining out on the missteps of the rest of the world. But that only added to his appeal, promising, somehow, that there was a human being under his chalky skin.

When he broke up with his girlfriend, he and I began an affair. I was intrigued by the studied pallor of his life. His studio apartment was furnished with an iron-frame single bed and a copy of Diderot's encyclopedia. He had a passionate moral/aesthetic objection to houseplants. I was sure that there must be a flip side to his minimalism, a carefully guarded enclave of superior things that he respected and loved. If only I were smart enough, hip enough, sexy enough, I might get invited into the inner sanctum (where I could what? copy his tastes?).

I recognized even then that this guy, with his glass-of-milk looks and his monastic appetites, was sexually and emotionally undemonstrative, to put it mildly. But at the time, the challenge of getting tossed a few table scraps of affection was a compelling project. If he touched my back while we were walking down the street, I wrote about it in my diary.

We were seeing quite a lot of each other, so I was pretty shocked to find out that he was also seeing another woman. We were at a party that I'd taken him to when I overheard him tell a mutual friend that this other woman was probably going to move in to his apartment within a few weeks. I confronted him and he looked stunned—like a clumsy albino deer caught in the headlights. In retrospect, I see that his critical fervor about manners and aesthetics simply didn't translate into a parallel fervor about honesty. Oh well. At least I hadn't thrown out my plants.

These events took place at a time in my life when the strange thrills my bad guys offered seemed greater than the disappointment that came in their wake. *Part* of the attraction was quite simply that these guys had qualities I envied: I lusted after men whom I would have liked to have been.

But to even begin to make any kind of sense of my interest in these men, I have to talk about my father, who was the author, John Hersey. He was 45 years old when I was born. By the time I was old enough to be even marginally cognizant, he had been a successful writer for over two decades. He'd arrived already—I never witnessed any kind of struggle. Everything he did was met with attention and respect. To my awestruck eyes, he was perfect.

My father was a loving man who was also by nature reserved. He wrote about the deepest range of human feeling in his books, but rarely talked to me about what *he* or *I* felt. From a very young age, I somehow knew that there were emotions underneath his Buddha-like calm, but I couldn't see these emotions in his face or glean them in his words (sometimes I did think I could hear them in a subtle catch in his voice). Because I'd already ascertained that my father was perfect, I concluded that the fact that we didn't communicate as deeply as I would have wished was somehow my fault.

There was so much that I wanted to tell him. To me the world was a place full of smell and color and feeling. I wrote songs and sang them loudly, despite the fact that everyone told me I couldn't carry a tune. I made up stories. I wanted to enthrall him with the poetry of my own observations. He was indulgent but he could only listen so much, he had his own work to do.

The second and third of my bad guys were as mysterious as my father. By striving to captivate them with my energy and my wisdom, I was plugging away at the old drama of trying to engage him. I inferred that both of them were full of feeling, even though they were really showing me the most opaque and emotionally closeted of selves. The deep thoughts that I read in their unhappy eyes and furrowed brows, I now see, began and ended in my own imagination.

As significant as the guys themselves was the role these early infatuations played in my life. They were a distraction. *The* distraction. By seeking to tap into the men's energy, approximate their depth of feeling, appropriate their aesthetic sophistication, I was avoiding facing what I see now was a vacuum inside myself.

I now believe that this vacuum, this inner emptiness resulted from a deeply held sense of my own powerlessness.

My father's life was structured around a foundation of intense personal discipline. He worked seven days a week, in an office at home. Our household pulsated to his rhythms. We stifled noise during his office hours, ate meals according to his work schedule, vacationed according to his journalistic assignments. My mother, a woman of many gifts, shaped her life around keeping the rhythms slow, quiet and steady, insulating my father from the destabilizing chaos of the outside world.

I don't mean to detract from the love and respect I feel for my father, but the message I got very early on was that his wishes were paramount. The rest of us had to accommodate, anticipate, even schedule our rebellions in such a way as to not disturb his work. From a very early age, the motivational mantra that rattled around in me was not "I want...." but "What can I do to help?"

The unquestioning deferral to a man's needs at home was repeated in my elementary school experience. In the early '70s, the electric energy of feminism was in the air on the Yale campus where my family lived. But it was still very much male voices that dominated in my classrooms.

I realized this one day in seventh grade Social Studies. I had an idea I was bursting with, but Andy, Aaron, and two guys named John were talking so loudly and insistently I literally couldn't get a word in. The (male) teacher made no effort to moderate. I remember noticing that day, when one of the Johns made, to great praise, exactly the observation I'd wanted to make, that none of the girls had added one word to the debate. I noticed this, but, surprisingly, I didn't feel angry. I now realize that I didn't feel entitled to be heard.

Variations on that experience took place all around me. We girls did our homework diligently and took home the top grades, but the boys grabbed the spotlight in class. Our impressive report cards, I see now, served to reinforce the status quo. No one questioned whether there were things we weren't receiving in our academic experience, because, ironically, we were doing so "well." In school, I ruled on paper (where there was no need to compete for the floor), but in a crowd, I let other, louder voices prevail.

It was only when sex entered the picture that the power balance started to shift. It happened about eighth grade. Suddenly, the boys who were drowning me out in Social Studies started showing up at my house. Their formidable verbal skills served them badly as they hulked nervously on my doorstep. For the first time ever, I was in some kind of driver's seat. I could choose who, if anyone, to relieve from his state of tongue-tied misery. I could choose who would be my boyfriend, and what "base" we would go to (*the moral/political question of adolescence*), and whether he'd still be my boyfriend the following week.

Of course, I realize now that this was a passive power. Real power would have been for *me* to be hulking awkwardly on some boy's doorstep, risking humiliation but pursuing what I wanted. But feminism hadn't trickled down *that* far. In New Haven in the '70s, my friends and I waited and hoped. We entertained offers, we didn't tender them. The power to attract boys' attention was the only power we knew. And for the time being, it was enough.

I felt a shock of recognition some years later when I read Rebecca Goldstein's *The Mind-Body Problem*, a novel favored in certain bookish-girl circles. Goldstein's narrator, a graduate student in philosophy at Princeton, muses: "Sex is essentially the same game for men and for women, but for women, most of whom are otherwise powerless, it assumes a life-filling significance. *La femme fatale, la belle dame sans merci*, is an otherwise impotent person who has perfected her one strength to an unusual degree."

Flushed with the illusory sense of power I felt when a man looked at me with lust in his eyes, I was able to put off for more than a decade the recognition that this was the only form of power I knew.

The quest of getting and keeping men's attention provided a more focused challenge than getting and keeping my own. So-called bad guys were particularly alluring, because they were continually receding targets. In some upside down way, they perpetuated an illusion (if I catch them, I'll feel whole) that more available guys didn't offer (I *had* them, after all, and I sure wasn't whole yet). It was through pursuing these men, uncatchable bicycle messengers of the spirit, that I could sidestep the challenge of pursuing myself.

What happened next was that, in my own backhanded way, I grew up. I stayed involved with one man for five years. I worked in magazines, and slowly discovered—truly to my surprise—that

I not only enjoyed writing, but that other people were actually interested in what I had to say (take that, Andy, Aaron, John and John!). Slowly, falteringly, I began to both identify my desires and feel that I could do things to realize them. I ended my long-term relationship, and began to seek out men who would mirror my feelings of growth. I wanted to love men who would stretch and expand my world.

Anyone who was remotely conventional was not a contender. I'm not sure where in my upbringing I picked up a pathological dread of things predictable, a conviction that nothing common-place would ever happen to me. Wherever the idea came from, for most of my life I truly believed that I would reinvent the relation-ship wheel. My goals weren't run-of-the-mill: I have never been, for instance, particularly focused on marriage. And the men I would care about, I was sure, would not only share my scorn of conventional goals—they would be free of conventional failings. The intimacy-fearing men I read about in magazines were off tor-menting busty Cosmo Girls on some other planet. My men would be different.

Of course, I was wrong. The clichés about relationship frustra-tions exist because they reflect a certain amount of truth—a point that the subsequent chapters will make again and again. I fell for a string of well-intentioned men, none of whom were "bad guys" in any of the clichéd liar/cheater/womanizer ways. But they were *bad for me*, in the sense that none of them could love me in the whole-heart-whole-body way that I wanted to be loved.

I've resisted caricaturing these men here: These weren't one-note relationships. But the gist of my frustration can be easily summa-rized: The men who were sexually available were unable or unwilling to deal with emotions, and the men who were emotion-ally available wouldn't have sex. I had difficulty accepting this, and was constantly pushing every man I cared about to give more, talk more, see me as a sexual being *and* a soulmate. No one was ever enough.

I careened from one version of this struggle to the next, begin-ning to wonder if what I wanted was illusory. Was there anyone out there *intense* enough for me? Or was I purposely choosing men whom I sensed would withhold from me, so I could continue the struggle for attention that had begun with my father?

Certainly, one aspect of these struggles harked back to my feelings about my father: If the intensity that I desired was missing, on some deep level, I was sure that it was my fault. Rather than accepting in my heart that these men were *unable* to be what I wanted in a partner, that they had very real limitations that I was right in considering "bad," I came away from each encounter fearing that it was because of my own limitations that the men had chosen not to take some fundamental plunge with me.

Almost exactly a year ago to the day I'm writing this, I found out that my father was dying. I was already feeling fragile, because two close friends were dying of AIDS. Two days after I got the news about my father, my boyfriend—who was very nervous around emotions, his and mine—broke up with me.

In the months that followed, during which time one of my friends, and then my father died, I experienced a new kind of loneliness—the loneliness that accompanies permanent, irreversible loss.

In *Nobody Nowhere*, her memoir of growing up autistic, Donna Williams describes how, as an adult, she knew how to comfort a disconsolate autistic child. Williams taught the little girl to tap her arm repetitively and hum a tune to close out the confusion of the outside world and restore inner focus and calm. What I did in those sad months was turn off the quasi-compulsive frenzy of activity that had been my life and develop my own forms of arm tapping.

This sounds corny, but here's the simple, life-changing thing I did. I made it a priority (more important, in other words, than taking on an extra magazine assignment, or going on another date, or returning every call on my answering machine) to do things that made me feel strong and good. I did yoga. I ice-skated. I began to learn to fix a car. I listened to music. I baked bread. I wrote constantly. I realize, oddly, that these activities are latter day versions of my decade-old interlude with *Anna Karenina*: I could find meaning on my own. Fulfillment didn't have to take the form of engaging the attention of someone else. By doing what I wanted, rather than what everyone else wanted or expected me to do, I diminished the strength of that inner vacuum in a way that professional success, and four thousand friends, and a handful of charismatic bad guys never had.

As time passed, I rediscovered men. Without conscious effort, my frame had shifted. I found that I now focus on what the men who interest me have to offer, rather than on what they can't give. If a relationship's all about sex, so be it. I'll go with it for as long as that suits my needs (which isn't usually very long). If it's an emotional connection, so be it too: how much richer I am for having such friendships in my life. To co-opt a cliché, relationships are half full, not half empty for me now.

Does this mean that the whole book's a moot point, that I'm throwing over the whole concept of "bad guys" for some "I'm Okay, You're Okay" Zen state of acceptance? Of course not. Deceptive or evasive or wishy-washy behavior still makes me insane. I'm sorry about men's limitations, especially those that keep them from being able to love. What's changed is that I'm able to label these shortcomings as *their* problems—not mine.

Researching this book and hearing other women's stories has provided me with a coda of my own: For a woman to say—and really believe—that a man was bad for her is relatively easy. But for her to know—and really believe—that she deserves better is where true empowerment lies.

Aggressive Men

✳

The men in this section are the "bad guys" of stereotype. Often charismatic, frequently forthright about their
selfishness, they do unto women according to their own
needs. The womanizer is a compulsive seducer with an
underhanded disappearing act waiting in the wings. The
possessive man is pathologically jealous, fiercely controlling and borderline violent. The hustler lures a woman
into a relationship so he can get something tangible from
her. The cheater may think of himself as looking for a
meaningful relationship, but his declarations of love are
built on deception—he's secretly sleeping with one or
more other women. And the cruel man systematically
inflicts pain on the woman he supposedly loves.

The effect on the woman is that of a frontal assault: That's
why I call these men "aggressive." He takes her money, or
controls her life, or betrays her trust. An underlying hostility
towards women is clearly at work in many of the stories in
this section's five chapters.

The narratives that follow, told as they are from the perspective of hindsight, reveal the degree to which these
men's interests are about things other than cherishing and
preserving the relationship. (At first glance, the possessive
men seem to be an exception. But witness how quickly
they replace the women who leave them: It's *a* woman, not
this particular woman, that they need.)

The intimacy-related problems that are so troublesome
elsewhere in this book aren't a big issue here, because
these men have not crossed the boundary from "I" to "we."
They don't have to grapple with the difficulty of merging,
because they're not interested in doing it.

While these men exhibit different behavioral patterns,
their manipulations are often very similar. Many lies are
told. Much infidelity occurs. And when the man is
"caught," he often asks for another chance. And often he's
given one.

In fact, these men get away with a great deal, using the simple "Just ask" tactic. Women may well want to ask *themselves* why they are so quick to accommodate. It may be that a woman in a relationship construes a "please take me back" request as a demonstration of her power, proof that a man needs her. It may be that she feels some culturally determined duty, or it may be that she's giving the man the loyalty and devotion that she wants to receive. It may simply be that she loves him, and doesn't want to have to give him up.

The women who succumb to this genre of bad guy are often young. Many of them share a fervent belief in romantic love, which leads them to see a flawed relationship as a grand passion. The effect is that they will fight hard—and deny much—so as not to lose it. As Joan Silver, who told about her involvement with a possessive man, put it: "Lots of women just see the good and forget about the bad. We forget we had a life before we met the guy."

These are stories of betrayal and disappointment. But they are not, for the most part, about abandonment (the stories about womanizers being the exception). In many cases, it's the man who wants to cling to the relationship—the interplay, defined as it is by his aggressive behavior, is working for him. There are 25 stories in the chapters in this section. In 15 of them, the woman left the man; in six cases (four of which are in the "womanizer" chapter), the man left. In four stories, who left whom is ambiguous.

Although these categories represent the traditional kinds of bad guy, they are, in fact, the least damaging relationships of those chronicled in this book, and the easiest to get over. (This is an oversimplification of course; a few of the stories that follow were brutally painful.) As compared to the two other sections, in which the men's behavior is often murky and unreadable, allowing the women vast leeway for self-sacrifice and self-blame, here it's very easy for the women to understand what went down. There are readily available labels for the experience. A woman can consider an aggressive bad guy to be the human equivalent of a hurricane that blew the roof off her home. He happened *to* her. And after a period of shock and mourning, she'll start to build something new.

The Womanizer

In the movie version of Milan Kundera's novel, *The Unbearable Lightness of Being*, Daniel Day-Lewis plays Tomas, a surgeon who explains his womanizing as an unceasing labor of love. "You want to know," he murmurs, "how she will smile, how she will whisper, groan, scream."

Tomas' credo embodies the myth of the womanizer as connoisseur. This is the Man Who Loves Too Much. He relishes what's best in every woman, and takes too much pleasure in discovery to halt his search. Although many of the men in this chapter are extremely charismatic, I don't take such a romantic view of their prolific pursuits. In fact, a womanizer is a man who is *compelled* to pursue women.

Most of the relationships that follow are fueled by the womanizer's need to act out an internally driven conquer-and-withdraw maneuver. He may genuinely like some of the women he pursues, but no matter how much the objects of his desire would like to think he's relishing them for their subtle and precious uniqueness, in reality, his women are interchangeable. Certainly, he doesn't waste time missing them, once he's moved on.

Womanizers do so well with women because they appear to offer them two compelling things. Good sex, for one. And, on a deeper, murkier level, they seem to gratify—without any complex or difficult negotiation—a women's yearning to be desired, to be sexually powerful, to be liked.

The sex thing is simple. Any womanizer worth his salt can make a woman go weak in the knees. It's two parts charisma, one part a series of almost choreographed moves. (The Burning Look. The Elbow Caress. The Even-More-Burning Look. The Kiss. The Post-Kiss Expression of Wonder. And so on.) And he makes all the effort. He masterminds the seduction. He has condoms in his wallet. He knows foreplay and afterplay. He's a connoisseur of the female orgasm. Just surrender, his look half-dares, half-begs, you won't be sorry.

Even when a woman instantly recognizes the kind of guy she's dealing with, this sex-charged come-on can be hard to resist. She's turned on. And he's a master of creating a sort of urgency, a climate of desire. Why not? I'll just have some fun, the knowing woman rationalizes. I'll take it for what it is. An affair.

But at the same time, the womanizer poses an implicit challenge. An experienced woman's thought process might go something like this: Men like me. This man, who clearly loves women, will really appreciate me. Unlike those model types he usually goes out with, I can make him laugh. Look how smitten he is. Look how much fun we have. I bet we'll have great sex. I hate to even think something I should know better than thinking, but I could be The One.

Or, as Carrie Fisher put it in her novel *Postcards From the Edge*: "I used to fall in love with homosexuals, because they had rejected me before they even met me. Womanizers don't reject you, but they accept you in a rejecting way, so it's similar. And just like I used to think with gay men, I thought, '*I'll* be the one who makes a difference.' I don't mean that I'll have a relationship with him, necessarily. I don't allow myself to hope for that much, but I guess underneath my nonhoping is the hoping thing...."

The hoping thing isn't restricted to womanizers, of course. It rears its head in many of the narratives in this book. Women hope that men will recognize, give in to, and therefore validate their power. Here's how one woman I interviewed described the denial implicit in this wish: "You're getting these grandiose visions of yourself as more important and powerful than you are, thinking that just the force of you is going to change someone. At the same time, you're denying. Denying how he ended it with the last girlfriend. Or how he's treated other people. You know that the chances that he's going to do the same thing to you are 99.9 percent. And yet you walk into it. And when you're one of the 99.9 percent, you're surprised."

With a womanizer, the denial has to be particularly blind. Not only is his behavior transparent, but the bodies in his wake tend to be both numerous and vocal. His reputation precedes him. A woman talking herself into thinking there's any real relationship potential with one of these guys often does the Carrie Fisher two-step: Of course I don't hope but, well, maybe I *do* hope.

Interestingly enough, a womanizer-prone woman is often attractive and willful. She considers herself something of an expert at men. She is experienced enough to appreciate his skillful button pushing, his practiced kiss and glitch-free seduction. She is confident enough not to fear being hurt, and has enough romantic success in her bank to crave a challenge. And she tends to feel quite sure she's in charge ... at least until she discovers she's not.

Amelia Chase, who told two of the stories below, is a good example. She usually has an entourage of suitors, but the ones who captivate her most are often womanizers. While she cites their sexual magnetism as their principal allure, she's also quite aware of how they play into her psychological profile. "A friend of mine said something interesting the other night," Chase said. "That people with low self-esteem cannot delay gratification. A womanizer gives you instant gratification. You are the world to him. So fascinating, so sexy, so desirable. I am an easy target for this."

With a womanizer, a woman is spared the strip tease of self-revelation that's often a part of a new relationship. She's more than good enough as she is, at least for that brief moment that his attention is turned on.

✳ **Amelia & David**
Amelia Chase is a fine-arts photographer who supports herself working as an administrator for a non-profit arts organization. In this, the first of her two stories, she explicitly discussed the way hoping crept in to her relationship with David Francis—a relationship which her good sense told her was an affair and an affair only.

David was a sculptor who was on the board of directors of the organization I work for. I'd always thought he was really attractive and we'd always flirted, but then I found out that he was married. His wife would go around New York and intro- duce herself as his wife, but he was never with her. He didn't wear a wedding ring. They lived in separate apartments.

We'd had this flirtation, and I went to see one of his shows and I just thought his work was out of this world. I have to say that's probably when I really fell in love with him. I mean "fell in love" very lightly. I <u>was very intrigued by him</u> and infatuated by him.

We ran into each other at an opening once and there was a def- inite spark between us. His wife was there. I remember talking to him and the wife coming up and making her presence known.

We basically flirted. And then he wanted to get together and talk about our work. I went to his studio, which was part of his apartment, and we looked at some of his new stuff. I guess that's when I realized he wasn't living with his wife. He seemed to be pretty much on his own, pretty independent.

I was being naive, thinking my visit was an art exchange. I later discovered this was a classic seduction thing he'd do with artists. I guess he was sending me a lot of signals that I wasn't really picking up on. I knew he was married, and so I didn't really think about it or let anything register. We talked about his work for a while, and I left some slides of my photographs with him. Then we said goodbye. I realize now that he really was coming on to me. There was even a moment at the door when he would have kissed me, but I kind of ducked out. I was feeling slightly sleazed out by it, that it was really inappropriate. I didn't want to think that he was trying to seduce me. I wanted to think that we were friends via art.

The next thing that occurred was that my organization had a big awards ceremony. His whole face lit up when he saw me. <u>He was a very seductive guy.</u> I felt like I liked him, but I wanted to keep the thing at bay. Every time I looked at him, he would beam. After the ceremony, I saw him in the hallway. A bunch of us were going out afterwards for drinks, and I asked him to come out with us. He agreed. But I remember beforehand he went around the block with this other woman—a pretty woman painter. They went walking off, arm in arm. And I wondered if something was going on between them.

We went to the bar of a nearby hotel. After a short time, David was eager to go. I went out to the ladies' room. He followed me out into the hallway and he said he was leaving. You could tell that there was a lot of electricity between us. I said, "Well, wait for me, we'll go together."

I don't know why my mind changed about him. I guess I was intrigued by him. I thought he was attractive. I figured he was separated from his wife, so they weren't really married. I was really intellectually drawn towards him. A group of us left the bar together, and it was clear that David and I were going to walk across town to get cabs. I remember the girl that he had gone around the block with looked kind of hurt. That really made me think that something probably had happened between the two of them.

We walked west together. I'd left him those slides, and he started talking to me about my photographs and their generosity of spirit. He was really focusing in on the work. It was thundering and lightninging, but it wasn't raining. I felt that feeling of becoming very infatuated with him. He took my hand as we were walking down the street. We were at the street where I was going to go uptown and he was going to go downtown. We were talking and talking and talking—about photography. And then he was playing with the buttons on my coat. And then before I knew it, he was kissing me. I remember saying to him, "I've never kissed a married man before."

And he said, "What's it like?"

And I said, "It's not that bad."

Then I got in a cab and went home.

Then we had a date. He suggested that we get together. I remember going to meet him at his apartment, and then we went to a restaurant in the West Village. The sun was setting and it was really pretty. And I remember we had dinner, and I didn't like him that much. I felt as if he was someone who was very self-involved. He wasn't listening. I didn't feel happy. I didn't feel seduced by him. I didn't feel much of anything.

We left the restaurant and we started walking towards his apartment and he walked me down this really pretty street that he loved. He brought me to this little tiny house, and there were these beautiful flowering trees, and we started talking and then we started kissing. And I said to him that I didn't want to get involved with him because he was married. And then, of course, I ended up going home with him.

We ended up fooling around. I got completely lured into it. At about two in the morning, I said I had to go home. He walked me out and we started walking uptown. I initiated not staying the night with him, but it turns out that he hadn't slept through the night with anyone—his wife included—for six years. If I had suddenly decided to stay, he wouldn't have wanted me to.

He had had a lot of sexual experience. He acted like I was Miss Innocent compared to women he had slept with. Which is also a very weird thing to have someone say to you, because it sort of puts you down. It made me feel really prim and proper. I remember he was teasing me: I was like a preacher's daughter. That he always had to seduce me and that I didn't seduce him.

David and I saw each other about once a month. I felt as if he was someone who I was very very attracted to, but he was some-one I wouldn't want to marry. It was almost like a wonderful sweet, or a drug, or a great bottle of wine. It was very excessive interaction, and very intense. Seeing him was like a drug: I'd need to see him after a month, but once I'd seen him, I didn't need to see him again for a while.

The bad thing about him was that he would lead me to believe that there was some future. I think that a lot of women who get involved with men like this feel like they're going to convert them, and fall in love with them and get married to them. David would say things about bringing me down south to Georgia, and he'd tease me about never having been married. He'd been mar-ried three times before. And he intimated stuff about if we ever were together.

He would talk about his wife, and their ups and downs, and how she wanted to be together, and he wanted to be apart. He was very much of a charmer and would say very seductive things. He was a wonderful crafter of sentences. I also felt as though we were friends, that there were no illusions about what was going on between us, that it was an affair. It was secret.

Things were very sexual, but he never ejaculated. He was 45 years old, so maybe it was a physical thing. When we talked about it, he said that he was "worried about the effect that it would have." My first interpretation was that he was worried about the effect on his wife and marriage if I had gotten pregnant, even though I was on the Pill at the time.

But as time went on, I remember feeling very frustrated by it. And feeling that there should be more of a culmination. To be having an affair and not really to be having a full-fledged affair.... The last time we were together, I think I said something to him, that I felt frustrated by it. He didn't really want to discuss it.

He made me feel that I wasn't exciting enough for him. Because he led me to believe that he'd had all these wild sexual experiences, and I was very straightforward and traditional. Whereas I'd felt other relationships of mine had been very passionate and sexy. But I think that he was just in this whole other realm of sex.

Because I wasn't seeing other people, David had become the sole focus of my romantic life. I was feeling more frustrated. I wanted to maybe spend the night with him. We were talking about the wife thing, and I was hoping that that would dissolve. At the same time, I was feeling all those other reservations, that this wasn't the right person.

He would say that he was going to call me, and then he wouldn't. And then I guess maybe I would call him and suggest getting together. Or we would see each other at a board meeting or something, and go out afterwards. I went to France and England one time right after seeing him, and I just remember feeling very connected to him. I felt like I wanted to write to him. I missed him and I wished he were with me. I'd said to him that I'd call him when I got back from this trip, but I never called him.

We had a board meeting in December and he didn't show up. He was sick. And then it was Christmas. In January, I spoke to him on the phone and he told me his wife had left him.

Then I think I saw him at a board meeting, and there was a spark between us, but he left. I was upset by that, so I called him. I felt like we had to clear the air. So I called him and said, "David, I just want you to know that I would have been happy to pursue the relationship with you, but you were married and it seemed like a dead-end street. I just thought I had to pull back, and that's why I never called you."

And then he basically said the most amazing thing. Which is that he was the equivalent of an alcoholic vis-à-vis relationships. That he was someone who would seduce women, and it was almost like a sickness that he had. He said that I was someone who was very special to him, and he said he could have seen going from his wife and getting involved with me. "I'm someone who goes from one burning village to the next," he said.

I felt like I was a vodka bottle that he was addressing. He was very objective about it, and very impartial, and it was like he was telling a story, forgetting that I was someone who was somehow involved with him. And I said, "Were there other people besides me?"

And he said, "Well, in the last several years there have been."

And I said, "What about just recently?"

And he didn't really give me much there: He didn't tell me if I was one of ten, or one of twenty, or one of two.

At that stage, I'd had some work that I wanted to show him, strictly platonically. And he wouldn't even see me. It was like someone with an addiction, who wouldn't see what they are addicted to. He said, "I've really got to be alone right now and pull myself together."

I remember I referred to a couple things he'd said to me. He'd talked about this one woman whom he'd known all of his life, and how they'd always had this affair, and whenever they'd see each other, they'd always get involved. And he'd said that he and I would always be involved with each other. We'd know each other when we were old. I didn't know if that meant that we would always have an affair, or always sleep together or what. I reminded him of having said that. And he was like: "Tell me what I said to you." As though he'd been drunk and said things to me and he didn't remember what he'd said.

I felt completely abandoned by him because it was sad that we couldn't be friends. I said to him that I'd felt like the last time I'd seen him that I'd felt the old electricity, and he said: "Yes, but that will pass in time."

I felt like he was treating me like I was an addiction that had to be conquered. I felt like I was one of many. One of many bottles lined up on the rack.

✳   **Sarah & Bobby**
Sarah Powell is now in her mid-thirties and divorced. Bobby Jenks was her high school bad guy. For the most part, I've omitted high school bad guys from this collection. Certainly they represent a common rite of passage, but the stories sound too much alike (well-behaved girl defies parents and goes out with scruffy, Jack Daniels-swilling rebel with the best record collection in town) and have too little connection with adult experience. But Bobby interests me for the light he sheds on womanizer evolution. By sixteen, he was entrenched in a womanizer pattern: He had not only mastered the art of attracting women, but had fallen into the habit of quickly moving on once he had completed his conquest.

Bobby and I were in high school together. I was fifteen. He was a year ahead of me. I have a theory that there are certain guys who come of age sexually earlier than others. As opposed to the guys who are nervous to ask you out, and when you do go out, they ask your permission for them to put their arm around you, these sexually confident guys lost their virginity when they were 12 or 13. Bobby definitely fell into that category.

The first time Bobby kissed me, I was babysitting. He kissed me after I put the kids to bed. It was mindboggling. It was the first time that someone had kissed me and my whole body went limp. It was very sexually arousing. Then crunch, crunch, crunch on the driveway, the people I was babysitting for came back. Bobby high-tailed it out the back door.

We went steady for six weeks, then he broke up with me because there was no chance in hell that I was going to have sex for at least another two years. I remember one time, in school, after we'd broken up, he came up to me in the hallway and kissed me on the back of the neck.

There was a certain adrenalin rush being around someone who was so male. Being with him gave me—a thoroughly good girl—

permission to break certain rules. We went on to have this on-and-off thing that continued until I got married.

He always knew when I was home from college. I'd always get a call from him within 24 hours of getting home. There would always be this period when he would treat me wonderfully. He always made me feel very sexy. I would sit on the arm of his chair while he played poker with his friends. Invariably, he'd end up ditching me. But equally invariably, he'd call me the next time around.

I always had to take the role of letting him call all the shots. If I called him and he wasn't in the mood, I got the coldest response in the world. And somehow I put up with the fact that there would always be other women. I even prided myself on the fact that I was cool about it.

One time, I went over to this house Bobby was sharing with these deadbeat friends of his. We were supposed to have dinner. He wasn't around, but his friends were acting funny. They told me he'd be there in a minute. I went back to his room, and I found him in bed with another woman. His whole reaction was to accuse me of making her feel bad. There was this core in me that knew this was bullshit, but my reaction was to crumple and cry and go home. And see him again the next time he called.

This went on till I got married. Even after I was married, he'd call every six months to feel out if I was ready to have an affair.

✳   **Amelia & Johnny**
*This is the story of Amelia Chase's other womanizer, Johnny
Andrews. It took place shortly after the affair with David.*

I'd met this really sweet French guy, Pierre. He was a banker, a little younger than me, loved literature, was attractive and sweet. We were taking a cab to a dinner shortly after we'd met, and I remember thinking to myself that there was definitely something wrong with me. If someone normal like Pierre is attracted to me, I just can't develop that internal stirring.

So we got to the dinner, and I was talking to Pierre. I looked across the table, and there was this guy with dark brown hair, who was staring at me the entire time. He was a ballet dancer, I found out. A whole bunch of us ended up going dancing, and somehow or other, after several drinks, I ended up feeling this animal magnetism attraction to the dancer, Johnny. I wished I could put these two men into one: I was attracted to both of them. To Pierre intellectually. And Johnny, I didn't even want to have him talk to me, I didn't want him to say a word, I just loved being near him. While Pierre and I were dancing, Johnny and I were shooting long, soulful looks into each other's eyes.

I was getting up to go to the bathroom, and Johnny said to me, "I would really like to dance with you."

I said I'd love that. At the time, I felt very much in control of the situation. I thought he was this very sensitive young thing. He was a young kid—twenty-five or so—and he was holding me like I was precious china. He said, "I can't believe I'm dancing with you. I've been wanting to dance with you all night long. And I can't believe you're in my arms."

It was almost like this very innocent, naive adulation. It was very charged. He took my fingers and started kissing my hand. I felt like we were making love.

I saw Johnny two nights later at a Christmas party. I was feeling very heart-fluttery, but also rational about the whole thing. Thinking this is a sweet guy, really sexy, but that Pierre was the right person to like.

Johnny looked a little shy. But at one point he asked me if I'd like to go out for a drink after the party. I had to cook dinner for a friend who was in from out of town. Johnny said, "Well, I could meet you at eleven."

It was a Sunday night. And I really wanted to play things slowly, because I felt sure something would happen at some point. So I said, "Why don't we get together after Christmas?"

We talked about our schedules and I gave him my number.

I went down to Florida for the holidays, and I thought about him constantly. It was a complete physical lust thing. I had a little premonition that he wasn't going to call me. And when I got back to New York, he hadn't called. I looked up his number in the phone book, and I called him and left him a message just in case he'd lost my number.

Pierre, in the meantime, was back from Paris, and he was completely gaga, and the more gaga he was, the less I liked him. He was a really sweet guy that I wish I could have liked. But all I could think about was Johnny.

I ran into him at the ballet. I tried to play it cool and friendly. I asked him why he hadn't called me. He said that his sister had been in town and that it had been really crazy. He didn't say he'd call me. I just played it out, and teased him, and that was that.

Another week went by, and in the meantime I'm just becoming heart-crazed. I started obsessing. Desiring him completely. It turned out that a friend of mine had dated him a while back. She told me, "He's very complicated. Very shy. He hates to call girls. You should call him again."

So I decided to give him another chance. In mid-January, I went to a party a mutual friend of ours was giving, thinking I would see Johnny. At around midnight, he arrived. I went up to him and I gave him hell. I said, "What happened? Why didn't you call me?"

And he said, "Well, I thought you rejected me. The first night we met, I wanted to drop you off in a cab and you got out of it. And I wanted to see you after the Christmas party, and you blew me off. I just figured you weren't interested and I should just forget about you."

I completely forgave him and assumed he was telling the truth.

We decided to go for a drink after the party. There was this bunch of ballet dancers, and one of them said to me, "Where are you going?"

And I said, "I'm just following Johnny."

And he said, "Be careful. Johnny's bad news."

So we went to this bar, and Johnny seemed kind of withdrawn. He wasn't coming on very strong. And then all the dancers came in and sat all around us. When Johnny went to the bathroom, I asked the guy who'd given me the warning why he'd said that. He said, "He's bisexual. He sleeps around. If you want a fun night, use a condom. Be very careful. He's really bad news."

Around three in the morning, Johnny and I ended up leaving and taking a cab uptown. He had this excuse about why people said he was bad news. His sister had gone out with so and so, who'd spread rumors about him. This whole conspiracy theory. And of course I again felt sympathetic. We went to my house, and ended up making out.

I was completely attracted to him. I'd been thinking about kissing him, and it was even better than I could ever have imagined. He was open and very verbal. All the stuff that I'd felt, he said he felt it too. I didn't feel like I was crazy, having imagined this stuff.

I was worried about getting in over my head physically. We were getting more involved. I said to him, "I like you, I can't judge you on your past actions, but I have heard that you are bisexual and I don't want to do anything that's going to risk my life."

He said that he'd never been with a man before. And that his father is a doctor, and he's always been very safe about sex.

Anyway, we didn't end up going the entire way. But we ended up fooling around a lot and it was really fun. I loved being with him. He was just so sweet. He kept saying things like, "I can't believe this.... It's so great."

I didn't necessarily want to have a relationship with this man, because I knew that he was unsuitable. I had been hoping to find someone to have a serious relationship with. And he certainly was not a lead candidate. But my guts, my passion was very drawn to him. We got two hours of sleep and then I had to go to work. He put me in a cab. The thing I misread was that I thought he was much more forthcoming, much more eager than I was. I thought he was really into me, whereas I was withholding. Wanting to keep everything at arm's length. He put me in a cab and said, "I'll call you this weekend."

At this point, I was in a haze. Paritally because I was exhausted, but also because I'd had such fun, and I liked him. My intellect told me that I would probably be saved if I never spoke to him again, because it would lead to trouble, because he was not suitable.

He didn't call. Which surprised me. Then I saw him a week later. I'd gone to this place where a zydeco band was playing. He and I had this little interchange where I could feel he'd pulled back from me. He said he'd lost my number. I said, "You did know my address. You could have dropped a note through the door."

He said, "Well, I really thought you would call me after not having heard from me. Let's talk about this later."

I thought the best thing for me to do was leave. As I was leaving, I ran into him. He couldn't believe I would leave without saying goodbye. He said, "Call me tomorrow."

I called him the next day, which was Saturday. He didn't call me back. But I kept making up excuses for him. I said to myself, "I'll do the final experiment and invite him to do something, and if he doesn't call me, I'll know."

So on Sunday, I called him and I left him this message saying, "I'll be free on Monday. If you want to do something, call me."

He never called. At this stage, I should have gotten the picture. But, typical human nature, I want something when I can't have it.

Then a mutual friend was giving a big Valentine's party. I was excited, because I thought that I was going to see him. And then I calmed down and realized that I shouldn't like him. We saw each other across the room, and he was giving me soul-searching looks. And I tried to avoid him.

We were seated at opposite sides of the room. He ended up weaving his way over to my table at dessert. He was talking to these other friends. I finally turned around and looked at him. He came over and said, "I've been very busy. Are you going to be around later at the party?"

I said, "Maybe we can share a cab back."

I didn't say this because I wanted to sleep with him. I just felt like I wanted to talk to him and resolve things. I had really felt like what happened was not a one-night stand. That there was something that existed between us. He didn't really answer me. He just nodded.

The evening progressed. It was about one in the morning, and I looked over and he was leaving. He had his coat on. He went around the room and said goodbye to everyone else, and not to me. All he would have had to do was come up to me and say that he was going. Instead, it just wrenched my heart. And I ended up humiliating myself. I got up and walked over to him and said, "Are you going home?"

And he said, "No, actually I'm not. I've got to go to a friend's house with this group of people. But I'll call you."

All I wanted was to talk to him for one second, which I knew was desperate. But I said to him, "Can you talk for one second now?"

And he said, "No, I really can't."

I became furious and upset. I ended up sharing a cab home with a friend in the ballet company. She told me that Johnny had been at the party with his girlfriend. A girlfriend he'd supposedly broken up with.

Men like Johnny know how to push the woman's buttons. How to charm her. They know the ropes. He was like an expert in something, as opposed to an ingenue. Poor Pierre. When he would take me home, he would say, "I want to kiss you." What could repel me more than someone demanding that I kiss him, and jumping up and down like Rumpelstiltskin if I didn't?

A womanizer knows exactly what to do and how to touch your elbow, and won't ask you but will just put his hand around your head and grab you. I'm attracted to the man who will just grab you and make out.

I also believe in falling in love at first sight. The question I ask myself is: Is this the man I'm going to fall in love with? While a womanizer is thinking about how he can seduce a woman, get her to bed.

✳   **Susan & Hank**

Susan Katz is a TV producer in her late twenties. The story of her flirtation with Hank Thompson verges on the absurd, but I include it to avoid giving the misimpression that all womanizers are slick and subtle.

I met Hank when I was walking my brother's dog—a very good move for women who are trying to meet men. I saw this guy walking a dog. He followed me around the block, came up to me, we started talking, and then went out. You know whose dog it turned out to be? I found out later it belonged to a woman he was living with.

I was very shallow and I thought he was beautiful. What was appealing about him? He had a different background. He hadn't gone to college. He wasn't educated but was worldly. Had traveled a lot, was a model. Had been all around the world. He was a good storyteller. Was into the scene in New York. I was 20 years old at the time, he was probably 32, but looked about 24. He was very fit. He was fun but he was crazy.

One date began at the China Club and I couldn't figure out how it was two in the morning, three in the morning, four in the morning, and this man was still going. Still talking. Obviously, he had a cocaine problem.

One night, I had some people over. Not only did he come over in a stupor, but he brought a drunken friend. They did the "refrigerator repairman" routine for us. They told the women to leave the room, and then to come back in, and they had their pants pulled down, making believe that they were fixing a refrigerator. Was that supposed to be appealing? What was I doing in this situation?

This one time, he'd wanted to come up to my apartment after we'd been out somewhere. But I didn't trust him. I said, "You can only come up if you promise ... We can make out but there's no way I'm going to have intercourse with you. Do you understand that as a condition?"

He was like, "Yeah." The guy was bombed out of his mind. He came upstairs, we were making out, very heavily, and then I said, "That's it."

There was a point where I had to physically repel him. I weighed 115 at the time, he was probably 205. I said, "You better take a shower." He did.

I'm sure I was one of the few women that said no to him. I had no interest in sleeping with him, and I didn't feel badly about myself for that. For this guy, I must have been number 250. Sex was a sport for him. Sport fucking.

On about our fifth date, we were at a club downtown, and we were dancing, and in the middle of the dance floor, Hank said to me, "I just want to know right now, are you going to fuck me or not? Because if you're not going to fuck me, I'm probably going to go."

I said, "I have no idea. I don't plan when I'm going to do that with someone."

And sure enough, he made a beeline for the door.

✳   **Me & Frank**
*What follows is my own story of a brief involvement with
Frank Reilly. It is followed by the account of another woman
who also dated him.*

I met Frank at a cocktail party and we talked all of ten minutes. Then, four months later, he called me out of the blue and asked me out.

Although I allowed myself a millisecond of thinking it was

incredibly romantic that this guy had called me on the strength of such a brief meeting, I knew in my heart that it probably really meant that he was an operator. But I could handle it.

Anyway, his timing was perfect. I was in the middle of a painful breakup with someone else. I was thrilled to have the distraction of a smart, good-looking man to go out with.

He seemed appealingly nervous the first time we went out. But we were both good talkers, and after dinner and a fair amount of wine, we kissed on the street. He was leaving town shortly for a job across the country and we both had heavy travel plans in the next few weeks, but we decided we'd like to see each other again.

We had another date, then he convinced me to postpone my departure for vacation by a day so I could come to his goodbye party.

I'd done some minimal research on him in the few days since he'd called me, and a couple of people had told me that he was a womanizer. So I was a little nervous that there would be other women that he was involved with at the party, and that things would be awkward. But that wasn't the case. The party was fun.

Because Frank was leaving town, at the end of the night he gave away his liquor to a bunch of his colleagues. I have this great vision of all these scruffy men hugging him goodbye, then gleefully running down the stairs, clutching almost-full bottles of scotch and vodka.

After everyone left, Frank and I put on Patsy Cline and talked about the party. I remember liking the fact that he described all his women friends very generously. And then we had sex. I can only describe it as athletic. I had this image in my head at the time that we were doing floor exercises for some gymnastics competition, with a panel of judges rating our performance.

But there was also something about it that felt clinical, impersonal. I'm not sure what it was: that we didn't talk, that he didn't smile or seem to be looking at me with any affection, that the nervous wonder he'd expressed the first couple of times he kissed me seemed wholly absent. It was physically satisfying, but it left me feeling kind of empty.

I left for vacation the next day. For the next couple of weeks, Frank and I spoke on the phone from different cities. On the phone, things were flirtatious and sexy. I partially forgot how hollow I'd felt actually spending the night with him.

Finally, we were both back in town at the same time. He had about two more weeks to go before he was supposed to report for his new job. I took for granted that we'd have a two-week-long affair.

We had dinner the night he got in. And we had sex, and it was very much like the previous time. I remember leaving his apartment, which was by now pretty much stripped of furniture, feeling a little unsatisfied by the lack of friendliness or warmth between us.

I can only describe what ensued as being dumped by phone tag. He called me, I called him back. I left specific messages on his machine about when he could reach me—he always called at times when I'd said I'd be out. He left me plaintive messages that I was hard to get in touch with, but he never called me at my office, where I was for ten hours each day. More than a week went by, and it slowly dawned on me that he was doing this on purpose. That he didn't want to see me, but, for whatever reason, he didn't want *not* to call.

We finally spoke and he made some vague excuses about how busy he'd been, trying to wrap up his life before leaving town. He didn't suggest that we get together, although when I mentioned in passing a dinner party I was having, he said he'd like to come. I hung up the phone, and this little wave of anger broke over me. I guess I felt resentful that he didn't seem wildly anxious to see me, but that he somehow felt that this party I was giving might somehow be desirable.

But mostly, I guess I just felt hurt. Because I'd gone into the tryst with Frank with my eyes open, I somehow presumed that we would turn into friends after our affair, which I'd presumed would end easily and naturally when he left town.

I called him back, got his machine, and—as politely as I could—I disinvited him from my dinner. We didn't speak again.

✳   **Wendy & Frank**
Wendy Lewis is another New Yorker. She dated Frank Reilly several months before I did.

Frank was pursuing my friend Monica. He made her dinner one night and charmed her. Then they went on some other nice date and he kissed her and left. She thought he had a lot of potential. She had a cocktail party and I went, and Frank chatted me up like crazy. Monica was upset. I didn't even know that this guy was the person in question, I was just in high flirt mode. Frank asked me my name and where I worked and a week later, he called me and asked me out.

I think we made a plan. Then I called him back and said I didn't feel comfortable about it because of Monica. Which was very awkward because nothing had really happened between the two of them. I didn't tell Monica he'd called me. I wasn't sure that he liked her, and I didn't want to reveal that she liked him. I said, "Look, you've gone out with one of my best friends, and it just doesn't seem right. If you want to talk to her about it, that's fine, but I'm not going to tell her that I'm going on a date with you."

He thought that I was right. He said, "Don't say anything to Monica about this. Let me talk to her."

I don't know if he did or didn't, but he didn't call me again. I sent him an invitation to my Valentine's party. In the meantime, he had gotten weird with Monica. I think by this time I'd told her that he asked me out. At the Valentine's party, he cornered me and asked me when were we going to go out. I said maybe later.

Then he had a party. He really flirted with me. He was very solicitous for the whole party. He introduced me to his best friend from college, and she told me that he was a womanizer and that I should stay away from him. I said that that wasn't a very nice thing to say about a best friend. She said, "It's just a fact of life. And he's not someone I would trust a friend of mine with, and you seem like you're a nice person."

At the end of the night, Frank and I kissed, and this all seemed to be leading up to the question of when were we really going on a date.

I told him that I was going to L.A. on business for two months. Maybe when I get back. He said that he was going to be in L.A. too. We ended up talking on the phone a lot when he was in New York and I was in California. When you're in a hotel room, your whole life changes. Your social life becomes the telephone. He ended up being someone who called me a lot. We became phone friends.

The phone conversations were pregnant with promise. He was

very straightforward about wanting to get involved. He talked a lot about why he hadn't been able to get involved in past relationships. Very intimate details about his relationships. So he seemed vulnerable and ready in a way. He projected something that made me think that he would be a good person to get involved with.

Seven months had passed since he first asked me out. He finally showed up in L.A. the night before I was due to leave. There had been all this prelude to our first date, and we went out and it was a complete downer. He was practically comatose. He wasn't interested in me. He talked about himself the whole time.

Since I had been so warned, and since I knew he had acted so weird with Monica, I was trying not to let myself get excited. I hadn't fallen in love with him, obviously, but I was pretty willing to explore what the potential was. But the date happened, and nothing.

I came back to New York, he was still in Los Angeles. He called me, and made all sorts of excuses. He said, "I was really tired that night. I was flipped out because I had all these work responsibilities. It was a bad night for me. I'm going to be in New York over Memorial Day weekend, and let's make plans to go away together."

So I said no to an invitation to go to Martha's Vineyard with some other friends. I tried to make plans for Frank and me to go away, but at the time he should have called, he didn't. Then he told me he had to work the Friday night of that weekend.

I had no plans on that Friday night because everyone else had left town for the long weekend. He called me late Friday night and said, "Let's get together late."

So I went over to his house, and we went out for a really late dinner. It was more romantic, but a certain excitement was not there. I really felt like it was missing on his part. We did have a sort of romantic kiss outside the restaurant, but we ended up sleeping together in a very perfunctory way. He just seemed to flip into auto-pilot. I don't even remember the sex.... I just remember that it wasn't very good. It was an out-of-body experience for him, I felt. He'd even taken his clothes off perfunctorily. He wasn't really interested in me. I could have gone home and it wouldn't have really bugged him. He turned over immediately afterwards and went to sleep.

The first thing that he did in the morning was get on the phone, then take a shower. He didn't say a word to me. It didn't really seem like he wanted me there. I started getting dressed to go home, because I was a little insulted at this point. I was ready to bail. And then he said, "What are you doing? Why are you leaving? I was just freshening up. Why don't we stay in bed? I'm just so freaked out that there's a woman in my apartment."

As if he'd never slept with anyone. But I thought, maybe I'm reading the signals wrong. Maybe he does like me. Maybe what he was saying is true. I mean we had planned to spend the weekend together.

So we had breakfast, then he went to work for a few hours. I met him and we went to a movie. When we got out, we goofed around a little bit. Which was fun. We walked downtown and went somewhere for dinner. But the whole time, I was very conscious of not being what he wanted me to be. I felt like I was not saying the right things, and I was not dressed right. I wasn't performing the way he wanted me to perform. I just felt inadequate the whole time.

We ended up back at his apartment, and again I felt like it was going to be one of those situations where I would be forcing him to have sex with me. And he told me he had to work again the next day. We were on his couch. I think he said he was tired. And I said, "Does that mean you don't want me to spend the night?"

I made him reject me. He said, "Well, I just wonder ... it might be a little too early for me. I don't want to rush things."

I said, "I'm going to go to my house. We can talk later."

At which point he started in, "It's so late.... How are you going to get home?... Don't leave now.... You could still spend the night and we could talk about it later."

It had only been 24 hours and he was already in a pattern of behavior. I had enough perspective on the whole situation that I was almost laughing a little bit. I wasn't really, though, cause I was angry. I thought about it all the way home on the subway. I'm mad, I'm angry, I'm hurt, I like him, I don't like him. God damn it, why should he reject me? And I called him up when I got home, and said, "I just don't think this is going to work. Let's just call a spade a spade. We can be friends."

What's interesting to me is how willing we are to overlook flaws.

I knew there was something weird going on with Frank. We kept having these false starts. When push came to shove, we'd finally get on that date, and nothing would happen. But always in the back of my mind there'd be the thought: Maybe it will work. Maybe he won't be as bad as he seems.

He told me later that he was impressed with the way I'd called things off, but he felt really rejected. I thought it was really interesting that he was so self-involved that he didn't realize that he had rejected me. I know I wasn't misreading it.

Womanizers are among the least dangerous bad guys in this book. None of the above stories are about real heartbreak. These "relationships" are not quests for a soulmate. So the loss isn't crushing. The sting lasts days rather than months.

And the woman knows that it was a womanizer that happened *to* her. She has a label for the experience. And it doesn't invite retrospective self-torture: If only I had done X, Y or Z differently, I would still "have" him today.

Are womanizers good affair material? Yes and no. The sex tends to be physically satisfying. On the other hand, these guys have a gift for conveying restrictive boundaries without saying a word. It may be as simple as their being unavailable on the phone. Or it may be a shorthand iciness with which they respond to any sign of initiative on a woman's part. In any case, she gets a message that the parameters of the affair—when they meet, how often, when they call it off—are his to define. She better not expect too much. Or complain when she's unsatisfied. Sarah went so far as to say that she was proud of how cool she was about Bobby's other women. The benefits of sex and adventure may or may not outweigh the self-negation implicit in having to play by his rules.

Who are these men? How do they justify themselves? It's rare that they're as candid and self-knowing as David, the self-proclaimed sex-o-holic. Frank is an interesting case in point here: My guess is that he was denying the compulsiveness of his pattern. He went through the phone-tag charade with me, which actually must have required quite a bit of effort. And he orchestrated his rejection of Wendy in such a way that he might tell himself and her that it was she who rejected him.

A host of books have been written about womanizers. All of them quote womanizers as saying that they have a greater-than-average sexual drive. Peter Tractenberg, a self-described compulsive lover, goes a little deeper, offering this analysis in *The Casanova Complex*: "At the center of every addiction, as at the center of every cyclone, is a vacuum, a still point of emptiness that generates circles of frantic movement at its periphery."

Although I presume that Tractenberg is referring to a vacuum of identity, I was reminded of this "still point of emptiness" when I noticed that several of these stories had in common an interlude of downtime: David at dinner, Johnny at the bar, Frank on his date in L.A. with Wendy. There's a passing moment or two when the pursuit juices stop flowing and the man is just a man, and a boring and self-involved one at that.

For anyone who's ever shed a tear or suffered regret over the evaporation of a womanizer, it's worth remembering how much of his charisma is linked to the intensity of his ephemeral desire, to how much his pursuit flatters the woman. The fact is, he may be erudite and well-informed but he's interested in himself, not the woman he's with. (Well, he's interested in making her like him ... but that's about it.)

Just pretend, for a minute, that he really did fall for a woman, and he really did settle down. She would have to listen to him talk about himself at breakfast, lunch and dinner. Feeling better now?

The Possessive Man

The cultural stereotype of the possessive man is rough-edged, macho and perversely appealing. Central casting might send someone like Sean Penn, a man whose virility is made interesting by an aura of sadness or anger. Possessive men, as this benign myth would have it, don't like other men hitting on their girl-friends, and they're ready to get into a fight about it. They're well matched with possessive women. Jealous fights give way to torrid sexual reconciliations. Possessiveness is a manly (read: unverbalized) manifestation of true love.

In fact, the possessive men who are described below are more pathetic, and at the same time more dangerous than the loose cannon of popular image. Few major movie stars would covet any of these roles. Their expressions of possessiveness are infantile, not macho. One man threw watermelon. Another called in a phony bomb threat to Pan Am. A third monitored the length and color of his girlfriend's fingernails. All this sounds pretty absurd, but the women who told me these stories weren't laughing. An undercurrent of violence ran beneath these seemingly silly tantrums.

Unlike the womanizer, who is an immediately recognizable type, the possessive man tends to come without behavioral warning labels. Chances are he's a man of the world (whatever world that might be). Whether he's sipping cognac or pumping iron, he does it with authority. If a previous boyfriend was timid or passive, this manly man is manna from heaven for the testosterone-deprived.

The possessiveness may surface when the woman gets a job or otherwise demonstrates independence. It may take the form of jealousy. It may show up in the sexual arena: Two of the women below described how their boyfriends insisted on having sex once or twice a day, almost as if they needed scheduled affirmations of their masculinity.

This possessiveness can cause knock-down drag-out fights. But the man tends to be apologetic afterwards. He promises to change. And change he does ... until the next episode.

Are certain women prone to relationships with possessive men? Obviously women don't consciously set out to find men who are going to isolate them, forbid them to talk to other men, and keep them in a state of suspended fear. But some women may well be drawn to the possessive man's vitality and decisiveness. These are men who invite a certain sort of surrender. Otherwise independent women—and men as well—often have a little corner of their psyche that longs to return to the "everything's taken care of" passivity of childhood. This covert urge may well be behind the initial allure of a possessive man.

After all, he takes the initiative. He's not ambivalent about wanting a relationship. He doesn't keep the object of his desire guessing, or force her to make the moves. Fusion is immediate—he seems uninterested in "are we right for each other?" testing. Instead, he zeroes in quickly, bearing gifts. Within a matter of days, the new couple is joined at the hip.

He may choose a woman whom he senses he can dominate— chances are he's not attracted to someone who seems too sure of her place in the world. (This is not always true. Joan, who tells the first story below, sounds fiery and assertive. But she only remained with her possessive boyfriend for six months. All the other relationships in this chapter lasted more than a year.) Most of the women I interviewed were very young when they got embroiled. One had newly arrived from abroad, and was financially dependent on her wealthy boyfriend.

But women change. A woman without a lot of experience or seemingly without other options may take a while to experience that epiphanic "I've got to get out of here" click. But the women in this chapter all reached it eventually. They adapted and submitted for a while, and then their independent streaks emerged—overpowering the fear and guilt and sense of obligation that kept them with these men after the initial bloom of love had faded.

✳   **Joan & Joey**
      Joan Silver, who is in her mid-twenties, lives in a midsize town
      in northern New Jersey. Her ex-boyfriend Joey Santanello was
      a member of the police force of a neighboring town.

I met Joey at a friend's wedding. He was short, built, dark hair, mustache, 48 tattoos. He had eyes like Al Pacino. There was something very sexy about him. He was a cop. I had always wanted to be a cop, so that interested me. At the end of the wedding, he asked me for my phone number, and he wanted to know if I wanted to go to a movie that night.

When he came to pick me up, he was very nervous. He seemed like a sweet guy, although my girlfriend had told me he had a bad temper. "I think you could be really good for him," she'd said to me. "You might be able to snap him back into being quasi-normal."

We went to a movie that night. From our third date on, he spent practically every night with me. It progressed very quickly. And I fell in love.

I had gone out with someone before Joey for about five years, and that guy was very passive. Joey was so different. He wanted to go out for dinner. He wanted to do things with my friends. That attracted me to him. And it was just so interesting to hear his stories about being a cop. He'd tell me about going on raids. We'd rent cop movies and laugh.

He drove a big truck. He had black hair which he slicked back. He had a whole testosterone thing going. He worked out three hours a day; his thighs were the size of roast beefs. My sister called him a bullet, because he looked like he was going to explode at any minute. He was so different from the men I had been dating. He was in control of his life. He knew what he wanted. He had money. And the sex was great.

One day, he stayed at my apartment while I was at work. When I came back that night, he was very pissed off. I asked him what was the matter. Apparently, he'd gone through my drawers, found my address book, and claimed that there were new numbers in it, even though he'd never seen this book before. He accused me of seeing someone behind his back. I said, "How could I? When I spend every living, waking moment with you?"

That was the first incident. I got pissed. We had a big blowout. But I forgave him.

My girlfriend had some friends over for my birthday. I had to go around and say hello to people and schmooze. So I gave everyone a kiss. There was this one guy that I had known for a long time. I just gave him a kiss on the cheek. Well, apparently Joey was watching me do this. He had a temper tantrum. He threw a piece of watermelon at me and stormed out of the party. In front of 35 of my friends. We had a huge fight about it later, and he was very apologetic.

Then at Halloween, a friend had a party. As we're leaving, I saw this cop I knew driving by the party and I started talking to him. All of a sudden, Joey came out of the party, saw me talking to the cop and came running over. He pushed me out of the way and grabbed the cop. The other cop got out of his car, and they started fighting. Some of Joey's friends came over and tried to break it up. The other cop was saying, "We're on the same team. We're both cops. What is this about?"

Afterwards Joey called me a few choice words. He dropped me off at home, and we had it out. At that point, he already had a drawer of stuff in my house. The next day, I packed up all his things, and drove to his house and said, "I don't want this stuff in my house. I don't want to see you anymore."

But he called a few days later, and I guess we started seeing each other again. Apparently I am a glutton for punishment. I was constantly justifying myself to someone who was very untrusting. In his mind, all women are liars. He called me a liar numerous times. Looking back, I think I must have been brain dead to take this, but at the time I thought it was going to get better. I thought he was going to change. After our fights, he'd say he was really sorry.

We broke up on December 21. It was a Saturday night, and I was waiting for him to call me. It got to be 7 o'clock, and I hadn't heard from him. So a girlfriend called, and I went to the movies with her. We went out for a couple of drinks afterwards. I got home around 1:30.

I was in my pajamas when the doorbell rang. It was him. He was pounding on the door. I didn't want the whole neighborhood to know that I was dating a psychotic lunatic, so I had to let him in. He said, "Who's here with you?" and then he ran to my bedroom to see if there was anyone there. He threw me on my bed, then threw everything off my coffee table and my wall unit. He started cursing me, "Where were you?"

I said, "What are you talking about? You didn't call me. I'm not going to sit around waiting for you."

He said, "I was out looking for your Christmas present."

I said, "I can't believe you pushed me." I had a cat scratching board, which is a piece of wood with carpet around it. I picked that up and smacked him over the back. At this point, I'd decided that we were not going to see each other any more because he had pushed me. That's where I draw the line.

We went outside. I was in my pajamas. I smacked him again, on the arm. He grabbed the board from me. He pushed me down the stairs, and threw the board into the middle of the street. He got in his car. I said, "I'm going to the police."

I got dressed and went down to the police station. It was three in the morning; I was hysterical. The sergeant beeped Joey. So by 3:30, he was there too, telling the sergeant I was a liar. I screamed and cried, but I didn't sign anything against him because he would have lost his job, and I didn't want him to lose his job.

So we broke up. I saw him New Year's Day and he gave me my Christmas present. I told him I wanted him to see a therapist. He said, "I'm not seeing anyone. I'm not crazy."

I'm not seeing him anymore.

Lots of women just see the good, and forget about the bad. We forget that we had a life before we met the guy. I gave it six months. If it's not getting better after six months, it's never going to get better. It's like an alcoholic. If he's not going to admit that there's something wrong, he's not going to get help.

My girlfriend told me Joey was seeing someone else after me, and it was the same thing. They've had screaming fights in the street. My friend told me, "It wasn't you. It was really him."

That made me feel better. The good things that came out of it all are that I know how to make homemade spaghetti sauce, and I've decided that I really want to go into some sort of law enforcement.

✳

Casey & Ben

Casey Anton lives in a small city in Illinois, as does Ben Carter. Although Ben's infidelity was a major theme in her account, his sometimes controlling, sometimes jealous excesses clearly identified him as a possessive man.

I was set up with Ben by a friend of mine who was going out with his best friend. He had a bad reputation and I think that's partly what made me like him. The friend who set us up thought he was really nice, but I'd heard that he would get into fights.

The second week we went out, he got in a fight with my old boyfriend. My old boyfriend got mad because I was holding Ben's hand, so he started calling me names across the bar. And so they got in a fight out in the parking lot. At the time, I thought: wow. It wasn't Ben's fault, and I thought he was my hero.

We were always together, and he was always nice. I thought that the stuff I'd heard about him was probably not true. He started buying me things. After we'd only gone out a couple of weeks, he came to my work with a huge Gucci purse.

At that time, I thought I was in love. But when I look at it now, I think I was just brainwashed. I was only eighteen—totally naive. When I first started going out with him, I would go to parties, and people would point at me, and say, "That's Ben Carter's girlfriend." I thought I was so cool. While they were probably thinking, "What a stupid girl."

We started going out in March, and everything was fine till right around Christmas time. He cheated on me. One of my friends heard from a girl that knew the girl that he cheated on me with.

I confronted him and he lied. I played volleyball with these girls, and one night after playing, we drove by her house. His car was out there. I went to the door, we got in an argument, and I ended up leaving. He was acting like, "What are you doing here?

But, of course, I took him back. He begged me. He bought me a

Gucci watch. He said, "I'll never do it again. I was drunk. I didn't know what I was doing."

I believed him.

He was a total meathead. Totally into himself. He drank protein shakes. Worked out all the time. We used to get in major wars, because he would want to wear tank tops and I hated them. Of course he would wear them anyway. And then he got tattoos—that was worse yet. I cried over them.

He always used to tell me I was overweight, and I wasn't. I was 5'5" and 110 pounds, but he wanted me 100 pounds. His old girl-friend in high school had been 95, so I could be 100. He used to tell me I was fat, and have me believing it.

He was real possessive too. I could never go anywhere. I couldn't just go the mall. I couldn't wear fingernail polish. I couldn't have long nails. I couldn't wear skirts. I remember I bought this jean mini skirt, and I loved it. It wasn't really mini. It came down to right above my knees. And I showed him, and he made me take it back. I couldn't get perms. Whenever I got a perm I would have to lie to him, and when he'd see me, he'd tell me how ugly I looked. I just believed everything he said.

I could never go out to lunch with my friends. One night I went to a mall when he was working, and when he found out, he threw a fit. But in the meantime he was working at a bar that he wouldn't let me into because I was underage.

He would do shots of Jack Daniels and—you could see it in his eyes—he would go psycho. I could never talk to any guy. I could not even look at old high school friends. I was even afraid to talk to my male cousins.

Every time I tried to break up with him, something would hap-pen. One time, I tried to break up and his mom called me up and told me he was in rehab for alcoholism. The family needed me. So I went. He quit rehab early. After I came back.

I broke up with him again, and then his dad got shot in the foot. So they needed me at the hospital. He called me at my mom's at three in the morning, and he was swearing at me on the phone, and my mom was listening. He was like, "Get your fuckin' ass down here."

My mom heard that. As I was getting ready to go, she said, "I wouldn't go anywhere for someone who talked to me like that."

But I just felt like I had to go.

Or I would break up, and he would follow me around. And cause trouble wherever I went. He'd start ripping into my friends. He'd make them cry. My friends wouldn't want to be with me. So the choice was either live in seclusion or get back with him.

He really got in the middle of me and my family. My family started to see through him. I remember my mom made me watch Oprah one time. She had a special on men who hate women and the women who love them. I didn't want to watch it. At the time I couldn't see it, but now I see that everything in it was about him.

The more my family sided against Ben, the more I went against them. He had me totally brainwashed against my family. I moved in with him at his family's house.

Once I went to a pre-season Bears game with one of my girl-friends, and he was mad that he didn't get to go. The next week-end was Labor Day. He went boating and made me stay home. I wasn't allowed to go, because he hadn't gotten to go to the Bears game. I waited and waited and waited for him to get home. Finally I called one of my friends and we went out to eat. And we stopped at a bar. I was there an hour. And all of a sudden, who comes pounding through the door? Ben had seen my car. He was scream-ing in the bar. My friend and I ran out the side door. He chased us in the parking lot and made me go home. His mom was mad at me cause he was so psycho when he got home and I wasn't there. It was my fault because I had gone out.

He would go out a lot but I had to stay home. Twice, he got all drunk and he and his friends went to the airport and took off in the middle of the night. One time, they went to Arizona and the other time, Florida. He would call me the next day at work, telling me that he was in another state. He'd say he was going to stay there for a week, but that I'd better not go out. He would call me every night to check on me, and I would stay home.

He cheated on me again. But this time it was like a dream come true. This was during the time when I was staying with him. My mom was in the hospital—she had a hysterectomy. I felt really bad going to see her, because I knew she was upset with me for living with him.

A lady that I work with, who's my mom's age, came up to me. She was crying, and she told me that she found out that Ben was cheating on me. I never cried. Never. She told me, and I'm like, thank you. It was my way out. That was it. I went to the hospital and I asked my mom if I could come back home. It was the happiest day of her life.

I went and got my stuff. He cried. Begged me to stay. When I met someone else, he started threatening him. Calling my new boyfriend's family at all hours and telling them that he was going to kill him. I had to change my phone number, get it unpublished. He'd call me at work to harass me. I'd put him on the speaker phone and everyone would listen. Then in six months, he got engaged. He came over one night, crying to me, saying he couldn't go through with his marriage. Then his fiancée came knocking at my door. And he wouldn't open the door, because he thought she would beat me up.

But they got married. It's been a year or two. Last month, he gave a message to one of my friends to give me. He would give me one more chance. If I didn't take him back, he was going to start having kids with his wife.

✳

Jody & Keith

Jody Christopher is from a midsize community in the midwest. Her ex-boyfriend, Keith Beatty, seems milder mannered and less overtly aggressive than the other possessive men. Instead of bullying Jody, he manipulated her with his insecurity and immaturity.

I must have been about nineteen or twenty when I met Keith.

I was working at a health club, and I met him there. He used to play tennis a lot. He was real nice-looking and real athletic, and I played tennis also, so that was our common bond. We started out as friends. He was really nice, really friendly. Fun. That's what prompted me to go out with him. I felt real comfortable with him. One thing that I couldn't stand was that he would have to be with me at all times. I was still in college, and I was commuting. If I was doing homework, he liked to be at home with me while I did it. If I was working at the tennis club, he'd have to be at the tennis club. I didn't notice this until I had already really started liking him.

One time I was working at the club, and one of the ladies that I was working with needed some help. So I offered to stay longer than I'd planned. He happened to be at the club. He'd been planning to come over to my house after work, but I said that I was going to stay a few hours later. He said, "Oh fine," and he ran out the door and just left. Rather than say he was upset, he just left. I was always the one who had to call and patch things up. He was very insecure. He'd throw little temper tantrums if he didn't get his way. I don't think he really meant to, but he tried to control me. I could tell he didn't like me even looking at any other guys or talking to other guys. I guess I was a little insecure at that time, otherwise I think I would have broken up with him. I felt like I was doing something wrong if I talked to a guy.

One time, I was going to school, I had homework to do, I was working, and I was playing on the tennis team and had practice. So obviously I was really busy. I didn't have two minutes to myself, because he was taking all my other time, if I had any. One Saturday I told him I had tennis practice. He later told me that he called some girl—I don't know if he used to date her or what—to play tennis on that day, because I was not going to be available. Obviously it was to make me feel jealous.

It's not that I think he was trying to be mean. I think he was so insecure that he couldn't handle not spending time with me. It was almost like I had to be with him all the time. I was a nervous wreck, wondering if things would upset him.

He never wanted to work. He would never hold a job for long. All he ever wanted to do was play tennis. That was another obvious concern of mine. That's where I felt like his mom. I was always telling him, "You should get a job." "Really you should be doing your homework, not playing tennis."

He'd respond, "Yeah, I'll do it after I play tennis." By then it would be ten o'clock. He didn't listen.

I guess I just got to a point where I couldn't handle it any more. I never had any time to myself. I felt nervous all the time because I didn't know how he was going to react. If I'd call him 15 minutes later than I'd said I would, he'd say, "Why did you call so late?"

I gave him absolutely no reason not to trust me. There was absolutely no way that I would have cheated on him at all. I think that was his fear. I think that's why he didn't want me to talk to other guys. I'm not the type of person who would give out that impression.

Plus, I got tired of being his mom. He was always around. It was suffocating. I never went to bars. He'd tell me I didn't "belong" in a bar. We didn't so much fight, it was just me taking care of things, smoothing things over.

I was commuting to my college, and I decided to move into a dorm. Because I was feeling isolated. We never did anything. We'd always just sit around, he never wanted to go out. I felt like I needed to broaden my horizons. Meet other people. I told him that, and he wasn't real happy. So he decided that he was going to go to school in Florida. I thought, this is great. It'll give me some time away from him.

So he went off to Florida, but first he had to borrow some money. So I gave him $150. He called a few weeks later and said, "I registered too late, they're not going to accept me. I'm coming back home."

Oh great. That's just how he was. He didn't plan this out before he went. By the time he had gotten back, that's when I had decided to break it off. The timing was bad because I never got my money back.

Actually, I had wanted to break up sooner, but I didn't want to confront the issue. I didn't want to hurt him. I kind of felt like he needed me. I felt sorry for him. I would bend to every demand, because I didn't want him to get mad at me. Now I look at it, and I'm like, I can't believe I put up with the guy.

He's probably still going to school. And I know he started dating another girl who plays tennis.

✳ **Marlene & Drazen**
Marlene Davis is a model who was based in London. She was in New York for a job when she met Drazen Silajdzic.

I was in New York for work, doing a press show for Gottex swimwear. We had a break and all of us young ladies went to Westhampton—to get a tan and meet guys. We stayed in this hotel. We met young men. There was Drazen. It was probably love at first sight. He was Yugoslavian. I thought he was really dynamic, assertive, direct. Everything an English man wasn't. I'd been living in London for seven years. I thought he was exciting and passionate and smart and good-looking.

So I came back to New York to do the show. I was staying at the Chelsea Hotel. And I gave him a call and said, "Why don't you come to the city?"

He said, "Why would I want to come to the city? What's there?"

And I said, "Me."

He said, "I'll see you in a couple of hours."

So it was a big romance and we both fell madly in love. But I was engaged to be married to another man in London. Drazen and I decided that I would go back and tell him that obviously the wedding wasn't happening. I did that. Then I came back to New York and I stayed with Drazen for about six weeks. And you can imagine, it was perfect. I was in heaven. This was the man I was going to marry. We were so compatible, and it was so romantic. We did all these things together, and he showed me New York. He loved opera, he loved theater, he loved ballet. He had tickets to the New York Film Festival.

And then I packed my bags and moved here for good. My boyfriend in London was devastated. And I was scared. I didn't know anyone. I just really knew Drazen. I had to go to an agency and find work. I was extremely vulnerable, because I was dependent on him emotionally and financially. And I didn't know him, really, did I? He was a stranger.

The first couple of months were great. He had money, so we travelled constantly. He wanted to show me Miami, he wanted to show me New Orleans, he wanted to show me white water rafting in the mountains. I have photo albums of pictures of us at Disney World. Here and there. Every week I would get presents. He was just fantastic.

I think the trouble started when I started to work and started to be more independent. I noticed that he didn't really like that. Actually, what he liked was to be the king. To control everything. Which he'd been doing, because obviously I'd allowed that to happen. But once I started to do my own thing, he became a monster from hell.

I started to get work. He'd say things like, "It's your choice to work, but I don't want to be deprived. I still want to have sex...."

The sex thing was very interesting. He really used that a lot to control me. If I had to go out to a job, he'd want to have sex. I'd say that I had to be at work in ten minutes. He'd say, "I don't care.

It only takes five minutes." And if I didn't go along with it, he wouldn't talk to me for days. He would say I didn't care about him. He'd go crazy.

In the beginning, I would get very upset. I would cry. And he would say, "You're absolutely crazy. You're just not behaving well. You're my priority number one. I'm your priority number one. You have to make me happy."

He wanted to do everything with me. He was one of those loyal swan types. He liked it when I had girlfriends, other models, with me, and we'd all go out. But he had to be the one that was the king of the castle. He needed a lot of attention.

Then he told me that I wasn't allowed to drink any more. Then he told me I wasn't allowed to use any substances whatsoever. He thought that probably I would have some kind of lapse of judgement. There were a few scenes. He would get completely carried away. Bash the wall. Throw eggs on the floor. A girlfriend came in from London, and asked me to meet her for lunch. And I went. And he just went berserk. You know why? Cause I hadn't invited him.

Eventually, I told him that I cared about him and that I thought he should see a psychiatrist. He decided he would do that. So he went, and then we both ended up going. And things did improve a little bit. The therapy did help.

But I still had to do what he wanted. And if I didn't, there would be hell to pay. He threw me out once because I came back from a lunch with my two girlfriends and we'd bought a bottle of champagne. I went to some women's hotel for a couple of days. I called him, and he asked if I was sorry, and I said yes. He'd already discussed with the therapist that he wanted a woman who didn't drink and who didn't do any drugs.

Anyway, I did what he wanted. I decided the relationship was more important. I stopped drinking, and I stopped the drugs.

Sometimes, things were still great, if we were going out and having a good time. And I was going along with what he wanted. But if I had a different idea or opinion, if I wanted to stay home and rest, there would be problems. It would usually result in a big fight.

One night we had a fight and he said, "Sleep in the other bedroom tonight. I don't want you to sleep with me."

I said fine. I felt completely helpless and I cried myself to sleep. Then I was aware in my sleep of something in the room with me. I opened my eyes and he was standing above me, and he was ready to piss in my face. I quickly sat up and he pissed on the pillow.

He said, "It's a metaphor." He felt pissed on in some way, and he was going to do it back to me. So I promptly packed all my bags to go back to London.

I was sitting on Pan Am thinking, that's it. I made a dreadful mistake. I'm leaving. An announcement came on the fight. "Everyone please get off." Someone had called, and said there was a bomb on the plane. And they had to search all the luggage. I knew it was him. And it was, I later found out. Which is a federal offense. I was sitting at JFK, knowing that the bastard was doing this to me. For four hours. So I was convinced even more that I was going to get away from him.

So I went to London, to my best friend's, and I told her what was happening. I spent about ten days in one of her bedrooms thinking. I didn't know what to do in London anymore. I'd made some friends in New York. I'd started working. I decided to come back.

So I came back, and I told him: "If it happens again, if you ever touch me, if any kind of abuse happens, I'm leaving."

We continued going to therapy. We went on a holiday, we were sitting on the beach, he asked me what I was thinking about, and I said, "Well, I was thinking about this time I had while I was in London."

He jumped up and got in the car and drove off. He left me there. He came back, and he rolled down the window, and he said, "There's only one word. What is it?"

And I said, "Drazen."

Wrong word. Of course, the word was "sorry." He wound up the window and drove off. The police came and drove me back to the hotel. Then of course he was always very good at apologizing. Washing me from head to toe. And buying me wonderful gifts.

It was very difficult, because he was a wonderfully vibrant, stimulating, great guy on one hand. Unfortunately, on the other hand, he was this aggressive, violent, paranoid, commanding, demanding tyrant.

So anyway, I was thinking, this is an experience. I'm learning a lot. I'm going to therapy. I'm getting tools that I've never had before. Maybe I should try to stick with it. Who knows what will happen in six months time? We'll learn about each other. Know what each other's issues are. That was one argument for staying in it. The other was that I think I really loved him quite a lot. I had already done so much for him. I think I just felt that I didn't want to give up.

He was very highly sexed. Even after a year and a half, he wanted to do it twice a day. I found that a little bit strange. I was basically most of the time doing things to make him happy. And then I thought, well, maybe this is what women do anyway. It's like part of the housekeeping. It's like a duty. If I had known what I know now, it would never have happened.

Another thing, I only had maybe $5000 in a bank account. I was terrified. New York was this huge place. I couldn't even imagine living in my own apartment, paying nearly a thousand dollars a month rent. Financial dependence was such a big problem. Which I see now constantly as a problem with women. Women put up with all sorts of things. If I'd had a child, I would still be with him.

Also, I was 29. Oh my god. Nearly 30. I started to get panicked because I thought of 30 as very much over the hill. I thought I should have been married with children.

I even had to ask him, like I was asking my father, if I could go home for the Christmas holidays. I remember being so terrified that he would just throw me out on the streets.

I could never relax. I always had to be on guard. He was always ready to attack. I would just be sitting watching a TV program, and he'd walk through the door and ask me what I was watching. I'd say. He'd say, "Why are you watching something like that? What's the point? It's not going to do anything for you. Why don't you give me one good reason why you want to watch that?"

I'd cry. And he'd say, "Why are you crying? Are you crazy?"

It was exhausting. An old friend of mine said, "If you don't get out, you're going to end up in a mental institution. He's going to drive you completely crazy."

And then I realized that things like that occurred when he was really angry and mad. He'd see what I was doing, and then whatever I'd do, then he could say whatever, and that would trigger my reaction, and then he could say, "God, you're so histrionic."

Once we had to go to the Film Festival. He was trying to take a nap beforehand. And the landlord's dogs were yapping. Drazen was like, "I'm going to kill those dogs." He went into the kitchen, and out came the poison. He made meat sandwiches, putting the poison inside. We went downstairs and he threw the sandwiches down to where the dogs were. I was like, "I can't believe you did that. Those poor dogs."

He said, "I'm not doing anything towards you. This has nothing to do with you."

The dogs lived, somehow. But I was starting to think that I had to get away. It had probably been a year and a couple of months.

There was one other fight where he did do something to me. I think he head-butted me. I think he put his fist through a wall. I pulled his hair. It was one of these really nasty violent scenes. I said, "That's it. If this ever happens again, I can't accept it."

So more therapy. More therapy. At this point, every job I went for, I'd say to myself, you better get this job. Cause I had to make money, because I had to get away. Money became the saving thing. I would literally lie on the floor to squeeze into Levi jeans that were too small for me, so that I could get that job. It was pretty intense. So then I made some more money, another five grand. I was starting to feel quite confident.

I was invited by a male friend and some other friends to go for dinner. Until that point, I'd never gone out by myself with friends. So I said to Drazen, "A friend has invited me and a whole bunch of friends to go to dinner, and I think it would be really good, and I'd like to do it."

He was livid. But I went anyway. When I got home, he said, "Admit you made a mistake."

And I said, "I really don't think I made a mistake."

He said, "I am your number one priority. And things have to be good for us. We are number one." And eventually he got so mad that he grabbed me by the neck with his hands and started throttling me. So I burst into tears.

He said, "Pull yourself together, I'll be back in ten minutes." And I'm thinking to myself: I better just agree.

So he came back, and I said, "Yes, yes, yes, I made a mistake. I shouldn't have gone." That was the third time. I thought, it's not ever going to change. Get away. Get out.

So shortly after that, I said to him that I thought it was better that we separate. And he agreed. He said something like, "Maybe it's good to have a couple of months by ourselves. And then we can review and continue." That's what he wanted to do. Meanwhile, in my mind, I didn't want to see him ever again. But verbally I agreed. I moved.

And the minute I was in my new apartment, I was like, I don't want anything more to do with this guy. He'd call me in the night, depressed, crying. Begging. He was overwrought. Said he'd made the most terrible mistake.

I joined WAC [the Women's Action Coalition], and I've been all involved in these women's issues. One day I came back from a march for the women of Bosnia ... it was great. We did this theater piece that got lots of coverage on all the channels. I came home and there was a telephone call from a lawyer, saying, "I'm Drazen Silajdzic's lawyer, and I would like you to call me."

So I called him. And he asked me if I would testify for Drazen. You know why? Another ex-girlfriend had him up on abuse and harassment charges. They wanted me to testify that he was just the sweetest guy. I said to the lawyer, "No, I'm not going to do that."

✳   **Jennifer & Peter**
Jennifer Davis got involved with Peter Wolfman during the
summer after their freshman year at a large southern
university, and remained involved with him for many years.

The first time Peter and I went out, we had drinks I had never had before ... things like Grasshoppers and Sidecars. And then we went driving around downtown Washington, which is beautiful at night. As we went past the Lincoln Memorial, I said, "I've always wanted to sit on Abe Lincoln's lap."

And he said, "Me too."

And we screeched to a halt and ran up to this monument. We were the only people there. We crossed over this velvet rope. The pedestal on which Lincoln's sitting figure resides was taller than we were. But Peter, in a feat of athletic prowess, pulled himself onto this pedestal, then leaned down and pulled me up. So we were standing at the pedestal at his feet. He had humongous statue feet. And his knee was above our heads. And we were looking up at this knee, thinking, "Oh, boy, how are we going to accomplish this?"

At which point we heard, "HEY, WHAT ARE YOU KIDS DOING UP THERE?" It was a cop.

He told us to get right down, which of course we did. And he said he was going to take us down to the station. We were both completely panicked. It was our first date, and we were being arrested.

Peter said to me, "You've got to sweet-talk him. Bat your eyes or something."

So I did. I said, "Oh, excuse me, officer, we're so sorry. We've always wanted to sit on Lincoln's lap. It's our first date, please let us go."

And the officer said, "Well, if it's your first date...."

And we went to Peter's house and we smooched like fury till three in the morning. And that was it. For eight years.

Peter was charming and smart. He'd traveled all over the world. He struck me as having the same sophisticated tastes that I thought my father had. We were eighteen, mind you. I was young enough to be impressed by a lot of what, in retrospect, I see was really pretense.

The first time Peter met my father and sister, we were at my father's farm. After dinner we went into the library. Peter knew my father smoked cigars, and he'd brought him cigars as a guest present. My father and Peter each lit one up, and Peter said, "Do you have any cognac? I always love a good glass of cognac with my after-dinner cigar."

I knew that in fact he did: He and his father used to sit around after dinner and smoke cigars and drink cognac. But my sister looked at him like: "How old are you?"

She hated him from that moment on. She said he was a pretentious little jerk. At the time, I couldn't see that. And I had a big fight with my sister about it.

We'd met over the summer, and then we went back to college for our sophomore year. Basically that year went pretty well. We were madly in love with each other. And then he went abroad our junior year. That was when things really started to mess up. We were too young to talk maturely in advance about how two libidinous post-adolescents would cope with a year apart. We didn't really deal with it. I guess we both assumed that nothing would happen with other people.

But in the end, there was a period when I didn't hear from him for quite a long time. I was very anxious. And I ended up having two or three brief relationships during that year.

He came back, and we never talked about it. We had this joke at the time: he used to tease me about "Bob under my bed." This fake boyfriend, who would come out and ravish me when Peter wasn't around. His name was Bob. Peter would say: "Has Bob been here?" I thought it was kind of cute.

So about four months after he came back, we were lying in bed and he said something about Bob, and we laughed. He said something like, "Well, at least it was just Bob when I was gone."

And I said, "Oh Peter, I figure while you were gone, you probably had a couple of affairs. And you probably figure that I had a couple of affairs. But it really doesn't matter."

He sat upright in bed and he said, "You what?"

I realized, with this sinking in my heart, that I had just made this horrible error. He ended up walking out, slamming the door. Before he walked out, he managed to call me a whole lot of nasty names. He said, "I can't believe you'd be so slutty."

I was completely devastated. It was so unexpected. But then I also felt bad, because part of me felt I'd been unfaithful. Another part of me felt, oh, for crying out loud, I'm 19 years old. I may marry this guy. Is this really such a bad thing to have done?

I didn't speak to him for four months. I knew I didn't want to put myself up for more abuse. I was not very good at dealing with emotional things. I avoided him if I saw him coming in the halls, rather than picking up the phone and saying, "Come on, let's be real. We've gone out for a really long time. We're in love. Let's talk." I guess it was a question of feeling small enough that I didn't even think that it was my right.

Four months later, I was writing an English paper and he showed up one night at 11:30, knocked on the door and said, "Can I come in and talk?"

I said, "I'm writing an English paper. Can you come back another time?"

He did go away, and he came back the next day. We got back

together, but we got back together with terms. He said, "We'll get back together, but one false move and it's over."

Ask me why I accepted this. I don't know. I guess because I figured I wasn't going to make any false moves. He told me that he missed me and still loved me, but that I was on probation.

For the next three years, he totally dominated the relationship. He continued to be horribly jealous of every man I knew. If I had a male friend, I basically didn't talk about him. But when I did, I would find a way to dismiss him as a potential threat. I'd say things like, "My friend Steve—he's gay," or "I was talking to David today—he's really happily involved with Sue."

I'd do this to avoid Peter being snide or making nasty cutting remarks about me. "What, are you sleeping with him too?" he'd say. "Did you ever sleep with him?"

It never went away. Sometimes things were fine, but basically I lived in total fear of his reprobation and disapproval for about three years.

Sexually, things were really horrible between us. He insisted on having sex every day. If I resisted, he would just push ahead anyway. If I said I was tired, he'd say, "You didn't seem to have that problem when I was away for a year."

Every day, I would have to sleep with him, or he would physically or mentally abuse me. Not that he'd beat me up. But there were times when he practically raped me. I wasn't fighting back, but I clearly wasn't interested and didn't want to have sex with him. But we had sex anyway.

Then it began being talked about between us as "my problem with sex." Because I didn't have much of a sexual appetite, what was my problem about sex? He bought me a vibrator.

He could have sex for hours. So imagine, not wanting to have sex, but having this guy who just wanted to go on and on and on. It would get to the point where I would be rubbed raw. And walking around limping, and the next night we would have to have sex again. I'd say I couldn't that night, and he'd say, "You didn't seem to have that problem when I was away."

It was useless to say things like, "God, that only happened a few times." Obviously, I must have had some kind of voracious appetite in order not to remain faithful. Obviously, he felt emasculated and was trying to prove himself.

Every time we had the littlest fight, it would turn into a fight about "it." I'd be five minutes late somewhere. He'd say: "You're late. And moreover, three years ago…"

After graduation, we both moved to Washington. And I got a job that I liked. My friend Molly at work had been in a very similar relationship. This guy had actually physically abused her. He'd beaten her up. I helped her get out of her relationship, and she returned the favor. We talked about Peter a lot. For a long time before I was thinking of actually breaking up, she and I would rehearse the speeches that I'd make to try to get him to change his behavior.

We'd go off to the bathroom and rehearse. She would play me and I would play Peter, responding the way I knew he would respond. He was a very good arguer—he later became a lawyer. He could always talk me into a corner, so I'd start to doubt myself.

Molly would be me, and I would come back with his repartee. And she was better at this than me, because she hadn't been driven into the ground for as many years as I had.

I was also just getting older and more self-confident. I had a job, I was doing well at it. I'd been promoted a few times. Molly helped me realize that I shouldn't have to deal with this anymore. She said, "Jennifer, you're incredibly attractive and plenty of people would like to go out with you."

We were in New Hampshire around this time with two friends. I burned a meatloaf. I told Peter, and he got mad about that, and in front of these people, he said, "You just can't seem to do things right. You can't even be faithful to me when I'm gone for a year."

I just remember thinking, "I've paid my dues."

So we broke up. I said to him, "I can't believe you're still obsessing about this. It's clear to me that you're not getting beyond this issue. You're making me miserable."

He was pretty devastated but we broke up anyway. I then ended up going out with this guy who was something called a "process facilitator." He was basically an organizational behavior guy. He would get hired by organizations to work out their problems. He was touchy-feely to the nth degree. He always wanted to "talk about it." I'd be a little tiny bit cranky and he'd go, "Do you want to talk about it?"

Before we went to bed for the first time, he felt like we had to "process" the whole thing before doing it. At first it was tremendously appealing, but he was so phony and I got very sick of him very quickly. I missed Peter because of the comparison with this guy.

I had lunch with Peter's sister. And his sister told him that during those three years when he'd been making my life miserable, and making me feel guilty, he'd also been sleeping with everything that walked. He'd had endless affairs on me, and I'd had no idea. Perversely, that made me understand him.

I could never understand how he could still be obsessing about my affairs after three years of perfect behavior on my part. I'd been saintly. I'd worn collars up to my neck. I couldn't believe he was still calling me a harlot after all this time. Suddenly it made sense to me. He felt guilty. So he was taking it out on me, and also leading me off the scent.

I guess I was relieved, because suddenly I realized that it wasn't about me. Because that's what I had been feeling all these years: that it had been about me. I must have been bad. I suddenly realized: He doesn't think I'm bad. He thinks he's bad. And I felt tremendous pity for him. And pity was an emotion a whole lot nicer than the ones I had been having. It made my heart go out to him. I thought, "Gosh, this poor guy is so confused."

So we talked, and we got back together. But it was never the same. It was a different relationship. It lost something because he didn't have as much power over me anymore. He wasn't being a bully so much anymore. But it had lost its excitement too. I think he was larger-than-life when he was being awful, and he wasn't any more. He was kind of pathetic in some way.

He went off to law school. I would go visit him on certain weekends. One time I was there, and he was off at class. I don't know what got into me, but I opened up a file drawer and I found a photograph of another woman. Framed. That had obviously been shoved into this file drawer before I came. I imagined it had been sitting out on his table, and then he'd put it into this drawer. I didn't know who this woman was.

And then I found this series of letters from her—they were pretty much love letters. I didn't have a clue who this woman was. The issue was not that he had had another woman, but that he had had one recently. That he cared enough to have a photograph of. But the oddest thing—and the biggest indicator that I was on my way out—was that I had to try to get myself to cry.

Then I put everything back. And I planned this whole thing. We were about to go to bed that night, and I was waltzing around. And I said, "God, you have the biggest filing cabinets of anybody our age. What do you keep in these things?"

And I pulled out this drawer "accidentally." He wasn't even looking at me. And I stood there. He turned around and saw that I was staring into this drawer. And I leaned in and picked up this photograph and I said, "Who's this?"

He was very awkward, and he confessed finally. And I sobbed. At that point I was able to turn up the tears. I said, "I can't believe you've got this person, and you've got her picture and you put it in the drawer before I came in the door for the weekend."

He said that she wasn't that important to him. I think they may have been involved during the period when I'd broken up with him.

I consciously thought to myself that this would be how we'd get over it. Because we were even. Even though I knew about all his women in the past, I just thought that if I could be hurt enough by this, we'd get over the relationship.

We just drifted apart after that. The night before I left for business school, I remember wanting to spend the night alone, but feeling like I really had to spend it with him. He got very drunk and kind of morose. He said, "I almost decided to give you a ring tonight. And ask you to marry me. But I sort of figured you wouldn't say yes. So I didn't."

I said, "I'm just going through a lot of changes in my life now, and this probably isn't the greatest time."

We spoke a few times after that. But it was clear that I had another life. And he did too. He started going out with this woman, who he's still going out with now. I hear stories about them now, and I think, "Better her than me."

Five years after we broke up, I invited him to my engagement party. I thought, after all these years, we really should be friends. He was talking to Greg, my fiancé. And my cousin went to take a picture. And Peter said, "Isn't this cute?"

Greg said, "Yeah. A picture of Jennifer's men."

And Peter turned to him and said, "Well, there certainly have been a lot of them."

This was more than a decade after "the thing" happened. He was still upset that in my junior year of college I'd had a couple of affairs. If Greg hadn't been so relaxed, it could have been a truly destructive comment. I think that's what Peter intended. I was furious and I'm still furious.

Despite the fact that possessive men exist by the multitude, they are something of an anachronism, standard-bearers of an outdated sense of male entitlement. He'll bring home the Gucci, as long as the little woman behaves.

But despite his swaggering, bristling exterior, this would-be macho man also quickly becomes dependent on his mate. Any gesture on her part that isn't about him becomes threatening. He reacts aggressively to his feelings of fear and dependency. He deals with powerlessness by cursing, breaking things, and worse. After the episodes, he's frantically sorry, but no matter how "well" the woman behaves, he'll eventually act up again.

So why does the woman stay? First of all, as unbelievable as it may seem having just read these grueling stories, she launches the relationship thinking that she's in love. Things start in a burst of romance (as in Jennifer and Peter's Lincoln-climbing adventure). And, chances are, when the man's not exploding (which he often manages not to do in the early stages of the relationship), the couple is actually quite compatible. Marlene and Drazen, for instance, both truly loved culture and travel. When they neglected the rest of their lives for their de facto honeymoon, their relationship flourished.

The relationship isolates the woman at the same time that the man is undercutting her confidence in her own judgement and sense of reality. In Jennifer's case, Peter wore her down with a two-pronged attack: constant verbal punishment and sexual terrorism. Casey's boyfriend estranged her from her family, chased her out of a bar when she dared to go out for a drink without him and, later, harassed her friends when she tried to break up. For a while, his assaultive strategy worked. He gave her no space in which she could have gotten some perspective on her situation.

In Marlene's case, she reached the point of knowing that she wanted to leave before she had the means to actually go. The fact that Drazen was financially supporting her gave her minimal leverage with which to fight back. Economic dependency keeps some women trapped for far longer than they would be if they were answerable to their emotions alone.

The woman feels stuck, and she feels alone. Often, she develops temporary coping mechanisms: She learns to drown out his verbal assaults, to smooth over rough patches, to edit her talk and her behavior to keep his anger at bay.

But then some line is crossed, and the woman wants out. Practical considerations may postpone her escape. But all the women in this chapter managed to exit.

I had strong impressions of all of these women. Although they spoke openly about their naiveté, their lack of firm identity and their compliance in the early stages of their possessive-man relationships, in every case, I was struck by their present-day confidence, and the sophistication of their perspective. These women were neither angry nor meek, they were simply glad to get on with their lives. My guess is that it's a relatively rare woman who makes the possessive-man mistake twice.

But I don't want to put too pat and optimistic a face on this. Not all women have such an easy time getting out. The stories in this chapter exist along the shadowy boundaries of domestic violence.

It's chilling to read that every single man described in this chapter has gone on to a new relationship. We can only hope that the new women in these guys' lives will find the internal strength—and the practical resources—that will allow them to take care of themselves.

The Hustler

Hustlers fall within the historical tradition of swindlers, con men, and gigolos. They come on strong and seductive, like the womanizer, but they're after something more tangible. These are men who fake love, or, at the very least, barter sex and attention for money or some other practical advantage.

As opposed to his historical role models, the modern day hustler knows that he's dealing with women too wise to hoodwink entirely. The men in this chapter wear the fact that they want something—money, a green card, whatever—on their sleeve. One of the secrets of a hustler's success is that he doesn't indicate to the woman he's scamming that he's in any way counting on her to come through for him. In fact, he manages to imply that he has other options waiting in the wings. To reserve her privilege as savior supreme, the woman better ante up immediately.

But at the same time that he's up front about his demands, this guy seems to have lots to give in return. He has gleaned exactly what it is that the woman wants—intellectual or artistic camaraderie, sex, travel. He manages to turn the exchange into something that approaches a consciously acknowledged bargain. You marry me so that I can become a citizen, and I'll take you to Peru for an incredible adventure. The fact that the deal is overt allows the woman to quell her slight suspicion that she's being taken for a ride.

In fact, the visibility of the bargain obscures the deeper level of seduction that's going on. Often, the man is also manipulating the woman to care about him, to have an emotional stake in the relationship that goes beyond the agreed-upon exchange.

One way a hustler sinks his hooks deep is by appealing to the woman's caretaker impulses. He occasionally lets his vulnerability show—allowing her to revel in the perceived satisfaction of giving him balm of the spirit. The woman's emotional involvement provides assurance for the man that she'll stick around and keep on delivering the real goods that he wants.

Adding to the hustler's appeal is the extent to which he resembles a culturally exalted stereotype, the entrepreneur. Wheedling, fast-talking and big plans are the American Way, after all. A woman without a robust sense of entitlement can hardly fail to admire a man who knows what he wants, how he's going to get it, and how she can help him achieve his goals.

What makes these stories different from the duped-widow sob-stories of lore is the extent to which women have changed. The women in this chapter seem titillated by the perversity, the danger of tangoing with a man with a not-so-hidden agenda. They see in these guys an opportunity for a horizon-broadening walk on the wild side. Choosing a man that makes parental hair stand on end can be the stuff of a delicious rebellion. As with the women who knowingly choose womanizers, these women feel sure that they can handle whatever comes up.

✳   **Betsy & Tito**

Betsy Sawyer was a sophomore in college when she met Tito Benavides, an illegal immigrant from Peru. She had no money to speak of, but he clearly perceived her as something tantalizing: a ticket to U.S. citizenship.

I got back to college the day classes started, and I didn't have a place to live. Through an ad, I found a thirty-three-dollar-a-month apartment on the wrong side of the tracks. I shared it with a girl named Mary, who was planning to become a nun. She did bongs every morning, and worked as a coat check girl at a local restaurant.

Tito and his brother Pepe lived downstairs. Pepe was older—he was quiet and shy. Tito was the troublemaker, the out-of-control one. He was dealing cocaine.

Tito and I started seeing each other. I was really attracted to him. Very early on, he told me about this predicament he had, which was that he was illegal. He wanted to find a girl to marry so he could become a citizen. Very early on, it became part of the picture that I was considering marrying him. He offered me money to do this. He also told me that he'd take me down to Peru and show me all this amazing stuff.

I was caught up with the idea that my younger sister, who lived in New York, led a wild life, and that I was such a home-grown safe person who never did anything exotic. I thought it would be a wild and crazy thing to do to marry Tito. I thought it would be really fun to play married. I had this vision it would be a light thing.

He was incredibly charming, but I don't think that he was at all attracted to me. He wanted to find a girl to marry, so he could get a green card, and I was an easy victim. He was so sneaky. He figured out the best way to convince me was to say things like, "You really don't have to do this," and then go on to talk about how much fun it would be to go to Peru and travel. He'd show me all these amazing things, he promised, and his parents would pay for it all.

He had this beautiful brown skin. He wore faded jeans. Once I found a sweater in the street. It was a lime-green Lacoste sweater. It had a little alligator on it. I gave it to him and he really liked it. He got it. He knew it was a cultural thing—something he didn't have. He wore the sweater a lot. And then the alligator fell off. He kept asking me to sew it back on. One day I came downstairs and he'd sewn the alligator on, but it was upside down. He hadn't known it was an alligator. I was touched by that.

I brought him home for the weekend once, when I was trying to decide whether to marry him or not. My father was really into him. My father was going on and on about how sick it is that the United States doesn't let immigrants in freely. I interpreted that to mean that, if he had known, my father would have wanted me to marry him, that my father believed Tito should become a citizen.

Tito told me that in Peru he'd had a girlfriend. She was like a well-to-do princess who was kept in her house, and he'd go and visit her every night from 7:30 until 10. Then he would leave and spend the rest of the night out at clubs, screwing other women, doing drugs. He'd gotten addicted to a raw form of cocaine.

He'd become a drug addict to the point that he started selling his mother's jewelry. Finally he broke down and asked his parents to save him, so they put him on a plane to America. In the beginning, telling me this stuff, Tito let me into his heart. He felt so guilty about what he'd done to his family. He told me about how hard it had been when he'd first come to America. His brother hadn't come yet, he'd been completely alone. He didn't speak the language. He'd been part of the upper class in Peru, and here he had no authority. He was shaken and scared.

I really responded when he let me see how wounded he was. Or how vulnerable. We went to New York for New Year's Eve. We were walking through Chinatown and there were firecrackers going off everywhere. He was scared of New York—it was just too big for him. He just wanted to go home and be safe. I loved him at that moment.

I finally agreed to marry him. But once we actually got married, he started getting freaked out by my idea that we would play house. I wanted to play out this fantasy, and he started trying to avoid me. After he started not to like me, all I wanted was for him to like me again for a minute. To be part of his world for a minute. And he got more and more freaked out, because we did have this legal bond.

He just rejected me more and more. It was torture to have him in my building. I'd hear him come in at two in the morning. I'd get ready for school, and listen for him leaving and try and come out at the same time.

He'd tease me, but it was really mean. He used to call me something like Potato Girl. He hated the way I dressed. He wished that I wore makeup and painted my fingernails. I remember buying tighter jeans, because I was so desperate to get his attention and to be the one he wanted.

I slept with him more and more rarely. I was completely tortured. He had been having sex since he was ten. I had only had sex with a few other people before him, so I was uptight. I had in my mind that he had never dealt with such a sexually uptight person. It made me feel awful.

One night, I was partying with Tito and Pepe and this woman Sally, who was married to a cousin of Tito's who was out of town. I really wanted to spend the night with Tito—I was supposed to be having a relationship with him. He said he was going to drive Sally home. I went upstairs to my apartment in a huff.

Then I came downstairs to make sure that he wasn't sleeping with Sally. And I caught them in bed. The pain was really great, but I continued to be obsessed with him.

He had a motorcycle. He never took me for a ride on it. Here I was supposedly having this bad guy experience, and he never took me for a ride on his motorcycle. He took Sally on the motorcycle a lot. They were obviously screwing all the time.

Things weren't working out, and the more I tried to control them, the more he wanted to get farther and farther away. In the meantime, I had to go talk to this lawyer with him, and go to immigration. Tito had to string me along enough to get me to go to certain meetings. I'm sure it was calculated. He had to drive me to school once every two weeks to keep me happy.

He convinced me to put a phone in my name in their apartment. He and Pepe made tons of calls to Peru on my phone. There was no way they were going to pay any of the bills.

Even when we weren't sleeping together, when Tito was being really mean to me, I was still hanging on to the idea of our trip to Peru. I'd always wanted to go there, but I was broke. His parents were going to pay for everything. But then he started talking about how it would be no problem for me to smuggle cocaine back into the States. He said an American girl would get away with it. I realized that a lot of the point of this trip was about me bringing drugs back.

I also slowly realized that there was no way I was going to have a good time. I would be stuck in the house with his parents, there was no way he was going to take me anywhere. This guy was out for himself.

I finally realized that I did not want to go. And that I better cash in on the money he'd promised me as an alternative to the trip. He didn't give me as much as he'd said he would. Maybe about $2000. And I left town for the summer—that was pretty much the end.

I made a lot of incorrect assumptions with Tito. I made the assumption that he was honest, because it had never crossed my mind until then that people weren't honest. Until then, when anyone told me anything, I thought they were telling me the truth. I assumed Tito was on my program.

Everyone I'd ever gone out with until I met the man who's now my husband had a character type that combined the wounded with the macho. Arrogance, combined with deep self-hate and insecurity. I wanted to take care of these guys and see them realize their potential, but they were impossible to attain.

The feeling is related to the maternal instinct. It's about wanting to take care of someone, wanting to be needed. It's about defining yourself through someone else's needs. Rather than serving yourself.

And then there's part of the culture that makes you feel like this is a way that women should be. That women define themselves through their men and the sacrifices they make for them. Men define themselves through themselves.

Tito and I lost touch. He moved to Miami. Then several years later, I met the man who's now my husband. When I realized that he might ask me to marry him, I flipped out, because I was already married. I had to get a divorce. I had to hunt Tito down, which was really complicated. I spent hours in the library, looking up his last name, and calling and writing letters to people who might have been his relatives. I finally found his brother Pepe in San Diego. He told me that Tito was in jail in Mexico.

He was arrested bringing drugs back from Peru. It could well have been me. I called Mexico, and talked to him on the phone in jail. He told me he was on the soccer team in jail. I got an English-speaking lawyer in Mexico City and got my divorce.

✳   **Evelyn & Charlie**

Evelyn Hensler was living and working in Boston at the time she met Charlie Mann, a rock music promoter based in New York City. Charlie "borrowed" money from Evelyn, but that was almost incidental. His prevailing interest was in creating and maintaining a sexual arrangement. Unlike a womanizer, who's drawn to the dynamic of seduction and abandonment, Charlie procured himself a woman who was available on demand, but who would make no claims on his freedom.

I worked with this woman, Laura, who had once been a groupie with a rock band. One day, she and I were sitting around the office talking about guys. I had just broken up with someone. She said, "I know this guy you really should meet. I haven't talked to him for years."

So she called Charlie, and he happened to answer the phone, and he happened to be coming to Boston the next weekend. So she said, "I've got this woman you have to meet."

I went and picked him up at the airport. We chatted. He was intrigued by me. By whatever Laura had told him about me. (She'd said I was single and available, which was probably enough for him.) He was very intriguing to me. He was an out-there kind of guy, who was just yakking up a storm. Mr. Hyper. Mr. Show Biz.

So we wound up sleeping together that night. It had been a given that if we were at all attracted to each other, that would happen. It wound up that he was a wonderful and passionate lover. Very experienced. Very into karate. Very strong. Lots of fun. We really hit it off. I'm really flexible. He was amazed. I was willing to do a lot of things. Experiment.

We started getting together a couple times a month. I'd go to New York and we'd stay in a hotel room for the weekend and never leave. It was very, very sexual. For me, it was the ultimate fantasy to be in New York City, in this hotel room with this wild guy.

We kept this relationship up for several years. He was in New York. I was in Boston. I was in my mid-twenties when I met him, he was fourteen years older. I'm sure there was some sort of attraction to that: He was my mentor and teacher.

The relationship was pretty monogamous on my part, although I knew he saw other women. One time, he called me and said, "I may die tomorrow. I don't know what's going on. You have to come here."

I went. To find out that he was living with a woman. She was really jealous of me, cause he would say that I was his number one. She was madly in love with him and wanted his baby. He'd wanted me to come to New York because he wanted her and me to have sex. He wanted to put her in her place.

So she and I did have sex. It was different. It wasn't my thing. I hadn't realized that he was living with someone. That threw me for a complete loop. But I had gone into the relationship with my eyes open. If I'd come into the relationship knowing that he was seeing other people, I needed to accept it. I'd get calls from her in the middle of the night, telling me to stay away from "her" man.

But finally they stopped living together, and he and I still saw each other. At this point, I had money and he had no money. He'd call and ask to borrow money, and I'd give it to him, wishing all the while that I wasn't giving it to him.

I'd come to New York, and sometimes he'd be moody all weekend. And I'd wonder why I'd even come. But I felt like I had to play by his rules. I felt like he was a stronger person than I was. I always felt like a little innocent next to him.

We did other funky things. We got together with this good friend of his who was a high-priced hooker. We had a weekend at her boyfriend's house, where everybody was coked out, and we had an orgy. That was different for me. I was this straight little girl from the Sacramento Valley, and I'd never imagined myself in those kinds of situations. I'm glad that I've had the opportunity to experience them, and I have no desire to experience them again.

We started seeing each other only once a month. He'd come for the weekend, and I'd have my period, and he'd be like, "Why did I come this weekend?"

I really wanted to feel like we had some kind of bond. But after several years, I just wasn't into it like I had been. I knew all along that I couldn't be angry at him. He moved to Miami. I visited him three or four times there, and each time felt less and less like I wanted to have a sex marathon.

We still call each other and yak on the phone. And he says, "You're really the only one that was ever for me."

But there was no way. He even admits, "I could stand you forever. But you could stand me for about a week. And then you'd be out of here."

✳   **Kelly & Teddy**

Kelly Kiernan scheduled our interview for a night on which her husband was out of the house—he has never heard the story of Teddy Gates, whom Kelly dated over ten years ago. While she occasionally asked the "what was I thinking?" question, she also admitted to having written Teddy in prison, and still having a soft spot in her memory for him.

Teddy was a real risk-taker. Very adventuresome. Crazy. He lived life on the edge. And I found that very exciting. My life was so predictable.

Teddy was a good friend of a guy I was dating at the time, who was a good solid citizen. Teddy, on the other hand, was the craziest guy in this group summer house. He drove too fast. He was into wild investments. He was always into the deals. The big money. He talked a really good story. And to a certain extent it was true.

I was breaking up with the other guy at the time.... I had always flirted with Teddy. He was one of those guys that any girl could talk to. He would listen to anyone's story, and would give you advice on what to wear to a party. He would be the first one to tell you that you're gaining too much weight, or that dress isn't the most flattering thing. My friends and I would have these girl talks with him. Teddy would get cornered, and he'd give us sex talks about what guys like and don't like in bed.

He was just adorable. He wasn't the most attractive guy. He was very unattractive, I guess. He was kind of roundish and he knew that he wasn't Joe Stud. Anyway, we ended up getting involved.

Teddy was a CPA and a lawyer. He got a lot of us into this surefire investment tax credit. We got a lot of money back on our taxes. What we didn't know was that Teddy and the people he was in business with were not investing the money. It was all going into their pockets. He was convicted of a felony, and eventually ended up in jail.

He was a very, very, very smart man. He was the brains behind this deal. I have to admit that I was very turned on by this guy's mind. How he could figure out all this stuff. Make it work. In the meantime, I and all of my friends were in these low-paying, steady, nine-to-five jobs. Here was a guy using his mind to come up with a big money-making scheme.

I remember my father saying to me once, "These guys are very seductive because they're gamblers. But by the time they're thirty, they're bums."

At the time, I was like, yeah, yeah, yeah.

If I had been smart enough, I think it would have occurred to me that the deal was too good to be true. He was pulling in big money. We would get on a private plane and fly to Pennsylvania for a party on Saturday night and fly back. It was the early '80s, and nobody thought beyond Tuesday. The parties, and the people, and the Hamptons. There was a lot of that that was fun.

When the shine fell off of what he was doing, the shine fell off of him. He just started getting a little bit sleazy. I'm trying to remember how the whole thing ended.

Oh, I know what it was. He took up with his secretary. Kitty. Whom he's still living with. He was seeing her on the side, and I found that really, really sleazy. I guess I shouldn't have been surprised because he was really flirting and seducing me when I was dating his best friend. We went in and went out of the relationship the same way.

✳

Angela & Sam

*Angela Holmes is a Manhattan-based artist, as is her former
boyfriend, Sam Logan. Angela had inherited some money,
which funded her "collaboration" with Sam.*

My friend Martine said that there was this show she thought I'd like to see. So we went by. The painter, Sam Logan, happened to be there. The three of us immediately got into this sort of intense painting discussion. It's very rare that you'll meet the painter at an exhibition and have a genuinely interesting engaged discussion about art. So I think we all went away thinking that that had been cool. I didn't really think twice about it. I don't remember thinking he was particularly cute or anything.

A few weeks later, I went to a dinner party and he was there. We had a nice time. Someone famous was there, a classic Hollywood beauty. We were actually having a really fun evening watching Sam try to pick her up. The night went on, and a group of us ended up at some club. And suddenly Sam and I started talking. We got very wrapped up in this intense discussion that I think went on for four or five hours.

It was one of those extraordinary discussions where we touched on a lot of mutually meaningful topics. He basically said everything I'd ever wanted to hear from a man. We had a great conversation about art. We had a great conversation about the concept of union between a man and a woman and what that meant. He said that he really believed that two people could be each other's best friends and lovers for life. It was incredibly engaging. And incredibly verbal. This flow of emotions and words just completely turned me on.

I had my car. It was really late. I dropped various people home and Sam was the last one. I don't think we'd gone another block before he attacked me. Sure enough, we went straight to his place. It was really intense. It was pouring rain. 5:00 a.m. I remember he put on Franciscan monks' music. A huge painter's loft. A bed at one end of it. These monks chanting. It was so great. We'd been talking for hours.

The next morning we had breakfast. He said, "I've got to tell you something. I've had this girlfriend, but it's over."

I remember a teensy weensy little red light went off in my head, where now a huge big blaring red light would go off. At the time, I had a love hangover. Who cares? I hadn't had that intense an experience in so long.

For the next two months, he would be with me for two weeks and then he would flip out and go back to the girlfriend. And then he'd flip out and come back to me.

At one point, he flipped out and disappeared and went back to her. I was very angry at him. Because he really had misled me. And I said, "I never want to have anything to do with you."

About a year went by. The girlfriend that he'd always fooled around on found out something and literally fled. Just got on a plane. He tried to commit suicide.

But it was one of these melodramatic things. There were people around. There was no way he was going to die. It was a huge cry for help. He did go to the hospital to get his stomach pumped out. He called me up, to ask me how I was and tell me that he'd tried to commit suicide.

I knew that he was in a desperate situation. He was very low, extremely lonely. You know how sometimes, when you have these weird epiphanies, you remember the sights and smells, the whole situation of when you had the revelation? I remember I was walking through some basketball court and I realized that I had loving feelings towards Sam. He needed me. So I needed to put my anger aside. Now I don't think I would do that in a million years. But I remember this mother-savior side of myself thinking that he wanted me to save him.

So in fact I did go about this concerted effort of taking on this guy who just felt terrible, that he was worth nothing. He'd fucked up this five year relationship, and he'd tried to commit suicide. I decided to love him and make him feel better about himself. I remember deciding to do that. So we started to spend a lot of time together.

At a certain point, he went off to do a painting show in Europe. And I went over to be with him. The first morning, he said, "I'm not going to have sex with you because it's too important to you."

For ten days, we traveled around together, and he just wouldn't. At that point, I was devastated. And cried a lot about it. But something was going on inside myself that I was going to fight and I was going to win. Somewhere inside me, I'd had enough feelings of failure in that arena. That for some reason I was going to fight back. I was not going to back off. I was going to win. I was going to show him. I didn't say: "Fuck you, I'm going to go find a man who desires me and shows me he desires me."

Instead, I was like: "I'm going to win you."

We must have been having good times too. He loved to eat well. And entertain. I'm sure we did lots of fun things. And we talked about art all the time. He was very engaged in my work. We would talk about all the ideals of art. Which is what I needed to do at that time. And then we started to talk about collaboration.

I do believe in collaboration. Although I now know, having done it, that it's of paramount importance that if two people are going to collaborate, they must have formed identities, separately. In their work. That wasn't something I understood at the time. We were so engaged with each other's ideas.

So Sam and I decided to collaborate. We decided that I would move my studio into his place, and we'd work together. Plus we were going to create a whole new art scene around us and what we were doing.

At one point when we were talking about this, he found out that Kathy, his ex, was in Paris. He felt that things hadn't been resolved with her. She'd found out that he'd been sleeping with somebody else, and had left. He felt he wanted to make it better between them. He had to fly off to Paris to do that. It was just fine with me. I really thought that if you loved someone, you had to let them do whatever they had to do. You couldn't control them. If you loved them, and they still had feelings for someone else, then fine. I absolutely accepted his need to go see his ex-girlfriend.

I remember he called me from Paris to ask me if they could go and stay in a friend of mine's apartment there because they didn't have a place to stay. That made me furious. He could tell. I remember he came right back to New York and made sure that things were all fine between us.

Then it was the collaboration thing that we were starting to work on together. He said, "I really want to do this, but I need some money. I need money to live."

In the meantime, my father called me from the car phone one day, and said that he'd found one of those Jewish ladies who hook people up together. He's calling me from the car to tell me he's found somebody who's going to find me a guy.

I said, "Dad, forget it."

He said, "Why, do you have someone?"

"In fact, I do."

And he said, "Oh really? What college did he go to?"

I said, "He didn't."

So you can imagine his reaction when I told him that I was going to give Sam some money. He completely flipped out. And actually in a way drove me even tighter into the arms of Sam. He basically said, "You cannot have this money."

I was like, "This is my money."

It almost got to the point of me having to hire lawyers. My father was completely beside himself, calling my friends, doing everything he could to stop me. It finally came down to a lot of people in the family telling him to let me make my own mistakes.

So Sam and I started doing this collaboration together that I was completely paying for. I was pretty completely estranged from my parents. And then in the meantime, Kathy came back from Paris and started living with him. At first, she started living with him in the space where he and I were going to be working together. I said, "Forget it. You've got to separate this." Kathy and I just hated each other.

As soon as I was in there and had put in a darkroom, and was ready to roll as far as working, the arguments started. All this wonderful theorizing was in a weird way all for naught because we were just not on the same track. He couldn't focus with me on the art-making stuff. He wanted to start doing fashion stuff. To have a commercial thing. He kept saying we could do both. I kept saying: "It's just not my interest."

We basically argued for a year. Most of our energy was taken up in arguing about what we were going to do. He just wanted to get in a good situation. He was not committed to collaboration. At a given point, I was like, "Alright, you do your thing. I'll do my thing. "

Meanwhile the Kathy-Sam-me triangle had gotten more triangulated. As far as I knew, it was mutually understood by everybody. That he was basically sleeping with me and her and other women. I thought it was fine by me, cause he loved me best. So I wasn't threatened.

I got pregnant once and he was such an asshole. That was the beginning of the end. I absolutely immediately knew that I would have an abortion. I remember knowing that meant something. If I had felt that there was any chance that I was going to stay with him, I would have thought much longer and deeper about it.

I remember when I told him that I thought I was pregnant. I was really upset. I remember he sort of collapsed. I remember almost going over and giving him a hug, and then thinking to myself, wait a second. He should be telling *me* it will be okay.

And then when I found out that I was pregnant, he did collapse, and he cried and said: "I can't believe this is happening to me."

Because he'd had five abortions with the woman before. And he had a child with his first wife. He said, "What if I'd aborted Claudia?"

I completely dealt with it, but any concept of me getting even an inkling of emotional support was out of the question.

Remember I told you that there was a triangle going on, and as I understood it, a mutual understanding that we all knew about it? One day, he let it slip that Kathy had no idea. Whenever Kathy asked him if he was sleeping with me, he said no. So I said, "Sam, you have to tell her. If nothing else, you've got to be honest."

We had a phone conversation where I didn't know she was in the room with him. I said, "You have to tell her."

And he said that it was his business. And I said, "No, it's not just your business. Not telling her negates me. If you don't tell her, I will."

And he said, in this very intense voice: "I'll kill you."

He and I had a screaming fight. Kathy said, "What's going on?"

And he said, "She told me to be honest."

She said, "What about?"

And he didn't say anything. So she literally ran out the door. This is someone he'd been having a relationship with for five years. So he was blubbering, crying. I'd ruined his life. And then Kathy called me on call-waiting, and was like: "Can I come over?"

She came over, and we went to some bar, and for the first time in two years, Kathy and I just talked. The things we each found out about the lies! Finally, we just told each other our respective stories. For the past two years, he had led two separate lives. With each of us.

I think it was great for her, because she made the break at that point. I started the emotional break. I knew it was going to be over, but the good parts were still there. I guess I wasn't strong enough. Then for a little while, for the only time in our relationship, it was just him and me. I think that felt luxurious. But very quickly he started another triangle. He got another woman in on the situation. That was when I broke up with him.

I broke up with him and I went out west for a few weeks. I came back, and we had to see each other, because we had all these practical things to work out. It was like a divorce. And we slept together.

I remember asking him if he'd slept with the other woman he'd started the triangle with. He said he had. I asked him if he'd used a condom. He said, yes, yes, yes. And then it turned out he got gonorrhea from her. So the last thing he did ... actually, he didn't give it to me. But I thought he did. And the doctor, when she gave me the test, said that because it's such a terribly dangerous thing for women to have, and there's some slight percentage of a chance that the test can be wrong, she wanted me to go through the course of treatment anyway.

He was a hustler. I understand the concept of hustlers and how they work. He had this ability to sense what I needed. And what I wanted to hear. In a chameleon-like way, he created himself in that mold. When we were together, he would fashion himself into the man that I wanted to have. He could really offer this intense outpouring of emotions and ideas. People in general don't do that. Pour themselves out. This was so attractive to me. I think I was just starved. When he paid attention to me, I was just completely rapt.

Even though his attention was false. It wasn't backed up by any real identity. His identity practically didn't exist. He would literally create himself to get whatever he needed. I was starved and this person just flooded me. He said these things and did all these things.

I have this very strong family unit. A very powerful father. My mom and dad both went to Harvard and got married when they were 18. My sister got married when she was 21; both she and her husband had gone to Harvard. And I was to be the next one. I was supposed to have met a Harvard man and gotten married when I was 21.

While I'd always felt very free, I have this image that I have this diamond-studded dog collar around my neck. On a very long nice chain ... that was hooked to my father. And I could go anywhere and do anything—as long as he approved. I had gotten to be 30 years old, and I think on some level, Sam was a gesture to my father. It was like: "I can do anything, Dad. *Anything* I want to do."

Even though I'm sure on some level it was against my better judgement to give a guy I loved money in the beginning of our relationship, I needed to make that break with my father. And show him that I could make the break and still be okay. I spent a lot of money on Sam, but to some degree it was money well spent. My relationship with my father is still very strong. And there has been this very profound experience of learning that I can do my own thing, and we can still have a relationship.

I recognize that I got in this debilitating situation. I really was with a hustler. For a couple of years. He did everything bad, and I kind of accepted it. But I felt a real range of emotion. It was very passionate, if nothing else. I came out on the other side having learned four million lessons. I'll never make those mistakes again. I think I had been a very protected, afraid little girl who just needed to have tons of bad experiences, so I shaped them for myself.

I grew up a lot. I had a mate-like feeling with Sam. And so Sam may not be the right guy to have that feeling with, but I've had that feeling and I want it again. I want to feel that committed to someone.

At first thought, it might seem as if getting over a hustler is comparable to getting over a womanizer: The woman has the comfort of being able to label and understand what just happened to

her. She knows the man was "bad," and that she's better off
without him.

But the fact is, in at least some of these cases (especially
Angela's, but also Betsy's) the man hooked the woman on a deep
level. He gave her a taste of a relationship that she wanted, and
whether the allure of that connection was based on sexual passion
and intense communication (as it was in Angela's story) or on the
pain of wanting back a dissipated closeness (as it was in Betsy's),
her attachment was profound, if not easy to justify.

At the same time, she has to face the fact that she ignored very
visible clues, and threw her lot in with someone who she should
have known was—to a greater or lesser extent—"using" her. When
a woman gains clarity about how she was manipulated, but still
feels drawn to a man, she not only has to undergo her feelings of
loss after the relationship ends, she also feels stupid for being
taken in, and stupid for feeling anything at all.

Still, many women would agree with Angela's conclusion that
these experiences can produce real personal growth. A defiant
romance with a guy who embodies one's parents' worst night-
mares can be an effective assertion of independence: an opportunity to claim one's right to make one's own mistakes, choose one's
own experiments, put the safety net away. Angela's realization
that she could operate outside her father's control was a develop-
mental watershed—and one she might not have reached through a
tamer form of acting out. So while the losses that these relationships entail may be substantial in terms of money and pride, the
gains in self-determination they offer may, in the long run, be more
profound.

But sometimes not. Sometimes a hustler/manipulator romance
is not about self-determination at all. In Evelyn's case, her situation more closely resembled that of a woman bound by the unstat-
ed but nonetheless rigid rules of a womanizer. She accepted the
notion that the "eyes open" nature of her relationship with Charlie robbed her of the right to ask for anything better than the treatment he chose to give her. In fact, she felt obliged to play along
with his more degrading schemes. While he did serve up some
dizzying experiences, the relationship didn't foster a sense of
independence—or power.

Betsy talked about how Tito forced her to rethink her assumptions about honesty: Until her involvement with him, she had assumed as a matter of course that people were being truthful. She also talked about how women who have had sheltered upbringings often don't realize what real danger is. "There's a fascination with the underbelly, a certain conviction that we can handle anything," she recalled. Fortunately, her sense of practicality kicked in before the Peru trip, and the pressure to smuggle that it would certainly have entailed. But our conversation made her remember a former roommate of hers, who liked the mild danger of buying drugs from some neighborhood kids. Liked it, that is, until the guys raped her, and held her boyfriend hostage while they cleaned out her bank account. "You have certain presumptions about human behavior," Betsy concluded. "You just cannot conceive of really horrible things happening."

A relationship with a hustler is likely to destroy youthful innocence. But after the initial conflagration, women often emerge with a greater sense of self. In the case of the women I interviewed, the burden of their new knowledge didn't metastasize into a systemic mistrust of men. Instead, they ended these relationships with a better sense of their own wilder yearnings, and a conviction that they should perhaps seek to satisfy those yearnings outside the realm of a relationship.

The Cheater

In the movie *The Addams Family*, the Addams' daughter Wednesday, clearly not in costume, is asked what she is for Halloween. "I'm a homicidal maniac," she tartly replies, "They look just like everyone else." The same might be said of most of the men described in the stories that follow. There is not an aura of danger about them. Although they share certain narcissistic traits, they don't broadcast behavioral quirks that foreshadow their untrustworthiness. When a woman falls in love with one of these men, she thinks she's found the genuine article. The discovery that he's involved with someone else comes as a total shock and a crushing betrayal.

The distinction between cheaters and womanizers may not be immediately obvious. Certainly, a number of men in the stories that follow are womanizer-like in that they jam multiple involvements into condensed periods of time. But while the womanizer burns through women, a cheater is capable of settling into a long-term domestic relationship and staying there. The cheater may in fact be quite conflicted about what he's after: He may genuinely crave the comfort that his primary relationship gives him (a major difference from the womanizer), but at the same time not be willing to give up his sexual liaison. While a womanizer's relationships are all about motion (pursuit, then flight), a cheater's relationship is more static. Tension, secrecy and deception are constants, but the emphasis is on maintaining the status quo.

Although some accused themselves of it after the relationship fell apart, the women in this chapter were not extraordinarily naive or gullible. They simply assumed, as most of us would have, that things were as they seemed, that the man who was professing love and a desire for union meant what he was saying.

In fact, he was lying. There are different kinds of liars in the stories below. A couple of the men fall into the pathological category—their lies seem to have been beyond their conscious control, extending beyond their relationships and into every aspect of their lives. Other men in this chapter were more deliberate, carefully crafting their lies for the sole purpose of carving out room for their extracurricular involvements.

✳   **M e l i s s a   &   H a r v e y**
*Melissa Schwabb's encounter with Harvey Kaufman could
serve as a definition for the phrase "two-timer." Seen in
hindsight, the clues she missed to what was really going on
seem overwhelmingly obvious, but she got involved with
Harvey at a stressful time in her life, and simply gave in to
the pleasure of being swept off her feet.*

I had met Harvey years before when I was working in the field of substance abuse, and he was a patient at the clinic where I worked. Even then, he was very professional, an executive with an entertainment company. Supposedly, when I remet him, he had gotten over his drug problem. He was sober.

He asked me out, and he was immediately very attentive and wonderful. I had been separated for a year and my ex-husband had paid no attention to me. So imagine how I responded when I came across this guy. He called me up every minute. Stared at me like I was the greatest thing in the world. Complimented me constantly and all that.

The first sign of trouble came one night when I was supposed to make him dinner. It wasn't our first date, but it was the night we were going to sleep together for the first time. It was his birthday. I'd spent the whole day putting up these happy birthday things, streamers and stuff all over my apartment. I made this great dinner. I was wearing lingerie. And he didn't show up. He called at 11:30. He said he was on a plane coming back from a business trip, and there had been a terrorist on the plane with a bomb, and they wouldn't let anybody leave or make phone calls. And they'd held the passengers on this plane for three hours.

I believed him and we actually had some wonderful dates after that. Then we were going to go away for a weekend. It was a Tuesday night. He told me that he wanted me to come up with the most wonderful bed and breakfast around, and we'd go there for Labor Day weekend. That was a Tuesday. I tried to reach him that afternoon and I couldn't. He was never at home or at work for the next three weeks.

Three weeks later, I get this letter. He was writing from rehab. He had slipped. He explained that there was a woman that he worked with, with whom he'd had a torrid affair that had broken up his marriage the year before. She was married. He really couldn't get over that relationship. He was trying to have a fresh start with me, he told me, but he couldn't. It upset him, and so he did drugs.

Maybe I'm a total idiot, but I took him back. He's a great con, I guess. I got about 20 letters from him apologizing. When he came back a month later, we started in again. I kept telling myself that I wasn't going to really trust him. But he started leaving songs on my voice mail at the office, taking song lyrics and changing them and putting my name in them. He sent me longstem roses at work. Amazingly romantic stuff. It was over the top. He seemed to be fine.

So we saw each other for a few months, and it was really great. He ended up infiltrating my family. My dad was really sick and Harvey was incredibly supportive. He became part of my family. He was there for Thanksgiving. He was there for Christmas. He bought everybody gifts. We had wonderful talks. Things were like that through October, November, December.

It wasn't just that he bought me things, it was the way he did it. He'd suggest going to Bergdorf's, and I would try on lingerie and underwear, and he would buy it all for me. This one day he bought me this perfume. He told me that it wasn't that he didn't like the scent I wore, but he'd smelled this one, and it was great, and would I wear it? That bothered me, but I accepted the perfume. I don't think I wore it too often.

At Christmas, he got me the most gorgeous watch I had ever seen. This was his favorite kind of watch, he told me, and he had always wanted to buy it for someone.

He wrote poems. He wrote little cards. He was always saying, "Hey gorgeous." He was always talking about getting married, and having babies, and saying that we should name our first child Elizabeth, after his grandmother.

In January, he started getting a lot of pressure at work. He had to travel a lot. I was so supportive. He started doing strange things. We went to see this movie one night, and then we went out to dinner, and in the middle of dinner, he said that he was sick. He went to the bathroom, and he came back and said that he'd thrown up in the bathroom. And he had to go.

He had given me the key to his apartment. This one night, he came back to my apartment after having left, and said, "By the way, can I have my key back? I seem to have lost my mine."

I gave him the key back. And I did think that was weird.

Two weeks later, again the same thing, he gets sick at dinner. And he says he really wants to go back to his apartment and be sick by himself. What are you supposed to do?

He told me he couldn't spend Valentine's Day with me. He told me that his mother had really, really rejected him after the whole drug thing, and it was very hard for her to trust him. And she'd actually agreed to spending a whole day with him on Valentine's Day. He was driving to New Jersey to be with his mother.

At this point I'm getting funny vibes. I'd talked to a million people about whether or not I should confront him about the key thing, and the fact that something about it didn't ring true. Everyone told me to go with my instincts. We went out to dinner, and I said to him, "This thing with the keys makes me feel weird."

He said, "What's your worst fear?"

I said, "My worst fear is that you just wanted your keys back. I know you're going to think I'm crazy, but I have this stupid paranoid fantasy that you and your ex-girlfriend are having sex at your apartment, and you think that I might walk in."

He was like, "How could you think that? Don't you think I would tell you if that were going on?"

He totally reassured me. I felt great.

Then one day I called him up and he wasn't at work, so I called him at his apartment, and this woman answered the phone. She said hello, and I just hung up. And I called back, and I said, "Who is this?"

And she said, "Who's this?"

And I said, "This is Melissa. Who's this?"

And she said it was Michelle. Michelle knew about me: I was Harvey's friend who used to be a counselor, who was helping him with his drug problem. Michelle is the woman from his office, the one who was going to leave her husband the year before for him, but whom he supposedly wasn't seeing any more.

I said, "What are you doing there?"

She said, "What do you mean? Why do you care?"

I said, "Well, I'm seeing him. I'm wondering why you're over at his apartment."

And she said, "I've been seeing him for years."

By this bizarre coincidence, I knew her from years before. I had gone to camp with her. We sort of had this bond, so I believed what she said. She told me that she had been going out with him this whole time. Throughout all of this.

There had been a period, she told me, when he had said to her that he had felt romantic feelings towards me, and had maybe told her that we had gone out on a date. And he felt so horrible, so guilty, that she forgave him.

She said, "Well, you don't sleep with him. You're just his friend."

I said, "Last Tuesday he was over."

It turns out that she was lunch, I was dinner.

They would leave work and go have sex during lunch at his apartment, and then he would go see me that night. All those times, that he had to leave, it was to go see her. Valentine's Day, he was with her.

Then we start finding out all the little things. I had the instinct to ask her certain questions. Like what perfume did she use. Sure enough, it was the perfume that he bought for me. So we would both smell like each other, if he had to see one of us after the other.

It turns out that the same lingerie that I picked out that day at Bergdorf's ... he ran back and bought her all the same stuff. The watch I had, he'd bought her the same watch for Christmas. He would call her and say, "Hey gorgeous." He wanted to call their first child Elizabeth. He was leading this double life.

In the middle of the phone call, he came home. And she started screaming at him. He obviously made some kind of bird-in-the-hand decision, and got on the phone with me and said, "You know

I broke up with you months ago. Why do you keep harassing me like this? It's over."

Afterwards, I called him up to yell at him. And he said, "You know, Melissa, I really wanted to break up with you before but your father was dying, and it would have been such a rotten thing to do."

If he were planning on ending things with me, I gave him plenty of opportunities. Especially that time when we were talking about his keys. I think he's satanic. Just think of the amount of energy it must have taken to keep all this deception going.

I saw what it was to be paranoid: It's this real feeling of thinking you're going crazy. Now, I have a really hard time believing anything anybody tells me. My biggest fear now is old girlfriends.

But you know what? Out of all the relationships that I've had, the ones in which there were many shades of gray—whether it was my fault or his fault—those were the ones that could hurt, that could go on for two years. As opposed to that kind of chronic pain, the relationship with Harvey was the most acute pain I ever had. I was a nutcase. I was shaking like a leaf. For a while. But then it got better. Even though the pain was acute, it was so obvious that he was crazy. There was no lingering torture.

✳ ### Nancy & Mark
Nancy Kobler was raised in an affluent suburb of Chicago.
She was in her mid-twenties and in the process of establishing
a journalistic career in New York City when she met Mark
Rubinstein.

I was on line to board a flight from Chicago to New York when I noticed that there was this really cute guy in line to get on my plane. He was pretty far behind me. The next thing I knew, he was right in back of me, and he asked me a question. So we got in a few minutes' conversation, and then boarded. He went into first class and I went into coach.

Mark was good looking, with blond hair and very blue eyes. Dressed impeccably. After a little while on the plane, he came back and asked if he could sit next to me. We ended up sitting together for the whole flight. He said all the right things; he was asking me a ton of questions. He was interested in my career. I told him that I had applied for a job at a magazine. He told me that he was getting divorced. We had a really great conversation. As we were leaving the airport, he said, "I have to rent a car. Do you want a ride home? I have to go that way anyway."

I found out later that he hadn't been going my way at all. He was going to New Jersey. But he went all the way into Manhattan.

I must say there was a real chemistry. I remember walking in to my apartment and telling my roommate that I'd met the guy I was going to marry. I absolutely knew. It was It. A couple days later, he asked me out. We went to Raoul's. We had a very good talk, and we made another date. And then he called me before that date, and said, "I have to cancel because I'm going to try to get back together with my wife."

What can you do? I totally put him out of my mind. And I got the magazine job I'd applied for. Several months later, Mark called me and told me that it was not going to work out with his wife. So we got together. I can't remember what we did, although he did subsequently do a chart for me, on yellow paper, of our first twenty dates: where we went, what I wore, what we said, what sexual thing went on. He charted our relationship. He was so into me. How could you resist somebody like that? We just knew we were meant to be together.

He had been living with his parents, because his wife had the place in New Jersey. And then he found a place in Manhattan. The day he moved in, I was helping him unpack and I stayed over there, and I basically never left. I just got all my clothes. It was really great. That New Year's, we went down to Florida and had a really romantic time. That summer, we went to Acapulco, to this honeymoon palace, where you have your own pool. We rented a little pink jeep and drove all over.

He had been working for a management consulting firm. I introduced him to a venture capitalist friend of mine, and my friend put together a proposal for Mark to start his own business. Which he did.

One of the things I did for Mark was that I compiled his bio, took off from work, and went around to the various business magazines, trying to get them interested in doing a story on him. One was actually published.

I didn't have a full-time assistant at that point, only temporary help. And one of the temps was this woman named Diana. She was really good, and she wanted to get into business. So I got her a job with Mark.

For the first year we were together, I was really hot to get married. I was not comfortable just living with him. When I first moved in, his divorce hadn't come through yet. I remember him saying to me, "The day after I get divorced, let's get married."

So he had gotten divorced, and we didn't get engaged. He really wanted a period of time to think about his divorce. I put pressure on him and was really pissed. Finally we got engaged.

I always had to prove my love to him. One time, he'd been away on some kind of business trip, and he was passing through Kennedy airport on his way somewhere else. He was going to be at Kennedy for an hour at 4:30 in the morning in the winter. And he wanted me to come meet him. He was like, "Of course you'll do this, if you really love me." So I went.

And he would do these incredible things for me. I'd hired an assistant that I really liked, but she didn't want to stay at the magazine, because they wouldn't pay her enough. So he supplemented her income. He paid her $100 every week. Out of his own pocket.

I was very impressed by him. I thought he was really classy. I really wanted a mink coat, and he bought me part of it, with my mother. He would never travel if he couldn't fly first class. He was a great cook. He had to have a silver Corvette that only seated two. If he ever smelled anyone wearing his fragrance that he found in Paris, he'd change it.

After we got engaged, my mother came to visit. My mother totally knew something was wrong. She told me before she left for the airport, "Just don't get pregnant."

We were planning our wedding, but something didn't feel right. We were more like roommates than a couple that was madly in love. He was always away on business trips with Diana, the temp whom I'd recommended to him. I accused him of having an affair with her. He started crying and said I was right. He said, "I can't help it. We were together in another life."

So we called off our engagement, but decided to try to work it out. I decided that I'd better go to a therapist. I found a guy—he was a real psychiatrist. He listened to my problems, and he said, "You aren't the one who should be here."

So I sent Mark to him. And he started going three times a week, talking about things that had nothing to do with me. His childhood. His wish to make things better for his parents. All this stuff. After he started going to the therapist, we both recognized that we had problems and we had to work on them. We were in repair.

He used to write me poems all the time. Really corny. When you're a professional writer, you don't respect stupid stuff like that. And then he told me, "I really want you to write notes to me and letters to me, like my old girlfriend from college did."

And he opened up these scrapbooks and photo albums full of her letters. "I love you like the sky and the sun...." Stuff like that.

I tried. I gave him one. But it just wasn't me.

He also wanted to save the world. He had a lawyer friend who worked with really helpless people. This friend called me once while Mark was away on business and said, "I have this guy that is wanted by the police, and he needs a place to stay for the night. Can he stay in your apartment?"

I said no. When Mark heard that, he told me that I didn't have any social conscience. He thought that showed my lack of moral character.

I decided I couldn't live like this indefinitely, so I found an apartment. We decided to live apart, date each other, and see where it went. That was the plan.

In the meantime, Mark bought a condo in Florida, and he asked me if I wanted to go down there for Labor Day weekend. I had just moved into my new place the week before, and I told him that I really wanted to stay in the city and get my new apartment together. He decided to go down anyway.

There was a health club in his building, with a masseuse. I made a massage appointment, and I thought I'd go into the apartment and pick up my records and books. So I let myself in—I still had a key. And lying there was a yellow pad. And the heading was "Mark and Susie's wedding."

I have never been so shocked in my life. I'd still thought he and I were going to get married. I knew who Susie was. She was the woman whom he always talked about, his college girlfriend, the one who wrote all those letters. She'd since become a nurse. I later found out that this friend of his, the one whose fugitive friend I wouldn't let stay in the apartment, got them back together. I guess they'd had a couple dates.

It was such a betrayal. I got the number of the condo and I called him up in Florida, and she answered. I just remember the last words I ever said to him: "I hope your flight back home crashes. And you die."

Then I called my mother sobbing. I was in Chicago in three hours. I didn't know where to turn. This is before I had really done therapy, and my whole world was centered around this guy. Looking back on it, I feel like I was in a cult. A cult of one. He had such a hold on me, and I was a naive kid.

It took me a long time to get over it. For years, I went out with guys that I was so much stronger than, so I would never have the problem of being under someone's thumb. I'd say it was three years before I could have a real relationship.

I did hear from him. He sent me a long letter about how he'd been flat on his back for five months and he thought it was from the pain of what he had done to me. He asked me to see him so we could talk about it. Of course, I never answered the letter.

✳   **Leah & James**
Leah Miller was taking a year off from college and living at home in Los Angeles when she met James Kramer, a musician five years older than she.

I was working at the Musicians' Union, doing contracts for musicians and band leaders. James was the musical director for a musical revue in a very cool theater. He was tall and really handsome. He had slicked back hair and a receding hair line.

We became friendly first, but it was always this very serious flirtation. He told me he had just broken up with his girlfriend, Annabel, who was the producer of the show. We started seeing each other, and it quickly became sexual. It seemed to be a really good relationship. I didn't think it was going to be the relationship of my life, because I was only 19. But we had a great time together. We sang all the time. He played the saxophone, the flute and the piano. He was learning the guitar. I really thought he was sort of a genius. He would write music. There'd be music paper all over the place. It was so romantic.

He was a workaholic, which at the time to me seemed really cool. He was really involved in his career, and I was just a student. I didn't know what I was doing. He was into food. We used to cook together. It was an important time for me, just learning about food, wine. He had these very wonderful friends, older people. One was a writer … that guy actually became a mentor for me for many years. I got involved in all these things I wouldn't have otherwise.

But there was always this constant specter of the ex-girlfriend, Annabel, whom I would bump into when I would go to his show. It was always uncomfortable. She was clearly jealous of me, and I couldn't figure out why, because they had broken up. I figured they had been together for a long time.

I was living at my mom's and he moved in too. My mom was crazy about him. And my little brothers were there. So there James and I were, sleeping in my childhood bedroom in the San Fernando Valley. It was great. At some point, the show closed, and he was staying home composing music. He didn't have any source of income. He started helping my mom redo some stuff in her house. Stripping woodwork. I would come home after work, and the three of us would have a cocktail party. A drink and little hors d'oeuvres. It was a very cozy thing. There was just no weirdness about it.

Then I went back to school. And he stayed on at my mom's. He lived there for four months or six months. The idea was that he would help her redo the house. The two of them cooked together and they were very palsy walsy. And then at some point my mom started really being down on him. He moved out.

He wrote me these long letters. He was old fashioned in that way. He had this very elaborate handwriting. He wrote about authors, which it later turned out he hadn't even read. But at some point, I must have started sensing that something was not quite right. I wouldn't be able to find him. He was living in a crummy little apartment in West Hollywood. I'd call him at three in the morning, and he wouldn't be home. Then there'd be some music-related excuse. It bothered me, but my denial level was high at the time. I just pretended nothing was going on. One day I got this weird panicked call from him, and he asked me if I had herpes.

I said, "You know I don't have herpes. And why are you asking anyway?"

He said, "Well, um, because Annabel accused me of giving it to her."

I said, "Aren't we talking ancient history?"

He explained that he'd slept with her once. I totally flipped out. I think it must have been about that time that I started to see other guys. But James and I still had a relationship. When I graduated, I moved back to L.A. and we looked for a place together. We found a place with a couple other friends. But in about three months, he decided to go to Japan for three weeks. He had a brother who was living there. He just never came back from Japan. All I got from him were two postcards. No indication of when he was coming back. I was livid. He was supposed to be living in this house with me and he disappeared. I decided, "Okay, this is over."

So I started seeing someone else. Several months later, I got a phone call. It was James, calling from Hawaii on his way back. Would I meet him at the airport tomorrow? It was my birthday the day he called, and he didn't bother to tell me happy birthday. Because he didn't tell me happy birthday, I said I would not pick him up at the airport. So that's the way we sort of broke up.

He came back, and he kept charming me, so we got back together. We'd been together for three years, and it just wasn't that hard for him to win me back. So he moved back in with me.

One day I got this weird phone call from Annabel. She said, "We've been seeing each other here and there for a long time. I thought it would be a good idea if we just got together and had a drink."

I said sure. She invited me over to her apartment. I remember that James was a little on edge about this. He'd always told me that she was sort of crazy. I went over there, and she was very nice, but she started telling me all these tales about how she and James had been having this ongoing relationship for the last four years. And that they had been sleeping together regularly. I really thought that she was deluded. She made it sound like it had been going on at the time James was living at my mom's house. When she told me, it seemed almost like a crazy person talking. So I sort of laughed, and said, "Oh, that's great."

And then I went home. James opened the door, and he said, "Well, what happened?"

I laughed and said, "You wouldn't believe what she just told me.

She's really out of her mind. She told me you guys have been sleeping together for four years."

I took one look at him, and he was white, and I just knew that it was true.

Everything came clear at that moment, and then we broke up. The reason my mom couldn't stand him anymore, it turns out, was that when he was living with her, he sometimes wouldn't come home until five in the morning. She just didn't have the heart to tell me.

It was totally, totally gut-wrenching. It must have been the most hurt I've ever been. The feeling of being deceived like that. The idea of any kind of love triangle. The idea of being that one person in the love triangle who didn't know. It's humiliating. My parents' marriage broke up when I was an adolescent because my dad was sleeping with his secretary. So this struck terrible nerves for me.

✳ **Evelyn & Duane**
Evelyn Hensler was living in San Francisco when she met and started seeing Duane Bennett, the roommate of a friend's boyfriend, who lived in Sacramento.

Duane and I started seeing each every other weekend or so, and we'd talk on the phone for hours, almost every day. Then it got so we saw each other every weekend. We were really close. He told me that he said things to me that he'd never said to any other woman.

I decided to move to Sacramento. Because of him and because of other reasons. Almost as soon as I got there, he hardly called any more. Rarely came over. When he did come over, he wouldn't spend the night. He'd say, "I left the sprinklers on," or "My cousin's at my house."

I was wondering what the hell was going on. But at the same time, we were talking about getting married. I even introduced him to my mother, who had major reservations about an interracial marriage [Evelyn is white, Duane is black], but she was trying to be open.

Finally, I called him on it one day, and said, "What the hell is going on?"

He said, "I'm really sorry. It's my ex-wife."

I was like, "What's going on? Is it the custody battle for your son?"

And he said, "Yeah. It's just not easy. I need time to myself."

I remember thinking: Poor guy. He's going through so much. I'll just back off.

One night he was working late, and he and I were supposed to be getting together afterwards. And he called and said, "Tonight I just want to go to bed early."

I told him not to worry about it. I had barbecued that day and I thought, "The poor guy's been working hard. He's gone through some tough stuff. I'll take him over some chicken."

We'd been going together for over a year, so I didn't think there was anything wrong with me just going over to his house. It was a hot summer night, and the front door was shut. That was unusual. He always left it open. I walked up with my little bag of chicken, and knocked. I heard laughter inside, and I think I knew what it was, but I just kept thinking that maybe it was the TV.

There I am, standing there like an idiot with my bag of chicken. I hear scurrying, a woman's laughter. And he opens the door. He's in his shorts. He said, "Oh. Hi."

I said, "Hi. What's going on?"

He said, "I'd invite you in, but I have company."

I threw the chicken at him, said something foolish, and went running off. I was seething mad.

I went home. I started thinking of all those other times that I'd called him up, and he'd said he had to go because he had company. I thought of all those times when I'd been over at his house sitting in the living room, and the phone had rung, and he'd gone off to quietly talk in the kitchen. How could I have been such an idiot? I was 32, too old to play this fool's game.

So he called. I said, "What's all this honesty stuff we've been talking about? Did you sleep with her?"

And he said no. And then later he said, "Yeah, of course I slept with her. But it was the first time."

And later on in the conversation, he said that it had been going on for several months. I said, "I want you to come over and get your stuff."

So he came over and got his stuff and said, "I never meant to hurt you. You're the best thing that ever happened to me."

Shortly after we'd broken up, I went to the doctor for a regular
Pap smear, and I found out I had venereal warts in my cervix.
The doctor said he was 99.9 percent sure that it was from sexual
contact. I had to have laser surgery on my cervix. I called Duane
and told him. His response was total denial: "Couldn't have been
from me."

But I hadn't been with anyone else for over a year.

The irony is that in my twenties I'd slept around. And here I
thought I was in a monogamous relationship. I thought I'd found
love. And then I found out from people we knew in common that
he was sleeping with just about anyone ambulatory.

✴   **Wendy & Chris**
*Wendy Lewis spent a semester in England while she was in
college, and looked up Chris Bingham, the boyfriend of her
college roommate. This story differs from others in this
chapter in that rather than being the primary girlfriend who
gets cheated on, Wendy was unknowingly cast as the
secondary girlfriend.*

My roommate told me to look Chris up. I think he came over the second day I was in England, and from then on, we were inseparable.

He was a commodities trader with the metals market, and traded
really early in the morning in England, from 2:00 a.m. to 7 or 8, and
then would get off work and come and see us. Us was this group of
Americans, who all lived in this great little flat that we had all rented. We had the greatest time. Chris would come over and show us
all the sights. I went to a couple of wild parties with him. We'd go
out drinking all the time. I kind of noticed that I would pay for
things a lot, but it wasn't a big deal because I was having fun. We'd
go on weekends in his car. Meanwhile he was also telling me that
his relationship with Martha was basically over.

One weekend we went away to the Cotswolds or somewhere,
and we ended up having an affair. I had fallen for him because he
was so charming and so nice and always fun. Always witty. I was
in a completely new place, and he was one of the natives. It was
really romantic.

But things started to get a little weird. He brought me home—he was living with his parents—and his mother was really strange. She took me aside at one point, and said, "What's going on with Martha?"

I pretended that nothing was happening. I said I didn't know. I didn't understand why she was asking me.

I tried to call him at work one morning, and there was no such workplace. The number didn't exist. So the next day, I asked him, "What's the name of your company again? The number you gave me is wrong."

He said, "Oh, I'll give it to you later. I don't have it with me. I don't know it by heart because no one ever calls me because it's so early in the morning."

One day Martha called me from the States and asked me if I had seen Chris. I said that he'd been showing me the town. I was feeling horribly guilty. Martha said, "He was supposed to be here last weekend. He told me he was going to come, and I even went to get him at the airport."

So I started freaking out. Not only had I deceived her—it had been convenient for me to believe that she and Chris had broken up—but I also started remembering all the things that he did and said that made no sense at all. At this point, I had spent quite a bit of money on him. And he was basically living in our house after he got off work.

His mother called shortly after that and said, "Have you seen Chris? He leaves here at seven in the morning, and we don't see him again until midnight."

I said, "What do you mean? Doesn't he work? What about his commodities job?"

She said, "He's been unemployed for a year."

The mother and I started comparing notes. Chris was 25. We had all thought he was 21. He'd told me that the car he was driving was his, when it was really his parents'. His mother told me there was a case of wine missing from their house. I'd recently bought a case of wine from him. I told her that when he left their house in the morning, he came to ours. Basically, he was a pathological liar.

I had really been charmed and taken in by him. That night, a roommate of mine and I sat down and tried to piece together everything he'd told us.

The money aspect wasn't that big a deal. I'd bought him dinner once in a while. He'd parked himself in our house for eight hours every day and used the phone, while we were all at work or in class. Which is when he called Martha in America. I later got hit with a huge phone bill. The equivalent of five hundred dollars. I sent it to his parents.

I confronted him and he denied everything. He said he would give me his work number, and he could give me references to call, people that worked with him. I said, "I know you're lying."

I never saw him again.

I worried that he had given me some sexually transmitted disease. Once during our affair he had said to me, "I have this funny thing on my penis that I think I should get checked out."

I looked at it and I didn't think much about it. It didn't look that bad, so I didn't take it seriously. After the fact, after I realized he was a pathological liar, I completely flipped out. I went to this clinic somewhere to get tested. I wanted to just wash myself clean.

I wasn't really hurt by Chris, but it made me suspicious of men. I've always said he should have been branded on the forehead, so he couldn't do this to some other person.

✳   **Kate & Lorenzo**
Kate Howe was a student at the University of Wisconsin, when she met Lorenzo Mariani, a student from Italy.

Lorenzo was being set up with my roommate, who was prettier than me, but when a group of us got together that night, he instantly zoned in on me. And I on him. He was dark and exotic, very intense. I instantly gravitate towards people like that. We spent that first night together. He went back to Italy the next day, and started writing me four, five letters a week.

He lied about every single thing in his entire life. And it started that very first night. He told me that he'd had a girlfriend who died of leukemia. He told me that he was a poet—which he was and is—but the story he told was that he was a poet who'd written lyrics for several famous singers in Italy. He told me that he'd been wealthy and that his family had lost its wealth. He told me he'd been a real rabble-rouser and that he'd lived a hedonistic life. And he hadn't. Ironically, he wanted to be more of a bad boy than he actually was. He painted a picture to me that was highly compelling, and it wasn't true.

He continued this whole letter-writing campaign. He sent me poems. Truly ardent letters. Based on seven months of incredibly romantic letters every day, I went over there. I didn't even know him. I'd spent one night with him. I stayed for about four weeks. He took me around Italy, and I stayed with his family. He was the first man I ever had an orgasm with. He opened up a world for me. Another culture, but also sexuality. It was quite amazing. I'm a diehard romantic.

One night we were in Florence and I caught him in one of his lies. I already knew in my gut that the man was a liar. I even suspected it that first night. Everything seemed to fit too perfectly. It was like he zoned in on my psychology and said everything that he knew would spark my interest. I can't remember what the lie was, but I remember a huge fight.

I confronted him with the lie, and he did what every liar knows how to do so well. He acknowledged that part of it was a lie, but he explained why he'd felt the need to lie. In the end, he made me feel bad for accusing him. He deflected it back on me, like it was my problem for being so scrutinizing. He was really skillful.

I was upset at the time, and it made me wonder. I knew that there was something seriously wrong, but it certainly didn't make me want to break up with him. I didn't even consider it.

I dealt with my fears about his lying by denying them. I just couldn't believe that someone would put so much energy into all this artifice. That was youthful naiveté on my part.

The lies got bigger and bigger as time went on, because I would be curious and I'd ask questions. When I was in Italy, he drove me by the house that he told me he'd lived in when he was younger, and that his family had lost. I asked, "Why aren't there any pictures of it?"

And he said, "It so upset my family that they burned everything.... And don't ever bring this up with them because if you do, they won't talk about it."

Some time later, he came back to Madison, where I was in school, and we lived together for an entire year. He was violently jealous of my past. The fact that I, as an American woman, had more of a "past" than he did had been a real sore point for him.

Which was ironic because he was trying to paint this picture of himself as a womanizer, drinker, etc. And yet he was getting jealous that he hadn't slept with as many women as I had men. He was feeling competitive, and at a disadvantage, and he set out to top me.

Unbeknownst to me, the same guy who would go into a violent rage if I made one allusion to an old boyfriend was sleeping with every grad student he could. Finally, at the end of the year, I'd become friends with a lot of the women he was sleeping with. One of them felt divided loyalty to the point that she had to tell me. So she spilled the beans to me three weeks before school ended. She told me that Lorenzo had been sleeping with everybody. Five minutes later I saw him, and he knew instantly that I knew. We had this huge blowout. He didn't have anything to say.

He claimed to love me and want to be with me, but I met someone else around that time. But even if there hadn't been someone else, I would have still broken up. I felt burned. I think the thing that bothered me the most was the heinous double standard: His jealousy of my past had been the biggest issue in our relationship.

Some time later, his sister Donatella came to see me. By that time, I knew Italian pretty well. She stayed at my house—Lorenzo was in Italy at the time. Some of these things he'd told me came up casually in the conversation. One afternoon, everything came out. The part about the wealthy family, the poetry, the dead girlfriend, all of that ... Donatella's jaw dropped to her knees. She said, "These are all lies."

It was very innocent on my part. I hadn't been thinking about trying to confirm these things. It just came up casually. And I found out that everything had been a lie.

Lorenzo entered this horrible period of talking about suicide. I think it was partly because everything had been found out. He didn't have anything any more. Everyone knew what was going on. The following year, he started analysis.

I thought I had him figured out. That he was feeling very inadequate and insecure. When he came to America, his remedy for that was to sleep with as many women as he could. You can't do that in Italy. I think part of the reason he came to America was to be Mr. Exotic Italian Stud. To be the person he always wanted to be, to cure the insecurities that he always had.

We were both symbols to each other. He wanted to become an expatriate. So I became a symbol of coming to America. For me, he was a way of getting out of my world. He was exotic, mysterious ... someone who was definitely different from my upbringing and my father. I don't think I was ever really in love with Lorenzo, but he opened so many doors for me. I'm thankful to him for teaching me so much about life. Had it not been for him, I wouldn't know Italian. I wouldn't have spent so much time there.

These relationships are destroyed by betrayal, and the result is, as Leah put it, "gut wrenching." The discovery of the man's infidelity instantly rewrites history. The passionate and/or comforting routine of the months or years together becomes a corrupted memory, to be picked over by the woman for clues she then blames herself for having missed. A woman burned by a cheater may have a hard time trusting subsequent men. She has become primed to look for the lie; she is braced for more hurt and disappointment.

There are certain qualities many of these cheating men share. They're men of the world, with actively developed interests and busy out-of-the-home lives. The self they present is often built on illusion: They labor over every detail of personal presentation, from their scent to their handwriting.

Many of them also have a tendency to dramatize or otherwise inflate their relationships, almost as if they need to convince themselves that it lives up to some vague ideal. Mark, the guy who picked up Nancy on a plane, is an extreme example, with his 20-date chart, and the various over-the-top love tests he devised. His inflated gesturing seems to have been his only relationship tool: As is the case with many narcissists, his capacity for genuine empathy was underdeveloped. He didn't delve into the couple's real problems, but continued to tend to appearances, to the point of asking Nancy for love poems well after his initial infidelity had compromised their bond.

An unusual focus on the trappings of romance is evident in the frequency of letter-writing in several of these relationships. Leah's boyfriend wrote to her about books he hadn't even read. Kate's lover inundated her with ardent letters from Italy. Melissa's boyfriend wrote poems and cards, as well as apology letters from rehab. And Nancy's boyfriend churned out those sappy poems. It seems significant that these men, whose lives lacked a foundation of truth, appear to have taken so much pleasure in allowing themselves to be extravagantly sentimental on paper.

To hear the women tell it, the men in these relationships didn't seem to be grappling too hard with the necessity of making a choice between women. Even as they talked of marriage, the ideal scenario remained one in which they proceeded undiscovered and didn't have to give anyone up. The breakups in this chapter were painful, but they were also crisp and conclusive. There was no ambivalence on the part of the departing women: No mental gymnastics could negate or excuse the betrayal.

The Cruel Man

The cruel man hurts, frightens or degrades his romantic partners systematically. His cruelty isn't just verbal—it's also conveyed through his attitudes and his actions. The provocation for his outbursts seems to reside in his own psyche, rather than in the behavior or words of the woman with whom he's involved. In fact, he seems to get pleasure or satisfaction from humiliating the woman he ostensibly loves.

I had one fleeting experience—mild by the standards of this chapter—in which a man's verbal aggression came out of the blue, in a moment of intimacy. He and I had just slept together for the first time, and we were lying around afterwards, talking. Apropos of nothing, he said to me, "You know, I tend to like women who weigh five to ten pounds more than you do."

My feeling of comfort evaporated instantly and my mind started to race. Why would anyone mar a warm mood with a remark like that? What was I supposed to do? Apologize for my body? Spring out of bed and start gorging on ice cream? Lash back?

What I did at the time—in order to avoid the necessity of getting up in the middle of the night and storming home—was to make excuses for him. Maybe the sudden intimacy made him anxious, and he had an unconscious need to push me away. Maybe he really *was* just observing my body, and didn't intend the criticism I heard. But in my heart, I didn't—and don't—buy it. A week later, he called me at my office, and proceeded to needle me with a series of personal questions. Then he said, "Do you think we should make another date now?" and went on to rattle off a prohibitive list of his professional and social obligations. I got off the phone quickly.

There was something gratuitously cruel about this man. I feel lucky that I got to see his acid edges before becoming more involved.

The aggressively bilious habits of the men in this chapter surfaced quite early on. In fact, they rarely made any effort to hide their belligerence. Marsha described taking her frightening boyfriend to her senior prom and being horrified by the way he strutted on the dance floor. This seems an apt image for cruel men in general. They project an almost defiant attitude: This is the way I am. Accept it.

The cruelty *isn't* a clever tactic to induce a breakup. Instead, love and the need to inflict pain are closely linked in their emotional makeup. As Polly Logan, one of the women interviewed below, said of her boyfriend: "He was so nuts that he only felt truly cared about if I was screaming at him."

It's tempting to write off the women who retain any interest in these bullies as masochists who somehow feed on the abuse. Certainly some of the women (Polly in particular, Kristin Kane to a lesser extent) were, for a time, complicitous in the dynamic. But the real quality that these women shared was youth. Experience hadn't yet given them tools for recognizing and dealing with a frontal assault.

✳　　**Polly & Henry**

"Do you have a category for psychotic assholes?" asked the chipper, friendly voice of this stranger, whom I had called late one night to interview. Polly Logan is a successful professional who lives in Minneapolis. Her relationship with Henry Preston began in 1976, but more than a decade and a half later her voice still resonated with anger and pain as she talked about it.

She singled out Henry's systematic cruelty as the story's central element.

I was working in a bank in Washington, D.C. and so was Henry. It was an office romance. Both our fathers were in the military, so we bonded talking about what it was like growing up being dragged all over the world by these really rigid authoritarian fathers.

This guy was extremely sensitive. Tortured, actually. I responded a great deal to that. What I didn't realize was that Nora Ephron was right when she said that sensitive men are really in touch with their feelings, but the only feelings they're in touch with are their own. The whole rescuing thing reared its ugly head.

I was 23, he was 27 or 28. He'd been married at 21, and his wife was some years older than he was. And she'd walked out on him. I went out with him for the first time three weeks after the wife had left. I heard all these stories about how she castrated him, and how vicious she was, and how she had tortured him. Poor baby, right?

The first time we went to bed, he was impotent. Poor darling, the wife had castrated him. But we proceeded to have a very intense physical relationship. I've never seen the movie 9½ Weeks, because I always thought it would be too close to the bone. This man was extraordinarily gifted in bed because he was sometimes impotent, and because he had spent seven years trying to please his frigid wife. He knew a lot of great tricks. It was the first time in my life that I was ever given head by a guy who didn't treat it like he was doing me an enormous favor.

We used to do it three or four times a day. We'd come home from work in the middle of the afternoon and have a nooner and go back to the office. It was wonderful. I was so young and so in love.

We had this wonderful intellectual rapport also. He was a reader, and he got all my references, and he was very professorial with me, which he could get away with because I thought he was so much older and so much smarter. He had a banter and a facility for intellectual conversation, especially when he was high, that I was riveted by. We used to read the same books and leave each other notes in the margins.

Then I walked in and caught him in the act of giving oral sex to another woman. I'd been basically living in his house. I only went home to pick up my mail. One night, his parents were having a cocktail party, and he told me that I was not invited because he had to bartend. He came home that afternoon and made love to me, and he showed me a box in which there were four corsages. One for his mother, and one for each of his sisters. I later found out that one of his sisters was not at the party, and the fourth corsage was for my rival. He'd expected me to exclaim over the corsages.

Some friends of ours who lived down the street from him had invited me over for supper and they were going to drive me to my house, but I ended up staying overnight with them. I'd left my purse and my raincoat sitting on his kitchen table. I don't think the door was even locked when I came by the next morning to get my stuff. He had hidden my purse and my raincoat.

I walked up the stairs, and I could see his ass, and it was moving funny, and I wondered why he was so far down on the bed. And as I took another step, I saw these other legs. Of course, I'm short and plump, and this woman was one of Hitchcock's blonds. Long, long, long legs, no breasts, long hair.

I was so ashamed—it was as if I had walked in on my parents. I turned around and I walked back down the stairs. If I had been able to find my coat and purse, I would have just left. But I had no bus fare. I had no money for a cab.

So I slammed the front door. And his feet hit the ground. He came downstairs still partially erect. He was horrified. He was caught. I asked where my purse was. He'd hidden it under the cabinet where the pots and pans were. I said, "I'm really sorry I've interrupted you," and I turned around and I walked out. And took a cab home.

People say: Is there one minute in your life that you would like to relive? What I wish I had done is gotten a pail full of water and put ice cubes in it, and gone back up the stairs and thrown it on them. And then I would have thrown her clothes out the window. She'd had to move my nightgown off the bed to get in it.

It turns out he had been lying to me all summer. He'd told me things like he was going sailing on the Chesapeake Bay and I wasn't invited because there was only room for three on the boat. When in fact he was taking someone else. This had been going on for as long as he'd been seeing me.

After this incident, my father came and picked me up and took me home. My mother said, "If you go back to him, we'll disown you."

Thank you very much. What set me up for the whole relationship with Henry was my relationship with my father. He was very verbally abusive. When I was a teenager, we moved four times in four years, and I gained some weight because I was so unhappy. My father told me that I was fat and ugly, and that no one would ever love me. And so I found someone who was going to make that true.

I got the bus back to Washington, and I called Henry up, because whatever I was getting from him was better and more satisfying than whatever I was getting from my family. The really sad part is that I stayed with him for another 2½ years.

He told me that his relationship with [the other woman] was a temporary aberration brought on by the trauma of his divorce. And that he had started going out with me much too soon after he'd split from his wife. I had come into his life, and he wasn't ready to make a commitment. I remember, even as young and as stupid as I was then, I said, "Well, this is not the way to do it. If you want to date other people, fine. Just don't lie about it."

She was the first of five affairs that he had during the years that we were together. I found another woman's banana bread in the refrigerator. I remember once I found another woman's hairpin in the bed. I was like, "What the hell is this?"

And he said, "It must be yours."

And I said, "I don't use black bobby pins."

He goes, "It probably belongs to the maid."

And I said, "We don't have a maid."

Fortunately, this was all happening in the late '70s, so AIDS wasn't a worry. This would be life-threatening behavior now. He lied. He was incapable of telling the truth. He was so nuts that he only felt truly cared about if I was screaming at him. Apparently his mother had been really weird, so he didn't recognize love unless the woman was frothing at the mouth.

We would have really intense wonderful honeymoon periods, with him trying to woo me back. As soon as he got me back, and as soon as I relaxed and felt in love with him again, something funny would happen. Tension would start to escalate, and I would suspect that something with another woman was going on. And he would lie, and say that I was imagining things, that I was crazy.

And what happened was that I would lose touch with my own reality. His reality was preferable to mine. If I bought into his, then I didn't have to leave him. So I would buy it, and then three months later, I would find out that no, I had been absolutely right in my suspicions. It made me nuts.

He had a little schoolhouse out in the country in Virginia that he was renovating. One weekend, he went out and said I couldn't come because he was going to be climbing down into the empty cistern to do some work. So he came back with mosquito bites all over his butt. Now explain that. I found out three months later that, yes indeed, he had taken one of my rivals out to the schoolhouse.

In order to compete with these other women, I had to do really kinky stuff. To be different. So I consented to a threesome with a woman whom he'd been having an affair with while he was married. I did not enjoy it. It was one of the worst experiences of my life. There's nothing like being in love with a man and watching him make love to another woman. And feeling like I had to do it to keep him interested, or else he would go off and screw one of my rivals.

Eventually, I started getting stronger, and I put my foot down, and I said, "This is not going to go on."

So he put a ring on my finger. He said he would marry me. Anything but change, right?

I said, "Look, I'm not going to marry a man I can't trust. If you lie to me again, it's over."

I remember sitting in my office at one point, planning the kind of wedding I wanted. I had a ring on my finger. I got into some kind of self-hypnotic state, and I was kind of trancing on what this wedding would be. We were going to have a country brunch, and we were going to have a mutual friend, who was a new age hippie minister, marry us. It was going to be outside on an Oriental rug. Country fiddlers. I'm picturing showing my family around the property. Opening the door to Henry's pottery studio and finding him in flagrante with another woman.

I realized, I can't trust this man to be faithful to me on my wedding day. Do I want to be married to someone like this? I realized, I don't want to marry him. I realized I could not trust him to tell me the truth about going to the corner store to buy cigarettes. It took me 2½ years to get to the point where I could see: This is not acceptable to me.

Why did it take me so long to realize this? For one thing, it was the first time that I was ever part of a couple and having regular sex. That was very powerful. The good sex continued all the way through the relationship, until the bitter end. The sex stopped when I realized that I had to turn off my mind in order to enjoy sex. I had to shut down the healthy part of myself that was telling me that this was not good for me.

I thank God I didn't marry him. But getting off him was like getting off heroin. I left town eventually because of this relationship. I had to get out of Washington. Our friends refused to choose, even though he had been so abusive to me. One of my best friends at the time said, "Well, you put up with it all this time, we figured it just wasn't that bad for you. When you guys broke up, he was the one who was hurting because you'd left him."

He's married now for the third time, and this man is so evil that he tortured each woman individually with a different thing. I was so insecure about my body—I'm short and rounded—and so insecure about my desirability that he tortured me with women who were tall and slender. He was so intelligent that he was just unerring in choosing his torture. The woman he married six months after I left him had two children, and he tortured her by being abusive to her children.

I didn't get involved with anybody else for years, because I was so afraid of being in another man's sexual thrall that way. I had been so much in his power physically that I didn't want to let anyone else close to me. To this day—I'm 40 years old—I've never married, and when my mother sighs about it, I can always say, "Look Mom, I could have married Henry."

That shuts her right up.

There was a series of letters that got exchanged years afterwards. He writes very well. His parting shot to me was, get this: "The true impotence is the impotence of a woman unable to engender love in others."

Don't you think that has rankled ever since? I had to admire him for hitting it right on the head. What a terrible thing to say, but you couldn't hurt me worse if you tried.

I was defenseless when I was involved with him. My nickname was Thumper, from Bambi. To trample on an innocent, the way he did on me, was evil. When he got high, we would have these discussions about whether innocence should be protected or not. And he would say to me, "Better I should do this to you than someone else. Because I love you and I'm doing it better."

✳ **Marsha & Vince**

Marsha Warren is now in her mid-twenties. Her relationship with Vince Taylor took place when she was sixteen. Her story differs from Polly's in that, rather than feeling emotional hurt, she felt physical fear.

I met Vince when I was doing research for a history report at the library at West Point. He was a cadet. They all looked so great and so patriotic in uniform. He and I started dating. They had dances, and my friends and I would go, and everything seemed fine.

In the beginning, he was larger than life. He seemed to be the perfect gentleman. He took me to places on the West Point campus that visitors don't usually get to go. The whole thing was very romantic. He was funny. He had stories. He was from the midwest. It kept giving me more excuses to go back to West Point, which felt like freedom. Too early, I invited him to go to my Senior Prom.

Then one day I had the day off from school, and he asked me to go to New York City with him. He showed up at my door in head-to-toe black leather. My mother nearly had a heart attack.

It was a shock, realizing that this man was totally different out of uniform. I just assumed—if you're picked for West Point.... But those boys love guns. They love the whole macho appeal. They like having someone to defend. I was young, and he picked up on that.

He took me to the city. He was buying gadgets at head shops and Harley-Davidson stuff. Knuckle gloves with spikes on them. He was on this whole power trip of how he was going to protect me. He was dragging me around by the wrist. I was shaking the whole time.

He was totally sexist, racist. It was day and night between the man I met and was attracted to and this very frightening, violence-prone man.

After that day, I began to see this side of him more and more. When I would try to reason with him, he was very forceful. He was Mr. Macho. I think my first response was denial. I thought I could change him. Or maybe it was me—maybe I was a prude. And then after a while I got frightened, and then I decided that I didn't want to have anything to do with him.

I didn't know how to break up with him. I had no experience breaking up. And I didn't want to tell any of my friends. Or certainly not my parents. But then I found out from his classmates that he was on probation at West Point, that he wouldn't last much longer. I just had to hang on until he was kicked out, which he was, quite soon. He still came to my prom. Just the way he danced was scary. He was strutting around. I was mortified, but I also got very frightened.

He finally left for his home in the midwest. He kept calling me. I guess he got prom pictures sent to him at home. He wanted to marry me. I said, "I'm not interested. We better break this off."

The whole thing lasted maybe six months. There was one time I was so nervous I threw up. I feel like I came out of it okay, but there are still nights when I wake up and think about it. I can't look at my prom pictures. My whole memory of high school ends with a sour note.

I'd gotten to the point where I would have done anything so there wouldn't be violence. Emotionally, it messed me up. I didn't know how to see my strength in the whole thing. I just counted myself lucky that I escaped.

✳ **Laura & Rick**
Laura Rohmer is a Manhattan-based journalist, with a husky voice and a wry sense of humor, who gives the impression of having leapt out of the womb ready and able to take care of herself. Her story is different from the others in this chapter in that the man she was involved with was more strange and unpleasant than outright cruel. Rick Brooks didn't hook her, he creeped her out. She says, "He's one of those people that I never admit that I went out with. Not a lot of people know and the ones that do have the decency to never mention it."

Rick wasn't very nice to me, or in general. He wasn't very attractive. He was sort of powerful in his chosen field and I suppose that attracted me. But I think what really attracted me was that I wasn't going out with anyone else.

I met him at a dinner party and he pursued me hotly. He was in the music business. He invited me to some big industry event that he was involved in. He was going to be a big cheese. That was very smart of him—it showed him off to his best advantage. It was a black tie thing, and I bought a backless evening dress to wear. I'd rarely been to events like that, and here I was, with the boss. (And I don't mean Bruce Springsteen.)

He was a pretty weird guy. I think I thought he couldn't be as weird as he seemed. He couldn't be as mean as he seemed. If I only looked harder, I would find something about him that was appealing.

He pursued me. He called me all the time. At the beginning he was reasonably charming over the phone. I really think it was more the pursuit than anything else. Even at the time, though, I sort of knew better. It's hard, when you're not seeing anybody, to remember that you get to choose too, if someone's making such a point of choosing you. In a way, the fact that he wasn't so terribly well-liked, that he didn't have many friends, made it all the more appealing that he would choose me. He didn't like 90 percent of the people he knew, but he liked me. That was flattering. I must really be better than 90 percent of the people in the world. When in fact I was just an easier mark for a lunatic.

He never let me in his apartment. For a long time, it wasn't an issue. We weren't sleeping together, so we'd meet in restaurants. Or he would come pick me up. Or I would go and pick him up, at his apartment and he'd buzz and say, "I'll be right down."

But then there was this time when we had to go to a party near his house. Which was uptown. And it really would have made sense to meet at his apartment and have a drink there first. Something like that. He said, "We can't do that. I don't want you to come up."

I said, "I've seen dirty apartments before."

And he said, "I really don't want you to come up."

And then it came up another time. I thought to myself, well, alright, he has an eccentricity. He has a thing about his space. But then it was getting to be more than an eccentricity.

It became pointed. I would ask him point blank why I couldn't see his apartment. And he'd say, "Well, I just don't do that."

At some point, I had told my parents about him. God only knows why. I guess because it was the 900th time they had asked me if I was seeing anybody. He had this big job. So I thought it would get them off my back a little bit.

I did tell them that he wouldn't let me in his apartment. I sort of told them as a joke. An aside. My father, God bless him, picked up on it, and brought it up several times. It was not like my father. He was upset. And worried. Worried about what was going on in that apartment. He actually told me that he had a friend, an old guy, who had hired a private detective to sneak around on this guy that his daughter was seeing. The detective had discovered that the guy was married. My father wanted to do this for me, because he thought that he was going to find out that Rick was married. It was so sweet and protective of my father, and so out of character. I almost would have let him do it. But I started to think, Am I prepared for what I might find out about this guy?

He was never outright mean to me. But he got less attentive. If the thing that attracted me was that he was pursuing me, and he wasn't pursuing me as hard anymore, it was like: So why am I doing this?

We started to talk about going on a vacation together. It was one of those things that started with one of us saying casually, "Oh, we should go there some time." The next time I talked to him, he asked me, "What do you think about these dates?" It was clear to me that I didn't want to go.

So I said, "I don't think we should go on this vacation, and as matter of fact, this isn't really happening for me."

He became incredibly verbally abusive on the phone. Stuff like: "After I've spent all this time and money on you..." And then he said: "Who do you think you're ever going to get? I don't know who else you're going to find that's going to be interested in you."

I was freaked out, but I wasn't hurt. I was scared of him.

He's one of those people that I wouldn't be all that surprised to hear something really horrible about. That he killed somebody. That he was found in his apartment with dead bodies.

✳ **Kristin & Carter**
Kristin Kane is in her late twenties. Her relationship with Carter James took place three years ago. She described how she kept on giving in the relationship, hoping things would improve: "It's like when you keep going back to the refrigerator, even though you know there's nothing in it. It's that hopeful thought: This time when I open it, something will be in there."

This story took place during a very lonely period of my life. I had moved to Washington, D.C. about six months earlier. I didn't have a boyfriend. I didn't really have that many friends. I was working in the Senate. And there was a coffee shop in the basement that I would go to a lot, just to sit and escape. There was an incredibly handsome guy who I would see in the coffee shop all the time. His hair was graying but he had a chiseled, youthful face. The kind of guy women would universally agree is gorgeous. I'd stare at him and catch him staring at me. I developed this huge crush on him.

I started thinking about him all the time. I'd go down there hoping to see him. My stomach would start quivering when I saw him. This went on for months. I sought advice from people. What could I do? How could I possibly find out who this guy was? How could I get to know him better?

One day I went down there for coffee, and he was sitting there with two other young guys. And the three of them were completely staring at me. Which thrilled me. And then this other guy walked in and started talking to them, and I was able to overhear what senator the guy I liked worked for, and exactly what his job was.

I was all excited. I got up and immediately went upstairs and I called the senator's office. And I pretended that I wanted to send some material to this person whom I'd met at a reception a couple of weeks ago, but I couldn't remember his name. So I found out his name: Carter James.

For a couple weeks, I sat on this knowledge. And tried to figure out what to do with it. I kept hoping he would talk to me. A couple times we were sitting at tables right next to each other, but he still didn't say anything. And I wasn't going to say anything.

Finally, I did this incredibly bold thing. I've never done anything like this before. I wrote him a letter saying, "You don't know my name, but I think you know my face. I see you a lot in the coffee shop. I'd really love to have a chance to get to know you better. Do you want to have a drink?"

I made this high school girl who worked in my office deliver it. I gave her all these elaborate instructions on how to do it. And I put my name and telephone number on it. I was sitting at my desk, and I got a call, literally ten minutes later. He was really gruff. Almost antagonistic. He was like, "Which one of my friends put you up to this?"

I was so shocked. I said, "What do you mean? No one."

He said, "Come on. I know this is a joke. Who told you to do it?"

It took me ten minutes to convince him that it wasn't a joke. And then he finally said to me, "Do you know what today is?"

I said I didn't. And he said, "It's April first."

I said, "Look, I'm completely embarrassed. This is the most embarrassing thing I've done in my entire life. But I swallowed my pride and did it because I completely want to go out for drinks with you. If you don't want to ever see me, that's fine. Please just don't tell everyone in the Senate about this."

We met for drinks that night. And as soon as he saw me, he knew who I was. He was totally gorgeous. We went for drinks at this bar. I was completely in love with him. We spent three hours at this bar. Talking. Laughing. We had the greatest time. I thought we were a match made in heaven.

But that night I noticed the first sign that something was kind of weird. We stayed in the bar until so late that all the subways had closed. I didn't have a car at the time, I was living with my parents. I was going to take a cab home to Georgetown. But he lived way out in the suburbs. He started putting all this pressure on me to drive him home, which I didn't really feel comfortable doing, because it was my parents' car. But I was so anxious to please him that we ended up taking a cab back to my parents' house. And I asked my dad if I could borrow the car to take him home. And he said that it was too late. And I asked to at least borrow the car to drive him to the subway stop. I was lying, because I knew the subway was closed. I borrowed the car and I drove him home anyway. My dad was furious.

I was completely obsessed with him. Over the next three or four months, we had this relationship. But he would never call me. I would always have to call him. I would ask myself why he didn't call me. Did it mean he didn't like me? But I would justify it somehow. Oh, he's really busy. Or he likes me, but he's just shy.

At one point, we made plans to get together on a weekend. He totally blew me off. He never called me. I called him and I told him I was really pissed. And he wanted to meet me to talk. I met him, and I said, "You just can't do that to people. Say you're going to go out with them and then never call them. It really hurt my feelings."

He acted so sincere. He was like, "You're right. I'm sorry. I'm not a bad guy. I ended up going away for the weekend."

We never slept together but a couple of times I ended up giving him blowjobs. One time, I did it in a car because there was nowhere for us to go. We started making out and he asked me. He said something like, "That really turned me on when you did that before. Can you do it again?"

We were parked on a street, and there were people walking by. I did it. Looking back on it, I can't believe how I debased myself with this guy. I really wanted him to like me.

He gave nothing back. He never did anything. I don't know if he ever even bought me dinner. He was fun and charming, but he was always a little bit weird. Volatile.

Another time we were in my parents' house. I don't know where they were. We were making out in the kitchen. And he started talking really dirty to me. In this really crude way. No one in my life had ever done this. I was so shocked. I was not turned on, but I remember thinking, well maybe I've just been with really staid guys. And I'm really naive, and this is what grownup people do.

The Senator I was working for at the time was trying to pass this legislation against violent pornography. I could certainly understand the First Amendment issues this raised, but anyone who is normal would say that the pornography itself was reprehensible. Disgusting. I was telling Carter about how I was doing research, and I'd had to get a hold of this one particular video. It was the most horrible violent thing. I'd had to watch part of it, and I hadn't been able to do it. I'd had to leave the room. I was telling him about this, and he was like, "I love that stuff."

I nudged him with my elbow—funny joke. And he was like, "No I think it's great. The more blood the better."

We went to a reception on the Hill. He flirted with other women in the room. The party ended and we were both really drunk, and we decided to go back to where he now lived, which was in sort of a dangerous area. Once I got there, I kept thinking that I should leave. He was doing nothing to make me comfortable. He wasn't sitting next to me with his arm around me. Nothing. But I was thinking to myself that if we didn't do it that night, we would never do it. We'd been seeing each other off and on for four months, and we'd never had sex. So finally I said something like, "I'm going to go," and he said, "Okay, if you want to." And I was like, "What do you want me to do?"

Anyway, we ended up making out and then we ended up having

sex. It was the worst sex of my life. It was completely devoid of feeling. He kissed me for 30 seconds, and then he was trying to have intercourse with me, and of course I was completely not excited at all. It was painful. I said, "You know, this really hurts me."

And he was like, "You love it. You love the pain."

Then he rolled over immediately afterwards and he fell asleep. He was totally asleep, and I was in this dangerous area, and I didn't want to stay there any longer. I felt completely weird. So I got up and left him a sweet note and I ran to my car, cause I figured a rapist wasn't going to get someone who was running. I drove home.

That was a Thursday night. I was thinking for sure he would call me to see if I'd gotten home okay. He didn't call me Friday morning or Friday afternoon or Friday night. I was seething. I was trying to keep my mind off of it, but I was so mad. Saturday morning, he still hadn't called and I just decided I was going to call him. I called him, he picked up the phone and was like, "Hey." I was trying to get some recognition that he had slept with me. I was like, "So I thought you might want to know if I got home okay."

He said, "Yeah, well, I figured you had. Look, I'm studying right now. I can't really talk."

So I hung up the phone with him. And something clicked. Literally. Something happened that morning. It was ten years of trying to make men happy, trying to appease men. Over and over again. Even though I wasn't getting anything from them. I snapped. I took a shower. I blowdried my hair. I got dressed. I was completely driven. I put in one earring but I forgot to put in the other. I was disheveled but so focused. I got into my car and I drove to his house and I banged on his door. He opened the door.

I had left this pearl necklace at his house. He opened the door, and asked me what I was doing there. I looked at him and I said, "I want my jewelry right now."

He went and got it and handed it to me. And I spun around and I walked away. I didn't even say goodbye. I never saw him again.

As I was walking away, I thought to myself, I don't need to do this anymore. That was enough. That was as low as I had to go.

And then I found out, like four months later, that I had herpes. And I knew it was from that guy.

Men are not inanimate objects. They think. They move. They

speak. You can judge them from the words they use. From their actions. You can make a judgement. You can say, this is not someone who is going to make me happy. This is not someone who has something to offer me. And likewise, you can say this is someone who is going to be good to me, who is kind, who is supportive.

I think the question that a lot of women fail to recognize is: How vigilant are you going to be about yourself? Are you going to set high standards for the people you're with? We need to say: I know myself. I know what I need. I know what makes me feel good in a relationship, and I'm going to demand that I have these things. And if I don't get them, I'm not going to be in one.

The manifestations of these men's gratuitous cruelty verge on the imaginative. Henry showed Polly her rival's corsage and pressured her into a sexual threesome. He talked almost gleefully about how his love for her impelled him to destroy her Thumperesque innocence. Kristin's boyfriend asked her for a blowjob on a crowded street, praised violent pornography, told her "You love the pain." Describing these degradations in retrospect, the women sound astonished. In the moment, they simply reacted, only partially registering the humiliation, while at the same time allowing their hopes for the relationship to mute their awareness of the cruelty.

Because these men were, in fact, offering something. Henry had a sort of dangerous brilliance: Beyond exerting simple charm, he appealed to Polly's newly awakened sexuality, her alienation from her family, her love of books and ideas, her wish to heal and nurture a wounded partner. Polly is insightful about the interplay between the good and bad aspects of the relationship. She describes having numbed her suspicions because she so badly needed the fulfilling things that Henry offered.

The appeal of the other men is less clear. Neither Marsha nor Laura can be said to have been in love with their boyfriends. But Laura's scenario—getting involved because nothing else is going on—is probably more common than traditional relationship discourse lets on. What single woman hasn't at some point said to herself: Well, okay, I'll go out with him. No one else is asking. What do I have to lose?

Kristin's story has such a delicious beginning that she went on to craft a great romance in her mind. She threw herself into the process of making it happen, and, in her flurry of activity, lost the perspective that would have allowed herself to wonder: Why does he never call? Isn't all of his behavior a little off? What am I getting out of this?

In each of these cases, the women were the ones to quit the relationship. What's striking, though, is not that the women left, but rather that they didn't leave sooner. Just as audiences want to shout out warnings to the woman in the horror movie who's descending into the basement, reading these women's stories provokes the urge to intervene. To tell them: "Get out of there. NOW!"

Polly clearly stayed with Henry longer than others might have: Many women would have been out the door after the first incident of infidelity. Even among those who might have forgiven him once, most would not put up with a second breach of trust. But Polly came to her relationship with a resounding loneliness, and credited Henry with keeping the void at bay. Although she eventually came to see, with crushing clarity, how damaging the relationship was, leaving him meant giving up the only family she knew.

Marsha was terrified, plain and simple. She was afraid that if she rejected Vince, she might spur him to violence. And Kristin was immersed in the hope that the relationship might grow into something approximating her fantasy.

Although these women suffered little ambivalence about making the break from their cruel partners, a bad taste lingered nonetheless. Given our society's propensity for ascribing to women an inherent masochism, it's not surprising that these women had to contend with a sense of self-loathing. As Marsha said, "I didn't know how to see my strength in the whole thing."

But as a woman's relationship experience accrues, her sense of what she wants tends to evolve as well. Kristin described the Carter relationship as a bottoming out. Shortly after her Saturday morning epiphany, she met and began dating a supportive and kind man, whom she said she might have completely dismissed before the Carter debacle.

Wounded Men

The wounded man is operating at a deficit. He needs to be given more than he's capable of giving out. The guy with sexual problems is incapable of satisfying sex. The nonfunctional man is depressed, unable or unwilling to hold down a job, often wallowing in self-pity as he lolls glumly around the house. Some crucial part of the addict's attention is locked in on the substance he depends on—meaning that the woman in his life can't expect dependability, commitment or growth. The immature man is so lost in his own wishes for attention that his partner's needs fall through the cracks.

These men have ceded responsibility for leading productive adult lives and for shaping mature, mutually supportive relationships. Their behavior often seems determined by the struggle with some deep-seated inner pain, which they are not identifying or grappling with head-on. The result is that they give only partial attention to the women in their lives.

Involvement with one of these men casts a woman in one or both of two undesirable positions. She may try to change the man. Or she may try to maneuver around his needs. In either case, she becomes a caretaker of sorts and her own desires—for good sex, for her partner's support of her career, to feel loved—take a back seat.

What's in it for her? Why does she stick around with a man who clearly has so little to give? In some cases, the women have fallen in love before recognizing the problem. Some of these men had genuine charisma and brilliance, and a portion of the connection was vital and real. And if the beginning was heady, the woman may have been slow to give up hope. As one woman said: "This was going to be the guy.... I had already cast him in the role, and when he fell short, I kept forgiving."

But love was by no means always present. In some of the stories in this section, it seemed clear that the woman was not all that smitten, but she was also not at all convinced that she deserved better. She badly wanted to be in a relationship—

and she feared that this was her only option. In fact, she may have considered this kind of man a "safe" choice—if he needed her so much, he wouldn't leave.

In these cases, the caretaking urge seemed to grow out of the *woman's* deep loneliness and internal pain. She craved love and attention, and she gave what she longed to receive. This impulse to give may also have been fed by cues from the woman's family history: If she grew up watching her mother put aside her own ambitions to support her father, she may, on some unexamined level, have believed that she should do the same thing.

The most common reason that the relationships in this section ended is that the woman simply got angry about or tired of putting her own needs on hold. In ten out of fourteen of the following stories, it was the woman who departed. She just became too frustrated, too unsatisfied to stay.

Of the four men who ended things, two were guys with sexual problems who just knew that things would never work out. More significant is the fact that both the men in the nonfunctional chapter were the ones to call it quits. The women who loved them are among this book's most long-suffering and their two stories demonstrate a harsh truth: Self-sacrifice may mollify in the short-term, but it's no guarantee that a relationship will last.

Unlike the stories in the "Aggressive" section, most of these women were not handed flashing behavioral signs that clearly signalled: Exit now. (The women who loved addicts are the exception.) Instead, they were confronted with men with potential, but with intractable personal blocks. Each woman had to take the measure of her own frustration, and come to her own conclusion about when to give up.

Looking back on a relationship with a wounded man, a woman may feel disgusted with herself. She may ask herself why she didn't trust her instincts or why she was so willing to accept such a third-rate romance. She may recognize, to her dismay, the ways that she transmogrified herself into a compliant (but quietly angry) creature in order to please her man.

To the extent that she uses these perceptions to develop a better read on the kind of relationship she wants, one of these involvements can be a life lesson. To the extent that she comes out of the relationship focusing on her own shortcomings, the experience is a discouraging failure.

The Sexually Troubled Man

In any given year, I have a couple dozen discussions about sex with close female friends. These talks incorporate certain unacknowledged rituals. We take for granted that we're comfortable trading intimate details. We show off a little as we detail our imaginative fantasies or our latest erotic experiments. We matter-of-factly allude to our lovers' ardor, and act nonchalantly wise about the ways in which we've come to understand our own sexuality. No one eavesdropping on these conversations would hear the slightest suggestion that sex can ever be indifferent, unincredible— or worse.

Women in their twenties and thirties have grown up taking the sexual revolution for granted. Sure, things have gotten more conservative over the last decade, as the risk of AIDS has eclipsed the allure of promiscuity. But if we've retreated from the rampant pursuit of experience, certain attitudes persist from those days.

Many women I know feel self-imposed pressure to have great sex all the time. Sexual inhibitions are supposed to be as faint a memory as the Eisenhower administration. Women should know what we want in bed, this line of thinking goes, and how to ask for it. The sheer joy and animal optimism of our sexuality should be enough to turn our men on in return.

In the stories that follow, the sex did not work. And the woman's forceful sexuality was not enough to fix things. These are the anecdotes that may well get buried or played down when we confide in our friends, because they don't jibe with the image of sexual confidence that we like to project. And because these stories aren't in common currency, women suffering from a bad-sex relationship don't necessarily have the ready "you're not alone" comfort usually available from female peers.

The result is that the damage these relationships can cause is magnified, as women take on themselves a large portion of the blame for the failure to connect sexually.

The actual stumbling blocks varied in the stories that follow. The common denominator was that each woman saw, in her relationship's sexual breakdown, her own deep insecurities reflected back on herself.

✳   **Sarah & Arthur**
Sarah Powell had ended her ten-year marriage about a year before meeting Arthur Pittman. His history (17 years in a sex cult) is unusual, but the psychological gymnastics he provoked—her shifting of focus from legitimate doubts about the relationship to an unremitting effort to please him—are common.

I met Arthur at a time when I was feeling that I had to try to get back into the world, and back into dating. I wanted to be with someone. I had no center. I started talking to Arthur at a book party. I knew that there was no way I was going to be in love with him, but he was smart and nice, and he asked me out for coffee right after the party. Then I left for a vacation in California, and he left me a message while I was gone, and I called him when I got back, and we started to date.

He was very encouraging of me. He kept telling me that I was smart, and that I should be more confident. Those were very big issues for me. And he was a very good kisser. The first time we kissed, it was really passionate.

But he also told me up front that he had been involved in a sex cult for 17 years. From when he was 18 until just a few years before I met him. He had been married, and he and his wife had both been involved. All the members lived in the same area, and the cult leader would dictate who would sleep with whom. They'd all have their jobs and their lives, but they would spend every weekend together, and have long discussions about who should sleep with whom. Maybe they'd all do it in the same room, or sometimes they'd go to different rooms. He'd be there with his spouse, and they'd each have sex with someone different.

He only got out of it because the cult leader died, around which point his marriage also broke up. When I met him, he was going to a shrink five days a week. I should have nicely bagged things when I found out about all this, but he was giving me so much in terms of helping me to look at myself.

As you can imagine, sex was a very loaded, bizarre concept for him. He was drawn to me in a sincere way. He felt something with me that he hadn't felt much before. But intercourse left him numb.

It wasn't like he was cold or unemotive in bed. In a sense he could be passionate, but it was anguished. There were times he looked like he was in intense pain. The theme between us became: Could we find ways to have sex that would excite him? We'd have sex, but when it came to actual orgasm, he'd say, "Well, my penis is numb."

I tried as hard as I could. I got to the point where I would have stood on my head if I had thought that it would make things work. I was forgetting that he wasn't all that attractive, that I knew he was wrong for me. I just tried. And cried.

I was in a phase when I felt like I had a lot to prove. I remember this time that I wore my prettiest, sexiest bra. We went to bed, and I whipped my shirt off to show him. He stopped cold and said, "I have to be honest. It really repulses me to see you in that underwear. You're trying too hard. It's too aggressive."

I was speechless. I think I hid in the bathroom and cried.

He'd work and agonize over having an orgasm. And every time he succeeded, there would be a period of evaluation afterwards. He'd say, "Well, that one was better." Or: "I actually felt a little something with that one."

He would acknowledge that our sex had excited him some. He was "strangely moved." Or "strangely aroused." He would just analyze it all.

He really wanted to get married. Not to me, necessarily. He'd been engaged before he met me, and they'd had the same problem. He would describe to me all the lengths they'd gone to, to try to make it work sexually. For her to arouse him sexually. They'd tried to make it work, and it hadn't.

The one thing that would really excite him was if I stimulated him anally. If I'm really attracted to someone, I'll do whatever two people can do in bed. But I realized that I wasn't that attracted to him, and I would be stimulating him anally when he was inside me. It was an enormous amount of work, but it was also a little humiliating. It grossed me out.

Very quickly after that, I ended things. It was actually very easy to end, because he'd separated me out: Weekends he could see me, during the week nothing could get in the way of his work. So it wasn't like life changed that dramatically. I also met someone else—thank goodness. Because I was in a vulnerable phase of my life where I might have gone on for a while, trying to make the unworkable work.

We had this nice, sweet conversation on the phone one night, where we agreed that it had been nice, but that it wasn't working. I've never had that experience before, where you basically know you're never going to see the other person again.

✳   **Roberta & Ralph**
Roberta Willard told the story of her relationship with Ralph Crane, which took place approximately three years ago. Despite his stated wish to have a serious relationship, Ralph in fact seems to have been deeply ambivalent. His complaints about sex served as an effective—if indirect—device to forestall intimacy.

I placed a personal ad in *The New York Review of Books*. It said: "Auburn-haired petite French-speaking beauty, 32, empathetic and eclectic, professional by day, artist/singer by night, seeks sophisticated, creative warmhearted good-looking beau, 29-41. Photo, not necessarily of you, optional."

I got some pretty good responses, but Ralph was the nicest one. He was a college professor, French speaking, had traveled a lot. He'd written a few books. He invited me out to a play, a proper date.

It was fun. I thought, I'd like to see him again. But things didn't progress in the way that they usually do with me. Which is pretty rapidly. Usually I know right away if I want someone to kiss me on the mouth. And I couldn't tell with him. We went out Saturday nights for about a month before we kissed.

He was smart. He had tenure. He was affectionate. Sweet. Gentle. He had beautiful blue eyes and a good sense of humor. But I wasn't in love with him at first sight. It's more like I said to myself: This one will be really good for me. I thought, this guy could be serious long-term material. I'll give it a try.

I do remember thinking that it was telling that most of the other women he'd been involved with had been much younger than he was. He reported having one girlfriend who had been about 19 years old, when he was 36. Her father used to drop her off for their dates.

It was when we started to make love that the trouble started. After a few nights together, he started asking me, "Why can't you come during intercourse, without clitoral stimulation?"

It came out that he was really feeling offended and upset by the fact that I couldn't do this. He said every other woman that he'd ever been with had been able to. It began to be a real issue. He said, "I've always made love and the woman has just gotten more and more aroused, and that's how it should be. This is hard for me."

When he first said this, I thought it was so old-fashioned and quaint. I couldn't believe it. All my other relationships have been centered around creative ways of reaching orgasm. It had just never been a priority for me. I *can* come during intercourse, but it's almost painful. I have to work so hard to do it that I lose the whole experience.

He suggested that maybe this was something I should look into. I did. I guess I thought, well, maybe he's right. I bought a book about how to arouse myself. As if I wasn't capable of that. Those books are for people who are frigid, for god's sake.

I went to his therapist with him to address the problem. I kept feeling defensive during the sessions, but they would end with some kind of resolution, and I'd feel like we were working on this. One friend told me that she thought it was weird that we were seeing a therapist together, and we'd only been going out three months. I thought she was being really opinionated, even though deep down I knew she was right.

In the meantime, I was realizing that he was really neurotic. He was very critical of the way I caressed. He used to complain that my toenails were too long, and I should be vigilant about cutting them. He was allergic to everything. When he came to sleep at my apartment, I had to dust really carefully, take away my ficus tree, and put away my down quilt. He used to imagine all these drafts all the time—he would sleep with a towel wrapped around his head. At one point, he wanted to put a Plexiglas wall around his bed.

But I wanted to be good to him. He was nine years older than me, but he had this vulnerable, childlike side. I was also responding to the fact that he was giving me a lot of attention. He liked my mind, he appreciated my wit. But as I began to really fall for him, he wanted to pull back.

I realize that things were so good with me that the sexual thing was his way of pushing me away. He had said to me, "I'm 41, and I want to settle down with someone, and you're what I'm looking for." And shortly after that, he suddenly had these problems with sex.

We got into this dangerous thing of talking about it in bed. He'd be very distant after sex. I would feel like he was going away. I'd say, "How was it?"

And he'd say, "Well, I had an orgasm."

One day in the early fall, he told me he didn't want to have sex anymore. At that point, I really should have said: "Ralph, go to hell."

I wish I had. But I was so destroyed by it. It was an insecure time in my life, and I thought there was room for hope, and that he was going to turn around. He was so intelligent; he was in therapy; he liked to talk about his emotions.

We talked about it later, and we didn't make love, but then we started to again. By this time, I was more aloof, and he was more into it. I was pulling away, and that was making me more appealing.

He became more tolerant of my need to have clitoral stimulation. And ended up being able to be very aroused by my arousal. But I just didn't want to see him so much. I realize, now, that it was my way of protecting myself. He called once and said, "When can we see each other this week? How many times?"

I said, "What, are you keeping count?"

He got really upset, and we decided not to talk for a month. At the end of the month, we said it wouldn't work out. I got bitchy at the end. I probably should have cut it off before I got bitchy. Consequently, he thinks that I really hurt him badly.

I still have so much annoyance that I didn't trust my instincts. That I let all this happen. Until Ralph, sex had always been unbesmirched territory for me. Now, his criticism goes to bed with me all the time, whenever I start a new relationship.

✳   **Nora & Hunt**
Nora Frost met Hunt Anderson her sophomore year in college. Meeting Nora a decade later, I was struck by her confidence and sophistication. Her story, though, reveals the painful isolation that can result when a woman doesn't have a community of peers from whom she can get relationship feedback.

I remember when I first met Hunt. He and his roommates and I and mine had dinner together the first night of sophomore year of college. I was making cultural allusions and he knew what I was talking about. At the end of dinner, we had wine. I knew that night that I was going to be having a relationship with this guy.

We all went out together a couple of nights later. We were walking back to our dorms and I was looking for a star to wish on. When we got back to where I lived, I said, "I'm sure I should invite you up, but I just don't know if that's a good idea right now."

He said, "You can hold me as close as you want, or as far away as you want, but I will always be here."

Then he kissed me, and pointed to a star. I thought we were made for each other. He knew about wishing on stars. We were smart. We were athletic. We were attractive. It was just a magic time.

In our own minds, we were a power couple. We made a scene wherever we went. He was very vain—he had a sunlamp in his room—and when we went out, me looking good was very important to him. Which I took as a compliment at the time.

We were both working really hard, but then we'd see each other after the day. We left notes on each other's bicycle spokes. I remember one weekend, we came to New York. We were walking down the street, holding hands, and we came to a post. You know when you're young, and two friends walk on either side of a post, and one of you says "peanut butter" and the other person says "jelly"? Well, I said "Theodora" and he said "Justinian," which were Byzantine mosaics we were studying at the time. It was great.

One night, after we'd been going out for a few months, we went back to his room after the library closed, and there was a note on his desk that said something like, "Cut the shit, hotshot." It was a note to himself that I was supposed to see. I asked him, "What does this mean?"

And he said, "Something is just not working. I don't want to go out with you. I want us to be friends."

Even though we were no longer a couple, we were both studying art history, so we kept landing in these three-person seminars with each other. I remember we were in one class, and he just never attended. He called me three weeks before the exam, and asked for my help. I remember going to the slide carousel, and walking him through the slides. And thinking to myself, "What am I doing this for?"

I just never said no. I had a car, and he didn't. We'd have a class together, and then I'd drive him to his dorm to get his stuff, and then I'd drop him off at his athletic practice. I remember thinking that if I just kept doing all these wonderful things for him, he'd realize how indispensable I was, and our relationship could go back to being the way it had been.

We had wonderful talks, sometimes, and wonderful walks, and hugs. But he kept telling me that he didn't want our relationship to go back to anything, and I just could not hear it. It was my pathology that I kept thinking: If only. If only.

But if he didn't want to be with me, why did he keep inviting me back into his life? You can break up with someone and cut them out of your life. Why didn't he do that? I see now that, for one thing, I was such a great, helpful little doormat to have around.

There were times when I was with him and things were okay and I was so comfortable. And so happy. When things were the way I wanted them to be, I was willing to put up with everything else.

He would call me up if he wanted something, or if he needed someone to talk to. I would never call him unless I wanted something very specific. There were lots of "don't bother me" signals that he gave off. It was always on his terms.

Sometimes I would call him up when I had had too much to drink. I would get brave, and I would want to connect with him. No one likes getting those kind of phone calls. He would listen to me, and then I'd hang up and feel like a big blub.

I do know that I was drinking more during that whole period. At times when I ordinarily wouldn't drink. If we were doing something together, I figured that as long as I had a cocktail, I would be okay, no matter what happened. I could take the good or the bad. I was anesthetizing myself.

I have more confidence now than I've ever had, but I still have less confidence than almost anyone I know. And he undermined me all the time. It's awful to have to ask in a relationship, but with him I always had to ask. I felt like I needed permission to move.

I remember once driving back from a party with this nice guy. And he said to me, "I've always been interested in you." And I remember realizing that there were people out there who thought I was attractive. But Hunt was the only person I cared about. Hunt was the only person who could validate me. And if he wasn't providing that validation, a million other people saying "you're smart" or "you're beautiful" didn't mean a thing.

I kept thinking that he would finally wake up and figure out that he wanted to be with me. In the meantime, I was like a sponge, absorbing all his unhappiness.

I made excuses—for him and about the relationship—to all of my friends. I never talked about some of the really horrible stuff. It was like being in a battered relationship—I didn't want anybody to know.

My father was manic-depressive, so my male role model was very hot and cold. I just assumed that this was the way with everybody. And my mother never said, "This is terrible." Instead, she'd say things like, "Well, you know, it could be worse."

We were lying in his bed once during the period I was involved with him, and he told me he was gay. I said, "Hunt, you know you don't have to tell me that if you want me to leave."

And he said, "No, I am."

I called my sister, who was also at college with us, and I said, "You're not going to believe what Hunt just said to me."

And she said, "You know, he told me the same thing. And I said to him, 'Right, Hunt. And I'm the queen of England.'"

I knew nothing about sex. And neither did he. We did not have sex. We kissed and hugged and everything, and I realize now that there were times that he didn't have an erection. Since then, there have been times when I've been around men, and done much less, and I've known they had an erection.

At the time, I thought I was completely unsexy. And that we were two absolute babes in the woods. But I now know that people who don't know anything can learn. It never occurred to me until right now that he might actually have been gay....

✳   **Amelia & Adam**
Amelia Chase, the photographer who told two of the stories in the "Womanizer" chapter, got involved with Adam Morrison about four years ago.

I had just broken up with a longish-term boyfriend. I went to stay with these friends of mine out in Connecticut, and we had spent the weekend doing tarot card readings and horoscopes. There was a horoscope in *Mirabella* that said that on August 17th I would meet somebody who would significantly change my life. And that we would have a relationship—it was going to be romantic and spiritual—and it would last a year.

So this date really stood out in my head. I was supposed to be with my family at their summer house during that part of August. And I knew that I wasn't going to meet anybody on that date, staying with my family.

So when my friend Erica invited me to come to East Hampton for that weekend, I went to a lot of trouble to get there. She had a dinner party on the 17th. And she invited her on-again-off-again boyfriend, Jack, and his friend Adam.

I just remember thinking that Adam was really attractive. I sat next to him and we talked and talked and talked. I remember we talked about Cyril Connolly. He was older, maybe 45. Very distinguished. We just completely clicked intellectually. I was intrigued by him, and thought that he was fascinating. And dashing.

As the night progressed, Jack suggested we go to the beach. I'm not sure how we shook everyone else. But the four of us left the rest of the dinner party, and we went off to the beach. I remember we had a bottle of vodka. I was drinking this vodka in the back of the jeep. We got to the beach, and Erica and Jack disappeared into the darkness with a blanket.

Adam and I stumbled out of the car and just started fooling around. Passionately. Just like that. It started happening when we hit the sand. We later went back to Jack's house, and I stayed with Adam in the guest room. I remember waking up that morning and thinking, what am I doing here? There were all these squirrels up in the rafters making a huge commotion, and I just remember thinking: What have I gotten myself into?

We had had sex that night, on the beach, and it was really fun and great. But when I woke up that morning, Adam seemed very old to me. Oh, my god, I'm with this old guy. Even though he was only five years older than my ex-boyfriend. I remember waking up and wanting to slip away. Thinking, oh, well, that was a good one-night stand.

The next night, Adam invited me back to Shelter Island, where he was borrowing a friend's house. He brought me upstairs to this huge master bedroom, with a four-poster bed. He put on music and we were dancing and it was very romantic and really really great.

I wasn't thinking anything else but that this was fun. Adam lived in San Francisco, and was going back there in two days. We had lots of sex. He quoted Molly Bloom's speech from the end of *Ulysses* to me. He was very literary and erudite. Very, very smart.

There was this storm brewing that night. The windows were rattling. I remember thinking of Prospero and *The Tempest*. It was very magical.

The next day, I just lollygagged in bed, and he got up and worked on a script, and went to the garden and picked some tomatoes. He was a wonderful cook. He made this delicious pasta with basil and tomatoes. Later we had clams with white wine. He just had impeccable taste; he was very cultivated.

I had to leave to travel back to my parents' house. I was just swooning. Dreaming about him. He called me from Shelter Island. He called me from San Francisco. I ended up sending him a note with some sand in it that said something witty, I don't remember what. And I think that note made him decide to move to New York. To go out with me.

He arrived in October. He was going to stay with some friends. But he really was saying he was coming over to see me. I was elated and terrified.

But before he arrived, I started hearing all these rumors. That he was this well-known womanizer, and had slept with practically every woman on the planet. And was really bad news. The poor guy, the night he arrived, I remember I gave it to him. I said straight out, "Listen, I've been hearing all these things about you."

He said to me that he had been like that, but these last few years, he'd been pretty quiet, and had had this one major love. Who'd broken his heart, a year or two years before. My sense was that he had gotten older, and he was reformed.

The beginning was very intense. It was scary because even though Adam moved into a friend's house, he spent every night with me. It was the first time that I spent every single night of my life with someone. That was exciting but scary. It was nice because it was really comfortable. He was a wonderful cook. The first month was incredibly romantic and physically charged.

The problems started around November. He and I went to Miami Beach. It was really beautiful. It was one of those situations in which it was really romantic, and suddenly I felt him pulling away from me. I remember being at a bar and we were surrounded by all these really young models. He started to talk to me about some girl and how pretty she was.

At the same time, this sexual thing started to happen to him. Which is that while he was able to have sex, he wasn't able to ejaculate. It turned out that he had had this problem before meeting me. When he first met me, he had overcome it. We had had this passionate sex. But suddenly the problem was back again.

I don't know if it was because he started to get to know me better and he started to realize that I wasn't who I seemed. I'd started to show him that I was possessive. From then on, our relationship became stressed and strained. We still spent every single night together. We kept trying to have sex. But it was inevitably really difficult.

We talked about it a lot. He had seen a psychiatrist in San Francisco. His theory was that the problem arose when he became very intimate with someone.

I just remember feeling very threatened. I remember feeling like he was taunting me. He was very smart, and he knew that one of my weaknesses was that I was very jealous. And I felt that he was really feeding into that jealousy. There were all these old girlfriends of his that he was very close to. And they started coming back onto the scene. He'd always have these little lunches, while I was at work, with different women friends. There was one in particular that was very threatening to me. She was the woman that had broken his heart. On my birthday, he had lunch with her. I felt as though he was torturing me. Getting back at me. I felt that he knew that those things undid me. And I was feeling insecure because I felt as though I wasn't sexually satisfying him.

He kind of moved out to Shelter Island to continue working. He was talking about going back to California, but he was also looking for houses to buy here on the East Coast.

Ultimately he went back to San Francisco. I remember feeling really sad. I was crying a lot. I kind of hoped things between us would pick up again. The idea was that he was going to go back and see a psychiatrist. We had just realized that our thing was not going to work. Something had shut off. He confessed to me that this was something that had happened to him before. But I felt as though I wasn't turning this guy on.

Neither Roberta nor Sarah was in love with her partner. Both women wanted to be in a relationship, and they willfully tried to downplay the ways in which Ralph and Arthur didn't measure up. But when the sexual difficulties arose, the women shifted their focus onto the new challenge: how to satisfy their partners. This new project displaced their earlier concerns about not being interested enough in the men.

Ralph and Arthur responded to the women's flat-out eagerness to please by analyzing their orgasms, and begrudgingly noting tiny signs of progress. ("Well, that one was better," was one meager bone Arthur threw to Sarah.) Their response to the women's effort was not gratitude, and it was not affection. It's tempting to infer that the men's anger at their own sense of inadequacy was exacerbated by the women's uncomplaining compliance.

But the women continued to act as if the problem were theirs. They kept trying. As Sarah said, "I would have stood on my head if I had thought that it would make things work." But then both Roberta and Sarah experienced self-protective impulses that caused them to disengage before their partners were necessarily ready to give up. Looking back, both of them wished that they had detached sooner. Roberta said she should have jumped ship the moment Ralph said he didn't want to have sex anymore. Sarah cited the moment that Arthur told her about the sex cult. But retrospective analysis is easy. It's only by going through the motions that a woman (especially a woman who's never been a quitter) learns that effort, understanding, even handstands in bed can't necessarily heal a man's wounded sexuality.

Nora's story suggests another pattern, in which a couple seems to form a genuine emotional attachment, only to have the sex never get off the ground. Nora and Hunt lacked the tools to talk about what was really going on between them (Nora's response to his comment about being gay—"You don't have to tell me that if you want me to leave"—is a good example. It reflected her own insecurity, but gave him no real safe haven in which to elaborate). They couldn't communicate, but they also couldn't quite manage to separate.

In telling me the story, Nora focused on her own lack of experience. She accepted, almost as if it were the best that she deserved, the frustrating quasi-relationship. Until she graduated from college and got some physical distance from Hunt, she was unwilling to him up. He represented her hope that justice might be served and she might be validated—if only he would change his mind and choose to be with her after all. She mentioned her increased drinking and the ongoing shame that caused her to hide her feelings from her female friends. The relationship eroded her sense of herself.

Amelia's relationship is like Roberta's in the sense that Adam's sexual problems seemed to arise when real intimacy threatened. But rather than listening to his take on what was going on, which he had apparently explored in therapy before meeting her, Amelia instead inferred that the problem was caused by what she feared the most: his discovery that she wasn't "what she seemed," that she was in fact possessive.

A relationship that stumbles or fails sexually often strikes buried nerves in a woman. We can attribute this pain to family history (a woman's frustrated erotic attachment to her father?) and/or to cultural constructs (the vestiges of the notion that a woman is only as good as the pleasure she provides to a man?). Whatever the cause, the upshot is that many women don't shrug off dysfunctional lovers, but rather pin their self-worth on trying to cure them.

Relationships with these men leave scars. The woman often goes on to future relationships feeling inadequate. As Roberta said, "His criticism goes to bed with me all the time."

Despite the pressure women feel to be the unfettered masters of their sexuality, many also feel vulnerable in the sexual realm, all too ready to judge themselves deficient or damaged. Both Roberta and Nora said it made them feel better to tell me their stories: The verbal light of day helped them get a perspective they lacked.

Know-it-all sex talk may feel bracing and progressive, but it doesn't tell the whole story. Think back for a minute to the women in the early '70s whose consciousness-raising groups pioneered the process of frank talk about sex. These groups didn't indulge in easy and unrealistic paeans to multiple orgasm. Often, the discussions of sex began with the halting process of women sharing the ways in which they were unsatisfied.

In the '90s, many of us share our triumphs and revel in our "openness," at the same time that we squirrel away other experiences, which we construe as personal failure. True strength lies in a willingness to talk about those relationships in which the sex didn't work. Speaking the unspoken makes those experiences less shameful.

The Nonfunctional Man

This chapter consists of two stories. In each, the man is handsome and compellingly artistic, with some demons that initially only enhance his stature as a romantic figure. He finds a sympathetic woman and insinuates himself into her life. Time goes by. He smokes pot, slowly abandons his vocation, and sinks into a depression of sorts, ultimately withdrawing from the world.

Because we are hearing about these men from the women who left their own ambitions unrealized to nurture them, only to be abandoned in the end, these stories are untainted by nostalgia. The men's charismatic veneer has been stripped away. We see that the dashing outlines of their characters were more imagined, projected, hoped for, than they were real.

On the surface, these men seemed to cede control to the more functional women, but in fact their elusiveness and passivity was what defined the relationships. Although the women had initially imagined that they were wielding a kind of babysitter's authority, they found themselves powerless to change or motivate their sullen and increasingly mute men. In retrospect, they saw the full extent of the men's selfishness. As one woman put it, "He took, he took, he took."

As opposed to many chapters in this book, in which women stumbled unwittingly into a bad guy's orbit, both women interviewed admitted that they played a role in allowing this dynamic to develop and continue. They allowed the men to wallow in the status quo. Fleeing from marginally stable homes, both women sought solace in the creation of their own families, and, in fact, were reassured by their mates' dependence on them. Safety was a major goal, and these quasi-emasculated men seemed to provide it.

Although in both cases it was ultimately the man who walked out, the women's resilience and inner self-protective power is of note. Lucinda's seventeen-year marriage caused her to lose potentially energetic and productive years, but her story is also a dramatic example of the internal evolution that occurs often in this book. A woman sacrifices herself, suffers a while in silence, and then, almost unbidden, her will asserts itself. She sheds her comfort-protecting denial and takes control of her life.

On one hand, her story is a grueling account of the costs of being committed to a nonfunctional man. But her story doubles as a portrait of a relationship on a generational cusp. She was an early convert to certain aspects of the late '60s lifestyle, but she remained bound by gender-related precepts from an earlier generation.

✳   **Lucinda & Ken**
Lucinda Swift met Ken Van Ost in 1968, when they were both college students: They quickly married and went on to have the longest involvement of any couple in this book. Now divorced and in her mid-forties, Lucinda told me her story in the hopes that "it will encourage other women to get out sooner."

Ken and I met as college students at a private college in California. We had both just gotten back from Europe. He had been on a painting fellowship in Italy. I had just gotten back from a semester on a ship traveling around the Mediterranean.

It was around 1968, and the counterculture was becoming quite fashionable. Our European experiences and our orientation towards art make us natural counterculture type people. We became silver-spoon, educated hippies. That's where our relationship was at the very beginning. We cut rather romantic figures to ourselves, and to each other.

The first time he ever picked me up for a date, he was really stoned. I didn't pay any attention to that. Pot really wasn't my thing. He apologized to me, and I said, "Oh, don't worry about it. I'm a really good sport."

I've come to rue the day I ever said that, because I know he picked up on that and interpreted it as "I'm a chump."

I started dating him. His painting was really extraordinary. He got a show with a really good gallery. The first few months I dated him, he seemed really focused, like he really knew what he wanted to do with his life. But as soon as I got super-involved with him, about three or four months into the relationship, I noticed that his behavior started to change.

But this was already after I'd started living with him, which I did after knowing him for about a month and a half. Back in those days, for a girl to live with her boyfriend was a very revolutionary thing to do. And I was one of the first "nice" girls on campus to openly do that.

And because I'd made this dramatic step, I felt really committed. But I also started feeling mildly uncomfortable about him, almost from the very beginning. Because his behavior became very childish and demanding. I started to lose my identity very quickly. He turned out to be an extremely self-centered person. He didn't know how to take turns. He didn't know how to share. He'd listen to me for hours and give me sympathy when I hurt, but he didn't know how to support a woman at achieving something on her own or having an identity of her own.

He was brought up by his father to believe that women were not supposed to have any identity of any kind. He continued to have that belief system the entire time we were together.

We wound up getting married after living together for about nine months. During that period, my grades kept going down because I started partying with him a lot, smoking a lot of marijuana. Because he told me that school wasn't important, and that I didn't need to go to class anyway. I quit school, planning to go back in a couple of years.

Well, that's not what happened. I got a really boring job at a bank. Ken was supposed to be going to graduate school in painting. But he never went to class. He never made anything. He basically drove around and partied with his friends all day while I was working at a bank.

Then he dropped out of school. It was everybody's fault but his own. The world was screwed up and he was an artist. I was young and stupid enough to buy that.

We were hippies. We lived in funny neighborhoods, and we wore funny clothes, and we didn't have middle-class values. After we'd been married for about a year, we ran off to Toronto. That was a real interesting scene because there were 30,000 expatriate Americans up there. Our baby was born in May of 1971. We got a cute little basement apartment. We had a rather idyllic time there. He got a job in an art gallery, and, in his own way, really tried. But he was constantly complaining about the fact that he had to work, because he was an artist. And he was resentful that I had this baby.

He basically stayed a very heavy-duty dope smoker the entire time we were together. It just got worse and worse and worse. There would be years when I would confront him about it, and years that I wouldn't. He was a very belligerent person who came from a family where the people were extremely belligerent and aggressive. I allowed that to overpower me an awful lot.

I was on a martyr trip, because I had been taught that women martyr themselves to their families, to their husbands, to their children. If you're a good woman, if you're going to be a transcendent angel, you're going to martyr yourself.

Now this was a time when a lot of women my age were choosing other paths. I feel like I was one of the last women of my generation—I was born in 1948—to choose the old way. It was a funny choice: While I chose a countercultural life style, I also chose to be a traditional wife. I chose to let a man dominate me and push me around.

We separated after we had been married four years. I went back out to California from Toronto, I took the child with me; she was almost two. I lived in a commune and had some time to myself for eight months. My baby and I lived in a little room. I even dated a bit. I had a chance to be the center of my own world. And buy myself some clothing. Married to Ken, I'd never had any clothes. All the money got spent on him being an artist.

I made the fateful decision to go back to him because I was really feeling like a failure. I was getting that from my family. I lacked belief in myself. I'd been told how terrible I was all the time.

I experienced some physical abuse from my father. He suffered from what I'm now convinced was post-traumatic-stress disorder from the Korean War. When he came back, I would hear him get hysterical with my mother in the middle of the night for no reason.

He would hit her, pull her hair. And he hadn't even been drinking. When I was 12, he turned on me and did the same thing to me. From the time I was 12 until the time I was 18, I was getting slapped around by him on a regular basis. My husband was a weight lifter, very thick and very strong. Even though he was psychologically abusive, he never lifted a finger to hurt me. I knew I would be safe with him. I married this guy whom I knew would physically protect me from my father.

The relationship gave me physical safety. But my self-esteem, my sense of my own power was so low that I didn't know how to get out. I would say I wanted to go back to college, and Ken would tell me I didn't deserve it. I was too neurotic and I had a baby and that's all there was to it.

I slowly but surely developed a concept of myself that was becoming stronger and stronger. After the eight months when we were separated, my attitude towards my husband really changed. I started seeing him as a screw-up. My late twenties were basically spent asking myself: What's the matter with this guy? He doesn't function.

I talked him into going back to California, because there were opportunities for us there. That's where our connections were. But once we were back, he didn't lift a finger to take advantage of anything. He was doing lots and lots of drugs. Every weird drug that came along, he tried. He had half-baked jobs, like working on people's yachts. But basically he was just sort of lying around and staying stoned. I wanted him to go to graduate school, so he could become a college teacher like he'd always said he was going to be. His father had some connections over at one of the local universities, and Ken went out and had an interview with the head of the art department. The guy said, "I'll let you in, but the kind of art you're into isn't the trip I'm on."

Ken came home and threw up his hands and said he couldn't deal with that. And that was the end of going to graduate school. He never explored any other avenues, any other schools.

I tried getting part-time jobs so that I could go back to college. I tried waitressing, hoping that I could make enough to fulfill my financial obligations to the family and go to UCLA. I was never able to find a waitressing job that paid enough to do that. Back then, a woman couldn't get a job at a restaurant where the tips were good—they only went to men. Here I am, an upper-middle-class hothouse flower, still a bit of a prima donna at age 28. I remember going into a nice restaurant in the Wilshire district of Los Angeles and having a couple of waiters tell me to go to the cafeteria down the street. Because that's where the women worked.

All Ken ever did was feel sorry for himself because his wife was complaining. And I was getting angrier by the day. He was getting me stoned when I would get home from work, to diffuse my anger. He would go out to his studio and never make anything.

When my daughter was three, I started working as a legal secretary. And I started developing a concept of success that I hadn't had as a member of the counterculture. Until then, I had never really been around people who had normal professions. And did something they really loved. When I started working for those trial attorneys, even though they weren't my type of people, for the first time, I was around people who loved what they were doing. There wasn't a conflict between having to make a living, and living for their art. I started comparing these men to my husband. And Ken did not look very good.

I started having to fix myself up really nicely to go downtown to work. I started feeling successful. The clients were classy. The attorneys were classy. And I started realizing that I was classy. This started making me even more determined to get my life under control.

I started getting ready to leave him. But right around this time, when I was secretly making my plans, his parents both got ill. I knew I couldn't leave him while his parents were dying. I didn't have the heart. First, his mother died, then his father died four months after that. He inherited about $300,000. Plus a couple of small trust funds that were good for about $1200 a month. This was in 1978.

I felt obligated to stay. Although I was in the process of falling out of love with him, we still had a child together. I was really into the concept of marriage and family. The amount of money he inherited was not such a huge amount that I would have money-grubbingly stayed to take advantage of it. But I mistakenly thought that after inheriting his parents' life savings, we would be financially safe. I thought we could invest it and that I wouldn't have to be a slave any more. Boy, was I wrong.

I talked my husband into moving to Santa Fe. Because I really loved being connected with the earth. It was still something of a hippie town in those days.

He would not put his money in anything but stock. That was very stupid. He had a college buddy—one of his substance abuse friends—who was just learning to be a stock broker. He didn't know what he was doing. He took our money. It did not go well.

Do you know what margining stock is? It's basically borrowing money so you can buy a large amount of stock. The point is to invest in something that you know is going to make a windfall. As soon as you make your windfall, you pay the debt back. Well, Ken margined most of our stock, and made a $50,000 windfall. Instead of de-margining the stock, he kept it in margin because he liked the huge numbers. We did very well for about a year. I didn't realize that he hadn't taken the stock out of margin. Then there was a huge stock market crash. We woke up one morning and we were worth one third of what we had been worth when we'd gone to sleep. We had barely enough money to pay cash for a rather modest house. There was no more nest egg. Basically, he lost his parents' life savings because he refused to invest his money wisely.

In the meantime, he wasn't able to find a decent job. The New Mexico economy was depressed, and neither one of us could find decent work. He stayed stoned all the time. No matter how much I begged him, he was writing checks to the tune of $3000 a month. On things like $400 sheepskin coats. Two hundred dollars for mari-juana every month. I couldn't stop him. I would make a budget, and he would never obey it.

When I realized that he had blown his parents' life savings, that I'd watched two people die in order for us to inherit that money so that my family would be safe, that really affected me very deeply. I did not have a callous attitude towards that money. I felt it was our spiritual obligation to make good on that. His grandparents had been immigrants. His father had worked his way through medical school. It was a kind of a legacy. My husband was such a bum, or so emotionally damaged, that he didn't know how to honor that. I remember having a conversation in the garage in Santa Fe—I was trying to talk to him about the enormity of having blown his inheritance. He just looked right at me and said, "Oh well ... easy come, easy go."

That's when I realized that I didn't love him any more. When he said "easy come, easy go," and two people died. What was this monster that I was living with? The crime I committed is that I stayed married to him for another four years.

In the fall of 1984, I was working another deadend job, and I decided I couldn't take it anymore. Ken had gotten a well-paying job. I made the decision that I was going to use being married to him to position myself so that I could take care of myself and my daughter. I told him that I was going to go back to school. I saw going to school as something that would help the three of us as a family, but I was also determined to be able to make a getaway, should I choose to do that. He kept telling me that I was going to fail. For the first time in the 16 years we'd been living together, I defied him and I went back to school.

I took one class. I had no belief in myself. After raising a child— children scramble your brains—I didn't know if I was going to be any good or not. I didn't know if I had a mind left. I took an economics class that I knew would be a real challenge. That class became the central focus of my life. In the meantime, Ken wanted me to quit school and go back to work, and I wouldn't do it. Much to my amazement, I got an A in that class, including an A-plus on the final exam. My daughter told me later that when Ken realized that I was not going to fail and he was no longer going to be the central focus of my life, she said she knew that was going to be the end of our marriage.

In the meantime, we had been sinking deeper and deeper into debt. We'd decided we needed to add onto the house. We were just barely getting by at this point, but our credit was good enough that we were able to borrow another $20,000. We really went out on a limb. But then my husband lost his well-paying job. We ran out of money halfway into the renovation, and our contractor left us hanging. The place was half-finished. It couldn't be kept warm. It couldn't be kept clean. We were not going to be able to make the house payments, and the house was going to go into default. When Ken had to admit to me that we didn't have any money for the house payments, he threw his keys down on the kitchen floor, and said, "I want a divorce."

From 1975 to 1985 I basically stayed stoned, because it was the only way I could handle the way he was. I lost ten years of my life. He'd wanted to make me financially responsible for the family, but he wouldn't allow me to become empowered to do it because he was afraid of being abandoned. As long as he could keep me helpless and downtrodden, he could keep me around.

I was emotionally destroyed by his leaving. I was losing my home. I was losing my land. I was losing everything that I had based my decisions around for 17 years. I was 37 and I had nothing but clerical skills. I had a fourteen-year-old daughter and I was being thrown out onto the street with nothing.

I was so destroyed that I would just sit on my bed and stare at the walls all day. I must have been having a nervous breakdown. This man had consumed my energy for 17 years for his own personal survival, and I'd given him what I now realize was a lot of mother love. It didn't do either of us any good. He really needed to learn how to nurture himself. And I wound up being, on some level, destroyed by this person.

After he walked out, I tried going for temp jobs. One of the reasons the temp agencies had liked me was I had been so presentable. They could send me to a big law firm, to attorneys that had gone to Harvard and Yale, and I would make a good impression. Well, I was no longer capable of doing that. I was having a nervous breakdown. I would wander into work 20 minutes late. I would get to a point where I realized I was about to start screaming or crying, so I would get up and walk away from my desk and walk out of the office. It would take me 40 minutes to get a grip on myself. I literally couldn't do any better.

I hadn't had a very good relationship with my parents in a long time. They didn't even know that Ken and I had broken up. A friend of mine said, "It doesn't matter how messed up they are. They're your family and you have lost everything. And I promise you that if you call them up and tell them what really happened, they'll come through for you."

So I called my father in California and I explained what happened. My family came through for me for the first time in my life. I went out and stayed with my folks for six months, because I needed to have a few months that I wasn't expected to provide for myself or my daughter. I had a walking nervous breakdown.

After six months, I got strong enough that my daughter and I came back to New Mexico and started all over again from scratch. And slowly but surely put everything back together again.

Ken and I have been broken up for about eight years now. He's just a memory. It took about five or six years for that to happen. It took me four years before I would have anything to do with a man.

I worked as a legal secretary. I'm not really made to do that. But I made my way in an expensive, difficult town. And I started taking classes again, one at a time, and started getting A's. My father got into a financial situation where he could help me a bit. For the last two years, I've been a college student, and I've been working part time. I will get my B.A. at the age of 46. I have 19 As and 2 Bs. I'm a Phi Beta Kappa. I'm going to go on to graduate school. I'm probably going to get a Masters in Social Work, although my father is trying to talk me into going to law school. My father is beginning to convince me that I need the money and I need the challenge. I'm in the process of deciding which moon I'm going to reach for.

✳   **Pam & Claude**
Pam Hitt, a Manhattan-based singer, met Claude Keiser several years after having moved to New York from the midwest.

Claude was very handsome. Exotic. When you didn't know anything about him, you could project all kinds of fantasies onto him. He was a member of a local theater company, but he didn't have many friends there. Basically, he was at war with many of the people he worked with. That should have scared me. But a flip side of this was that, after we got involved, he was immediately very joined into my life. We were together all the time. I'd been having a rough time when I met him. I thought, after all my suffering, I finally have mine.

I just wanted the fantasy. When I was a little girl, I saw the life my parents had. It was so hard. There was so much pain. So many kids. My parents had so little love to give us. My mother died when I was 17. And I just wanted ... I wanted my own thing.

He moved in with me really abruptly. Obviously, our communication skills were not totally in place. We'd talked about it, but then he just announced that he was moving in. I still felt it was my space. We did it, but it required a lot of compromise.

I began to notice that he was getting more and more withdrawn. His social skills were never that great, but now it was like he wasn't even present. I had all these friends, which I think constantly brought up in his eyes the fact that he didn't have any. We'd have a dinner party and my friends would notice that I would become the life of the party, and he was almost quiet. I started feeling that there was almost a competitiveness.

He liked to smoke pot, and at one point I found out he was doing heroin. He moved out, but then he promised he was off it, and he moved back in.

We'd talked about marriage, but we hadn't decided anything. And then I heard him talking to his mother on the phone. And I heard him use the word marriage. We hadn't decided anything, but at the same time, I was kind of like, yeah, okay. Now I would go: Wait a minute! But I was kind of enjoying being passive. There was some part of me that was willing to give up who I was, if I could be taken care of. But the result of that is that my soul got squashed.

Planning the wedding was one of the most collaborative fun times we had. He was really good at it, and I was good at it. We had a huge wedding outdoors. That was almost like the highlight of our relationship. And then it was over, and that was that.

We came back to New York after getting married, and we got this apartment and started working on it. I think he felt trapped, closed in. He was not happy to see me in the morning. He wouldn't talk. He became more and more withdrawn. I became needier, trying to bring him out of it. So he had this power. It was so oppressive. I'm a bit long-suffering. The anger in me is buried. I was in a state of depression, and I didn't know it. I talked about us going into therapy together, but it didn't happen.

I was singing, and doing other work as well. I had different interests. I knew that I had to make a living. And I felt like Claude just wanted to go sit by the ocean and stare out to sea. What did he want to do? Was it acting? It didn't really seem like it. He had a lot of anger.

It goes back to his family. He was broken. His father was stern, his mother really cloying. His parents still sent him money. He was one of the most selfish people I've ever met.

We had this place upstate that he was working on renovating. He was spending a lot of time up there. I had a singing engagement, and I remember I called him. I was supposed to go up there on a certain date, and he told me not to come. I had introduced him to some friends of mine, who had kind of adopted him and he had fallen in love with one of their daughters. Sixteen years old.

When he told me he was in love, I said, "Let's deal with this."

He said, "No. Either it's happening between us or it's not."

Everyone has to work on things. If a relationship isn't working, let's go in. Let's not throw it away. I really loved him. Those girls were provocative. After he liked one daughter, he liked her sister.

Finally, we just got divorced. It took us so long, because I couldn't deal with him. I had to let the place upstate go. I just didn't have the fight in me. He took, he took, he took. He owed me money for the balloon payment on the house.

I was devastated. I drank a lot for a little bit. I didn't leave the house. I stopped communicating with a lot of different people. I was so wounded that I didn't trust anyone. My friends would come over, but I could only handle it if one came at a time. If two came together, I felt threatened. I was so fragile, it was like it hurt to walk through the air.

Slowly, I started to make phone calls to find a therapist. And I started the process of crawling into the black void and pulling away the layers. It was like exercise. My parents had a terrible marriage. How was I to learn to have a good one? The school where I was raised had sadistic teachers. I didn't get any loving guidance. I took care of myself. I was a survivor. Which doesn't mean that I was a healthy survivor. I had so many wounds. So many needs. Only now am I starting to realize myself.

I really got married thinking that I was getting married for life. I'd made that real strong commitment to him. For me, it was like something sacred that was broken. It didn't take me one year to get over him. It took me three. But I got better and better.

Ken blamed everything on everyone but himself. He got stoned rather than painted, while counting on his wife to pay the rent. Claude just sank deeper and deeper into an impenetrable funk. And meanwhile, the women stood by their men.

First of all, they believed in the guys' ability and bought the tortured artist myth. As Pam recalled, "When you didn't know anything about him, you could project all kinds of fantasies onto him."

But even after the romance faded, Lucinda and Pam stayed the course. One reason is that both were wounded by their own family experiences. Pam talked about the powerful deficit she brought from her childhood, during which her parents didn't have enough love to go around. When she talked about the strange way she and Claude edged towards marriage, she said, "There was some part of me that was willing to give up who I was, if I could be taken care of. But the result of that is that my soul got squashed."

Lucinda's father had hit her. For all his emotional abuse, Ken made her feel physically safe. Plus, the message she'd grown up with (while watching her mother also being physically abused) was that "women martyr themselves to their families." Her family condemned her when she temporarily left her husband. The combined force of all these motivators kept her with Ken.

It's almost as though these women believed themselves to be making deposits in an emotional bank. The women gave the love and caretaking that they themselves would have liked to receive, as though they were assured of getting it back one day. Of course, their husbands had never agreed to this unspoken bargain.

Another woman who was briefly involved with someone she labeled a tortured genius, talked explicitly about the link between her caretaking urges and her more subterranean wish for power. "It was creepy how unhappy he was," she recalled. "He drank all the time. Once we were in bed together and he sort of tried to strangle me. I remember him having his hands around my neck. It was so drunken. It was out of anger. This guy was wounded and frustrated, and I remember thinking, he needs me."

Even his violent impulses were impotent—he didn't manage to hurt her. But they shaded the relationship with a certain dark poetry. Although the couple broke up shortly afterwards, the woman continued to monitor her ex-boyfriend's progress. He went on to get involved with a woman who "straightened him up." She recalled, "I remember having the deepest envy for the woman who cleaned him up. I wished that I could have won over his heart and taken care of him and made him change. If that isn't a Beauty and the Beast fantasy, what is? I wanted to bring out the potential of this brilliant guy. I wanted to have been so powerful."

The trick, of course, is that the caretaker's power is illusory. She can give as much as she wants, but a man this depressed, this self-loathing is largely incapable of love. The woman may become a walking reminder of his failures, of the ways in which he is inadequate. It may trigger childhood anger about being dependent. His anger at her may remain latent until some external catalyst (a missed house payment, another woman) impels him to depart.

Both women were shattered, but ultimately emerged full of fight. When I spoke to Lucinda, she was only a couple of credits away from finishing college. When I interviewed Pam, she reported that she was in a solid relationship, and was contemplating starting her own business.

The Addict

The addict may be charming. He may be the life of the party. But he also has a secret, which may or may not be well-concealed. The women in this chapter got involved, only to discover later that the men in question had substance abuse problems (or, in one case, a problem with gambling). The stories that follow are about how the women discovered the problem and left shortly thereafter.

I should say that I don't mean to imply that a woman *must* leave an addict. I'm just describing the choices made by the women I interviewed. But at the same time, I've made the conscious decision to exclude long-term relationships with alcoholics and drug abusers from this chapter. The reasons women endure them are too complicated to explore in a few pages, and the consequences too potentially devastating to treat as mere boyfriend problems.

Although one woman professed to be in love with her boyfriend (when she met him, he was, for the time being, drug free) and another recalled a "glowing" courtship, reading between the lines, there seems to be something missing in the relationships described in this chapter. Each woman was able to enumerate the attractive qualities of the man, but none of them shared a lot of detail about how the *couple* related. There wasn't any indication that the man paid particularly close attention to the woman. Part of the reason for this, I'm guessing, is that each guy was preoccupied with his addiction. Even in the early days of the involvement, his romantic interest had an absentminded quality.

The stories that follow also shed light on the ways in which the woman couldn't or wouldn't see what was going on. Wanting to keep her relationship going, she justified the man's actions to herself, downplayed anything disturbing that she noticed, and just kept plugging ahead. One woman, admittedly at a low and lonely part of her life, remembered thinking, in the midst of her relationship with someone she has since labeled an alcoholic: "Is this what love is?"

✳   **Kate & Terry**
*Kate Howe was working in Tucson when she met Terry
Komar, who had recently come out of rehab. Years into their
relationship, she began to suspect that he had gone back to
heroin.*

Terry chose me. One day there was an accident outside my office building, and I went out to see what was going on. Terry was being questioned as a witness. We took one look at each other and knew … something. He was my exact type … dark and gorgeous. I ran into him later when I was shopping, and he approached me and asked me where I worked. Later, he called my office, based on having seen me those two times, and asked me out.

The first time I went out with him I didn't trust him. He seemed smooth, very slick, with a veneer that I couldn't get under. I was attracted to him, but I didn't think that I would end up with him. But then one night we had dinner at his house, and from that night forth I was in love with him. I don't know how, but he won me.

He was a former heroin addict from Los Angeles. When I first met him, he was just coming out of a rehabilitation house for addicts. The bad boy image appealed to me. I liked the fact that he had this checkered past. He'd been arrested for heroin. I love these addictive personalities. Because I don't have one.

And he was also very well-adjusted in the worldly sense. He had a job, he was making money, he dressed well.

I fell deeply in love with him. We never really had an intellectual connection, but there was an incredible sexual thing between us. He was totally different from my upbringing. He brought up marriage at a very early point. He talked about marrying me throughout the entire relationship, which went on for several years. We moved in together. We even got sort of engaged. He gave me a ring.

Things started to fall apart several years down the line when I got pregnant. He had been pushing me, month after month, to go off the pill. He wanted me to get pregnant. And the month I did, I got pregnant. And didn't know what to do.

He instantly reversed himself and didn't want me to go through with the pregnancy. But I decided to keep the baby. I had this condition on my cervix that they were going to have to operate on, but since I was pregnant they couldn't. The doctor said, "You might as well get pregnant, because you might have to have a hysterectomy."

So I decided to keep the baby. I started to really want it. He conversely became more and more afraid of it. He threw me down on the floor once, and he pinned me down on the bed another time. He never actually hit me. He restrained himself from becoming violent, but there was that edge.

I spontaneously aborted. I was crushed. We were both kind of in shock. We went through the summer and then at Thanksgiving, he went back home to L.A. I called him a couple of times, and I sensed that something was different. When I met him at the airport, I knew something was wrong the instant he walked off the plane. What had happened was that he had started shooting up. I knew it. I knew in my gut. I said, "Terry, something's different. What's going on?"

Finally it came out. "I met up with these old heroin-addict friends of mine," he told me, "and I started shooting up again, and I realized the mistake and I'm never going to do it again."

But once a heroin addict goes back, he's gone back.

What ensued were five or six months of me knowing in my heart that he was shooting up, but he never owned up to it. There were these weird people coming through the house. There was a bottle of bleach that I knew he was using to clean his needles—the level just kept going down. There were bleach spots on the rug. Every weekend I would scour the house looking for needles, and I never found one. So I never had the positive evidence.

And then finally he went to a program. He told me he was on this medication that keeps people off heroin. In fact, he was on methadone. If he had admitted it to me, he would have had to admit that he'd been lying the whole time about not shooting up. Finally, it came out because I started going to see his counselor. His counselor let me guess, because he couldn't tell me, that Terry was on methadone.

He was moody. His whole personality changed. The most marked thing was that we never slept together. His sex drive disappeared completely. Everything he did was suspicious. In fact, he would even nod off once in a while. He was temperamental. He hadn't been like that.

I was in another world. I knew this was happening, and I was obsessed with verifying it but I could never verify it. I was in a trance. I knew that things between us were coming to a conclusion, but I couldn't make up my mind to leave him. It was torture.

I was just putting one foot in front of the other. I'd confront him every weekend, and he'd deny everything. He developed a pattern of lying, which is a pattern of every drug addict.

What broke the camel's back was one day he needed cash and asked if he could borrow my money card. He had my money card for two or three days. The next time I went out to get money, I was five or six hundred dollars short. So I got the printout from the bank. I confronted him. I said, "Terry, you're stealing money, here's the evidence."

He said, "Yes, I did take money out, but that was to buy you an engagement ring."

I already had an engagement ring. That's what addicts do. In the face of being caught in a lie, they will lie more. Their sense of reality is so skewed.

At that point, I had enough evidence. I decided to move out. I found a place and I had friends come and move me out. The day before I left, he broke down and cried and said, "I don't want you to do this. I can stop. Give me another chance."

But I was resolute. I was finished. I had been through too much. I was so relieved to have an excuse to move out. It was just such torture to be living around that kind of stuff.

It took me a year to get over him. It was a very deep love. I'd really thought I was going to marry him. I mourned the loss of the potential—what we *could* have had together.

✳   **Kelly & Patrick**
Kelly Kiernan got involved with Patrick O'Donnell shortly after breaking up with Teddy Gates (see page 76). She was part of a partying crowd, so the extent of Patrick's drinking was not immediately apparent.

This relationship started out being about a good time and a lot of laughs, but Patrick turned out to be a raging alcoholic. At that point in my life, I was in a very self-destructive mode. I'd just broken up with someone. I certainly wasn't pining over him, but there wasn't anybody else around. Patrick was part of the crowd. We'd go to parties, and Patrick would always drive me home, and eventually we started going out.

I knew he drank too much, but I felt like everybody did then. It was the time of margaritas on the weekends. What I didn't realize was that, with Patrick, it was going on seven days a week, and it wasn't just because we were at a party.

The day I realized the extent of the problem was the day we had to go to his brother's wedding. Patrick was the best man, and he was so cold drunk from the night before that I almost had to call the police to break his apartment door down. He wouldn't answer the door, and then he blamed it on me, because I hadn't gone out with him the night before.

He drove like a wild man, trying to get to the wedding on time. I remember thinking, where are the cops when you need them? I was crouched in the back seat of the car, because I was sure we were going to die in a car accident.

At the wedding, he yelled at his mother in a way that I've never seen anybody yell at a parent. I couldn't believe that he would treat his mother the way he did. I started getting a little bit scared about that.

But the relationship went on for a couple more months. I visited him up in Vermont, where he had bought this ski house. It was a snowy day. I agreed I would go to the store and get some stuff. I was trying to make the house nice for him. I came back, and he hadn't done anything that he'd said he was going to do while I was gone. And I decided that he had been drinking while I was out of the house. And I said something like, "I went out in this bloody blizzard for you, and you can't even do what you were supposed to do."

That's when he just started in on me. Screaming and screaming and screaming. I don't even remember what he said. Verbal abuse. He became as abusive to me as he was to his mother. I walked out. The storm cleared and I was gone.

There had been lots of signals that I hadn't wanted to see. Because frankly I didn't want to be alone at that time. My two sisters had gotten married within three months of each other that winter. I remember feeling so desperate and so lonesome and thinking that he was the best I could do. I knew that it wasn't a good relationship and I wanted to get out of it, but I was so afraid to be alone.

Everything with him involved drinking. I don't know why it took me so long to realize that Patrick was alcoholic. I had an uncle who died of alcoholism, but I had just known him as a young girl. He'd been the family bum, really a desperate alcoholic. I thought that's what alcoholism meant. I didn't realize what leads up to it. I just didn't get it.

I don't know where Patrick is today. I do know that he was in a very severe car accident. I'm sure he was drunk.

I did a lot of growing up right after that. I thought, I don't need to be with anybody. And I wasn't for three or four years.

I was so green. I was so young and so inexperienced. I had gone to Catholic girls' schools. Men were from another planet. I didn't understand them. I'd grown up in a single-parent family, so I never saw a loving relationship.

I'm amazed that I put myself through that. My relationship with the man I'm now married to is so loving and protective. So comfortable. His arms around me just feel so secure. And then I think about the time that I spent with this maniac. Thinking: Is this what love is?

✳   **Laura & Kevin**
When Laura Rohmer started her affair with Kevin Farbar, a professional blackjack player, she thought there was something vaguely glamorous (vaguely bad) about his lifestyle, and only gradually realized that his approach to gambling was on the magnitude of an addiction. Years later, married to someone else, she began her interview by saying, "The whole notion of bad guys to me ... that's what I liked."

I went out with a guy once who was a professional gambler. He was a professional blackjack player. He used to travel all over the world—to Monte Carlo and places like that—to play. It's how he supported himself. He was very handsome too.

I met him on an airplane. He was sitting across the aisle. It wasn't any particularly glamorous flight—it was from Miami to New York. He was my age. You know how you just start talking.

He wouldn't tell me what he did at first. We were talking about living in New York, and I asked him where he lived. He had this address that was kind of Chinatown-y, a downtown address. I asked him if he was an artist. He said yes.

We shared a cab from the airport. He used to play at a gambling club at a midtown hotel. I dropped him off there. He said he would call me, and he did. I knew by this point he was a blackjack player.

I went out with him a couple of times, but it was weird. We would go to a movie or dinner, but then he would have to go to work. He would go and play blackjack all night. He would work from ten at night until three in the morning.

As the relationship progressed, I would go hang out at his house or at my house, and he would come to whichever place when he was done. And then I would get up at 7:30 to go to work. I would say to myself, "Oh, you know, he works nights."

I didn't get the fact that at least 50 percent of his income—which I think was fairly considerable—came from betting on things. He slowly revealed that to me. I remember once talking to him about the Oscars. He was a big movie buff. He was like, "The odds on so-and-so winning the Oscar are whatever."

That was sort of when it dawned on me: this guy bet serious money on the Oscars. It was slowly revealed. He had gambler's disease. He bet on the horses. He bet on every sporting event. With bookies. Serious stuff. Not with his office pool.

He had a lot of problems. His mother had committed suicide. Now I realize that he was a psychologically damaged person who dealt with it with this disorder. He might as well have been a drug addict. But there was something Cary Grant-like and dashing about him. I never went to Monte Carlo with him, but I heard about it. Maybe he made it up. I don't know.

He read a ton. He went to the movies all the time. He read a lot of books. He was sort of like a gentleman hippie. He was a big reader, and he was really interested in the fact that I was a writer. He wanted to see stuff that I had written. Over my dead body, basically. I had translated a novel at that time. It was a Latin American novel. And I gave him a copy of it, and he read it, and he was sort of impressed. We had conversations about Latin American literature. Suddenly there was another level. It wasn't emotional, particularly. There was a sort of social-intellectual camaraderie that we had. Briefly. I think he was a person who was not capable of having any kind of emotional relationship.

But he was really Mr. No Commitment. I once asked him how he had done one night, and he told me to *never* ask him that. I gather, because it could have been so great ... or so terrible. He could have won $50,000, or lost $50,000.

It's interesting, because he's very similar to people I know who are in high-stakes Wall Street jobs. Traders, sales people, particularly commodities traders. This guy Kevin had a mathematical approach. He didn't just sit down and play cards. He had strategies and systems. It was as scientific as a lot of the stuff could be. I think that he was a math genius. He knew a lot of people who had given up playing blackjack and gone to work on Wall Street. He didn't believe in that, because he thought that was too straight.

I was attracted to the weirdness of it. It was so glamorous. Even though it really wasn't, of course. And the most glamorous stuff was stuff I had only heard about. Who knows if it was even true? I would meet him at his apartment at three in the morning, and he would come out and pay the cab driver. And then after a while he moved to this hotel. There was something about going to see this guy who lived in this funky but cool hotel. It was pretty sexy.

It started to get a little weird. It became unavoidable even to me that this guy ... I think he genuinely liked me, and I genuinely liked him ... but this was not someone who was ever going to have anything even vaguely approaching a normal relationship.

It got to the point where he would start to call me at one in the morning and say, "Well, I've got a couple more hours to go. You want to meet me at my house at three in the morning?" And I would do it. I knew, even when I thought he was It, that it was not going to work out. He'd call me at one in the morning, and wake me out of a sound sleep, and I would haul myself out of bed, put on my clothes and go over to sleep with this guy that I really didn't know. It went from being incredibly cool to seeming sleazy.

This was in the mid-'80s. It was starting to dawn on me that I was probably not the only woman he called up at three o'clock in the morning. And that when he was in Monte Carlo he probably had other people that he slept with. It just started to seem dangerous, AIDSwise.

I remember meeting him one night, late, for a drink at the hotel where he played blackjack. And there were a whole bunch of his friends there. And for the most part, they were very nice. They were surprisingly eggheady. They were serious brain people. It was mostly men, but there were some women. They were perfectly nice to me, but I just got the feeling that they'd been sitting at tables with Kevin and different women for years. They were like, you seem nice, this week. They weren't unpleasant to me at all, but I just got that feeling. Maybe I was projecting. But it just seemed like well-worn territory.

I can't remember exactly how I ended it. I just started letting the machine pick up when he called in the middle of the night. It wasn't like I hated him. It wasn't like I wanted to completely reject him. I just wasn't up to it any more. What can you say? I think you're as sexy as can be, but you're not what I want any more. In fact, maybe I think you should go to Gamblers' Anonymous.

He was the way he was. I didn't begrudge it to him. I just didn't want to be around him anymore. It wasn't serving any purpose. One time, he called me up. It probably was after a couple of times when he'd called and gotten my machine in the middle of the night. And one time he called me at a more normal hour. Like nine o'clock. And said, "I really miss you. I really wish we could see more of each other. I really think that we could take this to the next level."

I remember having this feeling: I don't think so. I don't think you think so. I think it was that I hadn't been around. Typical. It was late enough in the relationship that I didn't fall for it.

✳ **Caroline & Thaddeus**
*Caroline Marone, a Manhattan-based artist, had known
Thaddeus Leigh very vaguely when she was in graduate
school. She ran into him again several years later at a friend's
wedding in Boston, where Caroline had grown up.*

We met at the end of a stuffy, stiff wedding. We got in this hilarious conversation about Jimi Hendrix. I felt like I had found a kindred soul. We were both really drunk. I talked to him for a while, and then I decided to go home. And I got in a cab, and I thought, that was really fun. I'd like to see him again.

But I had no way to track this guy down again. I didn't know where he lived. And I couldn't call my friend, because she was on her honeymoon. I stewed over it for a while, and I finally got in touch with her and found out that he lived in Boston. The wedding had been in August and it wasn't till shortly before Thanksgiving that I called him. We spoke for a while, and had a really nice conversation, and I said, "I'll be home in a few weeks, and I was wondering if you have some time."

That's when we really got together, over Thanksgiving weekend. We went out Friday night, then I went to his place on Saturday night, and then we had brunch on Sunday before I caught the train back to New York. It was all this glowing beginning courtship.

He's a writer. He's a Southern gentleman with a little spark of craziness in his eyes. Very imaginative. He used to talk about literature in really wonderful ways. It was fun being around him. He was cute. He dressed well in a tweedy way. He's a very warm person. When I first called him, he was so receptive. It was like getting a big hug over the phone.

He came to New York two or three times before Christmas, then I saw him at Christmas when I went home. He came back up a couple weekends. I went home for Easter, and he came over to our house for brunch, and he had liquor on his breath. It was like ten in the morning on a Sunday. I remember being mortified. I remember thinking, my parents are going to see all this and know something is wrong.

When we were at school, I'd seen him drink really heavily—there had been parties where he'd been really looped. But when he was visiting me all those weekends, he either wouldn't drink, or we would just have wine at dinner. He really controlled it. He was really a Jekyll and Hyde. I guess he was really good at concealing the bad stuff in order to survive with me.

Later on, I put all these clues together. Like the fact that he didn't have a phone for a period of when we were together. He didn't pay his bill. Many alcoholics have real problems with money.

Then one time he was supposed to come up to visit me in New York. He was supposed to come on a Friday evening. I'd made all these plans for us. He called and said that he didn't have any money, but that he really wanted to come, and he would figure out a way. He never showed up. Nothing. Didn't come. Didn't call. He had no phone, so I couldn't call him. I did my little thing of walking around New York crying.

By about Wednesday, I was really panicked. I thought something had happened to him. I didn't know what to do. I called his brother, whom I'd never met. I was very composed. The brother said, "Okay. You sound worried. I'll get in my car and go down to his apartment and see what's going on."

It turned out Thad had been on a drinking binge. His brother pushed him out of his apartment, brought him back to his place, and I think was standing next to the telephone making him call me. By this point, it's eleven o'clock at night. He's still drunk. He said, "I felt so guilty when Friday came and I didn't have the money. I felt too horrible to call you."

He'd passed out, blind drunk. He said, "There were a couple of moments over the weekend when I came clear, and I really missed you."

I took all this in. I was in shock. I said, "It's okay. I'm not going to give up on you." After we hung up, I stayed up all night. And thought: I can't go through this again.

The next time we talked, I said, "Look, sorry, but it's over. I think you should really get help."

He said, "What's the point? You've given up on me anyway."

What had happened was that I realized that I just couldn't get towed under by him. I'd had a boyfriend who was a junkie before that. It had just been too painful, being around someone who wasn't there. And I didn't really have any illusions about being able to help Thad. When Andreas, my old boyfriend, and I broke up, we broke up *because* he got better. He had gotten very sick, and had gotten professional help—counseling and detox and all that. As a result, we broke apart. So I didn't even have any hopes that if I did stick it out with Thad, he'd still be with me.

Self-preservation finally kicked in, after a lot of dubious relationships. That was a landmark, now that I think about it. That may have been the first time I ever broke up with someone. And it really started with that awareness of, hey, I can take care of myself. I deserve better.

Recalling her long-term relationship with a junkie, Caroline said, "It had just been too painful, being around someone who wasn't there." The absence that she describes is one of the common threads in these relationships. After coming back from L.A., Kate's boyfriend's focus changed. Suddenly he had new friends and new errands to do, and when he was at home, he was moody and withdrawn. Laura's gambler boyfriend was similarly not present, and she was able to see that things were never going to evolve. "It became unavoidable even to me that this guy ... was not someone who was ever going to have anything even vaguely approaching a normal relationship."

Next, the women often began to experience the more severe consequences of the men's addictions. Kelly found Patrick's drinking life-threatening, and his hostility brutal. Caroline spent several days in hideous suspense when Thad just disappeared. Kate searched her house for needles and watched the level of the bleach bottle go down. She was obsessed and "tortured" by her suspicions, but lacking proof, she didn't have the strength to give up on the "potential" of her relationship.

Her reaction to catching Terry stealing reminds me of Casey Anton in the "Possessive Man" chapter, who was thrilled to discover that her pathologically controlling boyfriend was having an affair, so she had an ironclad justification for making the break. Having unequivocal evidence relieved Kate's ambivalence.

Kelly had stuck it out with Patrick for a while, knowing it was not a great relationship. "I was so afraid to be alone," she explained. But once he became verbally abusive, she left immediately. Laura left Kevin almost instinctively; if there were sophisticated thought processes involved, she didn't report them. When, after she'd begun to withdraw, he made a last ditch play—"I really think that we could take this to the next level"—he was offering too little, too late.

Caroline had already had a serious multi-year relationship with an addict. When she saw what she was up against with Thad, it was earlier negative experience that convinced her that there would be no reward to nursing Thad through to sobriety. But even more significant was her innate "self-preservation" kicking in. She knew she wanted more for herself than to be cast in a self-denying caretaker role.

The Immature Man

Calling a man immature carries the ring of a schoolyard taunt. It's an accusation that we've heard so often that it almost sounds meaningless. But relationship immaturity is actually a syndrome, with a set of symptoms that affect the women who love these men in specific ways.

I should stress that this chapter is *not* about men who are chronologically young, whose immaturity grows out of the fact that they have not had—and changed as a result of—certain formative experiences. The men described here are in their mid-twenties and older.

Once an immature man has targeted an object of his affection, he can not stay away from her, even if he is involved with someone else. In the moment, this lack of restraint masquerades as romance. It makes the man seem certain and decisive, when in fact these are precisely the things he's not. In the stories below that feature men with preexisting girlfriends, the men were suspended between two strong and opposing desires—to get involved with the new woman, who offered excitement and sexual passion, and to preserve the safety that the old relationship provided. This tension is only human, but the fact that these men sidestepped the need to choose is a hallmark of their immaturity.

The clarity of hindsight makes it tempting to theorize that these immature men should have been recognizable from the start. Despite the intelligence and professional aptitude shared by the men described below, there was a common lack of decisiveness about them, a perceptible gap between what they said they wanted and what they actually did.

But as Stephanie, one of the women interviewed below, said, "When you first meet somebody, they're their own ideal." For the first phase of the relationship, the man's on best behavior. It's only after some months have passed that the woman starts to register troubling observations. He's been promising to leave his girlfriend, but it just hasn't happened. He is moody and undependable, and simply doesn't come through in the clutch. He's not inclined to go out of his way to accommodate the woman. In fact, he's philosophically opposed to doing anything he doesn't want to do.

When the woman confronts him, he blames himself. He's working on it with his therapist. He's "depressed." It's as though, by naming his problems, he abdicates responsibility for his actions. It slowly but surely dawns on the woman that the man's affection for her is largely defined by what she does for him. Her needs aren't getting met.

Is there a certain sort of woman who's vulnerable to the lure of an immature man? The women below all craved relationships. They were initially seduced by how badly the man in question seemed to want them. Once they became enmeshed with the guy, they wanted things to work. But these women were not interested in losing themselves. When they realized what they were not getting, they spoke up, tried to get what they wanted, and—when they didn't—they bowed out.

✳   **Amy & Jerry**
Amy Brown had gone to high school with Jerry Larsen, but they had not known each other well. Amy was in her mid-twenties when she heard from him again: He was now living in San Francisco, but was in New York City visiting his parents for the holidays.

When Jerry called and wanted to have dinner, at first I kind of dreaded it, because he was one of those guys from high school who had been nice but not a great, great friend. I had never been alone with him, ever. He ended up coming over to my apartment because I didn't want to go out. It wasn't a romantic gesture at all. It was just practical. He came over, and we had this really wonderful dinner.

He talked about this relationship that he had been in for five years. And was sort of on the way out of. I talked about this relationship of mine that had just ended that had been incredibly intense. Which I really had ended. Which was already a huge difference, as I was later to discover.

And then we sat on a couch and watched a movie. Already on the couch we were sort of touching legs, and then he leaned against me. We were under a blanket. Hands began, and then he sort of looked up and kissed me. And we didn't watch much of the movie. No matter how much I later grew to dislike him, I will always say he was sexy.

And then it was not going to continue, because he had this relationship. He was going back to the west coast, where he was clerking for a judge. He stopped the fooling around at a certain point, because he'd felt guilty about Melissa, this woman he was involved with, and we said goodbye. I thought that was going to be it, a fun thing.

It was New Year's and I went out of town just for the night. And called him when I got back, and invited him to a party. He was very weird on the phone. He called back later and said, "I'm really sorry. I would have loved to have talked to you and to have gone to the party, but Melissa was in the room when you called and I felt strange about it."

So I went to the party. And I got home, and there were a hundred messages from him, just wanting to talk to me. I had taken all my makeup off, and I was sitting in my pajamas, and he called, and said, "Can I come by?" It was his last night in the city. And I said sure. I went into a tailspin and put my makeup back on.

I was totally excited. It was so romantic. He couldn't stay away from me. There was another woman, but he wanted me. He showed up. I was really cool, in my jeans with ripped knees. He was clearly into me. We totally fooled around. He said, "It's so weird. I feel a lot. I don't feel light about this."

He was talking big. It was the second night. He still had this girlfriend. He was still going away. Nothing had changed. So he went out west and called me a hundred times. We basically had a phone relationship for a very, very long time.

He was most romantic during this period. This first month. We were apart, and we had had this intense connection. But he was living with Melissa. So he couldn't talk to me. He would call me when she was in the shower, and then when she was getting out of the shower, he would hang up.

Finally it became clear that he wasn't moving very quickly about breaking up with her. I said, "Look, it's clear that this isn't happening. Let's not talk for two weeks." It was sort of game playing. I also thought that it would give things a certain heat. That he would have to make a choice. Well, as it turns out, that was a mistake, because the short time we'd known each other wasn't enough groundwork for him to miss me. He'd been spending day after day with the person he's been with for five years. How could he make a choice to opt for a person he didn't know at all?

During the two weeks, I wrote him a letter. Saying that I felt like I already missed this person I hardly knew. He called me after that letter. So we started talking all over again.

Things went back and forth, back and forth. And began to really frustrate me. He called me and said, "Look, I realize I just can't choose somebody that I don't know."

He admitted an insecurity. He basically wanted to know that *somebody* would be there, and choosing me would leave him out in this abyss without Melissa, who has been his security blanket for so many years. Although the relationship hadn't been good, and they hadn't been having sex. This romantic thing could totally fall through and then he'd be alone. So he said, "Let's not do this."

And I said, "Okay." I hung up the phone. I was in pain. I was like, this is over before it even had a chance. His inertia bothered me. And his playing it safe bothered me. What is life for, except to find somebody you're going to be crazy about?

So I did 15 minutes worth of thinking. I called a friend and she advised me to call him and say that we should see each other one more time. So that's what I did. I called him back. I went out on a limb and I told him that I thought we should see each other just once before making any decisions. His reaction was incredible. He was like, "I'm so glad you're calling." The coldness 15 minutes ago was so clearly about him being hurt too, and helpless about what to do. So he came for a weekend and we had an incredible time.

We started having these weekends. But he was still living with Melissa. I gave him some ultimatum and he told me that he couldn't ask her to move out. I hung up the phone and I was really upset, and he called me back that night and said, "I did it. I told her."

He had told her about me. And she said she should move out, all in one shot. I was really impressed by that. I was like, okay this is real. He's finally acting. He later admitted that they were having an argument when he told her. He later regretted it, I think.

That relationship was very much built on him feeling needed, and needing to feel needed. She did move out, but she would call him constantly and be crying a lot. And whenever she would call, he would get off the phone with me. It was like call-waiting hell. We would be on the phone and I'd hear that click and my stomach would flip. In the beginning, I was like, I'm going to be strong. I'm going to be understanding. I'm going to be generous. That was my posture. But the other side of this was like, this is bullshit. Something's wrong here. He was indulging every fit, every breakdown she had.

He was not in New York where all his friends were, so he had the excuse that she was the only person he knew there. If he didn't have dinner with her, he'd have dinner alone. What am I supposed to say? That he should have dinner alone? But there was constant anxiety. On any given night, was he seeing her? I would ask him what he was doing that night. Or I wouldn't be able to reach him on the phone and I would know that he was with her. We would have a weekend together, we'd just have had all this wonderful sex, and he'd get back on a Sunday night and then they'd go have dinner. It was horrible.

I never admitted to anyone how bad the moments that were bad were, and how much there was that really disconcerted me. This was the beginning of nine months of breaking down my security. My parents had always taught us that a lover should be crazy about you, should treasure you. I never felt that with Jerry. If I were to preach about relationships and who you should end up with, it's somebody who makes you feel like you're on top of the world.

The whole relationship started in January. He came back to New York in May, and we had an incredible three weeks. We went to shows. We had Passover with his family. I was so seduced by his life being so similar to mine. I felt like I was safe again. His parents loved me. They thought I was smart and funny. We were a great couple.

The three weeks were fabulous and then he went away to a work commitment in France. He was miserable there. There was all this romance in the distance. We were writing a postcard every day. His postcards were all informational. I would scour them for tenderness.

Then he came back from France early. And that's when the real trouble began. I think he was glad to be back, but he felt like he had failed. He came out to my parents' beach house right away. He was jet-lagged and I was in a tennis tournament, a once-a-year thing. He was clearly not that interested in watching me play tennis. If you love somebody, you cheer them on. You want to be there. And he was clearly not into it. It affected my playing. Afterwards, I asked him what was wrong, and he said, "I didn't come back early to watch you play tennis."

He had problems with his family. I went out to their country house and I felt more warmth and interest and attention from his parents than I did from him. It bothered him that his dad liked me so much. Jerry and I took this walk on the beach. It was a nightmare. I remember feeling that I could not get through to this person. There was this scrim between us. I felt helpless. I began to feel completely unattractive. Not funny enough. Not anything enough. I was pretzeling myself to be lovable.

He was completely self-indulgent. His moods, his depressions, his frustrations about things. Things would get him down that I didn't even know had gotten him down. The walk on the beach was pathetic. It put me in the worst possible cliché situation of saying, "What are you thinking? Tell me what's wrong. What can I do?"

"It's not you. Don't worry about it." His answers would stop the conversation. There was no engaging or working through this.

On the other hand, there was constant future talk. As if I was absolutely going to be in it. Before we fell in love, we were talking about marriage. Before we were passionate about each other, we were talking about logistics. And that was bizarre, but that was also what kept me in. When I look back, I see that all the seeds of trouble were there, but I was blinded by the desire to have it work. And also a faith that the goodness was there.

He was smart. He was funny. Sex was very good, very tender, very loving. I really thought that was where the love was shown. I was seduced by that. There was tremendous sweetness physically. He clearly wanted to do things with me, we were seeing each other a lot. He wanted to stay with me. But he quickly settled into inertia.

So then we went to the south of France for vacation, and he didn't seem to be enjoying things. We had this horrible meal where we were silent at lunch. I felt like I was alone. And I said, "How are you feeling about us?"

He said, "Frankly, not that great." Here we were in Avignon, my first vacation in two years, and everything went black. There was all this beauty around me, and it was like this black curtain came down. We went to this waterfall and just sat there, and I was just crying and crying. And saying, "You don't love me. I don't know what it's going to take to get you to love me. I don't feel loved, I don't even feel liked. I don't know what you like about me. I couldn't tell anyone what you see in me."

He said, "You're wonderful." But he wasn't really rising to it. This is the time when he should have come through and kicked himself and told himself to stop being an asshole. He said, "It's my problem. I'm depressed. I didn't want you to know this about me, but I live in this kind of depression. I didn't have a good time with Melissa when I was on vacation with her."

We got so wrapped up in his revealing his neurosis that I was in a position now of helping him. We were again affectionate, and sex was good, but it never really was a fun vacation.

I had a liberating thought: This can end now. I can leave this relationship. I was just going to see France with this guy. I think I basically severed it in my mind then.

My sister and her boyfriend were going to come to France after us and stay in the same apartment. So I was noting things in the guidebook for them. "You can skip this." "You've got to go there and have this meal." And he thought that was totally fucked up.

He told me that my family was so controlling. "I wouldn't want anyone to do that for me. I would just want to come and explore a place." Making it as if I was this neurotic compulsive, designing this vacation for my sister, instead of it just being a caring thing. I kept doing it, because I knew I was right, but I was feeling like an idiot. He made me feel stupid. Our last night there, he picked up the book that had all the notes in it and started reading it and I grabbed it out of his hands. "Why are you reading that?"

He said, "I just want to read what you wrote."

And I said, "Why do you want to read what I wrote when you've already criticized it? You're just looking for more to criticize." I started crying, and said, "Why are you looking for more?"

He said, "There's a basic gap. I don't understand you. I just would never do something like this. I don't get it."

I started crying, and he was on the bed, and I was talking, and he fell asleep. While I was talking.

When I got back to New York, I asked myself what the hell I had been thinking. Crying, adjusting myself to make the relationship palatable. I broke up with him. That's when he flipped out, decided he loved me, cried. And we went back and forth.

I tried again twice more. My parents, who had hated my last boyfriend, thought Jerry was wonderful. And that had an effect on me. This guy had the good in him. He just had to get there. He went into therapy and I thought that was a really big effort. I was completely taken by all his acknowledgements of his fuckedupedness. He admitted to selfishness and self-absorption. And somehow he seemed to always be vindicated by his own self-deprecation. That seemed to get him off the hook. But then I thought, I've been in therapy. I know how long it takes.

While my previous boyfriend had been a man, Jerry was a boy. It's really true. I felt like I was dealing with a child. I spent so much energy focusing my attention on him, that there was nothing left for me. And even at the end, when he told me that he loved me, it was so empty. It didn't stir me. I even said it back, and it was totally manufactured.

Three months into the relationship, I remember thinking, what could possibly go wrong? This is going to be the guy. I was sure. I planned it in my head. The right in-laws. And when you do that, you have more reason to make it work. I had already cast him in the role, and when he fell short, I kept forgiving because I thought he would rise to it.

Until my new relationship, I didn't realize how cut up I was by Jerry. Little slices were taken. In very subtle ways. Jerry didn't make me feel like a good person. Having really fallen in love [several months after ending it with Jerry], I feel so whole now. I feel so built up every day. I could go on a speaking tour, like Marianne

Williamson, and say what love is. When you have it, it is unmistakable, and you should settle for nothing less. It's so worth waiting for the real thing.

✳

Stephanie & Paul
Stephanie Horowitz, who works in public relations in New York, also had a relationship with a guy she'd known slightly in school. She was in her late twenties when she ran into Paul Cross at a party.

I went to a party and in walked an ex-boyfriend of mine from college. And he was with this guy I'd known in eighth grade. Paul. Even back then, Paul had been gorgeous. Mr. Unattainable. I was like, oh, great, an ex-boyfriend and a guy who never knew me from a hole in the wall.

Paul and I started talking. By the end of the evening, he'd stuck his Visa gold card in my pocket. And said, "I don't have a [business] card, so how's that?"

Then he took it back, and said that next time he saw me he'd buy me dinner. My socks were charmed off. He said he was single because he'd just broken up with someone. When you hear that someone was in a long-term relationship, you think that they're capable.

He walked me to a cab after the party and we kissed on the street. I was floating. I knew his background and I knew his friends. He was the ultimate trophy. Immediately "Stephanie and Paul" went through the grapevine. I had five women call me the next day and say, "Watch out for him. He's a heartbreaker."

I thought that they were just jealous.

He called me the next day and we talked for hours. I said, "I'm getting all of these warning calls about you."

He said, "I'm not like that at all."

We went out on Monday night. We went to a movie and then to dinner. We were both so nervous, it was adorable. I knocked over a drink, and he knocked over a drink. We were both shaking, and finally he took my hand and we stopped shaking.

Immediately, it was overkill. There was no way I could have been seeing anyone else. Night and day. We were going steady. We didn't sleep together though. I was ready to, but I told myself it was okay to take things slow.

He would never let me see his apartment. He would tell me it was a mess. And that he hadn't cleaned it in six months. He hadn't worked through business school and was completely supported by his parents. So although he hated his parents, he needed them desperately. He owned his apartment. He lived like he made about $150,000 a year. But when he talked about his parents, he'd get this dark and disgusted look on his face, like an angry little boy. I more and more got the sense that he was a little young. Realizing that as much as I liked him, he was almost a little brother.

He told me that everyone thought he has a perfect life, but that that was all on the outside. On the inside, he told me, he was really fucked up. He was so thrilled that I knew he went to a shrink and I didn't mind.

We went to Nantucket for the weekend. We still hadn't slept together yet. On Saturday night, we're making dinner and he toasts me in the sunset. And he asked, "Is there anybody else I need to know about? Or is it just me?"

I said, "It's just you. How about you?"

He said, "I've gone out with some women I'll probably go out with again."

I looked at him and almost fell off my chair. I stopped speaking to him, and I was upset and he was sorry. He was crying. He'd bought this swordfish and it was horrible and the evening was ruined.

I checked my machine, and there was a message from an old boyfriend, and I laughed out loud. And I said, "Look, Paul, it's fine. We've only known each other for a month, and you're quite right to say you'll date other people, and you set me up. If I'd said I was seeing other people, you would have looked wistfully off into the sunset."

"You're right," he said. "I'm a bad person. It's just that I'm afraid. When I get into a relationship, I lose sight of myself, and I do everything the other person wants me to do, and then when I realize that it's not what I want to do, I turn on a dime and I walk away. And I get accused of breaking women's hearts."

To show him that I forgave him, I said, "Let's make love."

Sexually speaking, he had a lot of hangups. He used to tell me that he really didn't like chests. He was a butt man. Waist down. As soon as we'd start making out, he'd slide down. Put his head on my bellybutton. Everything was lower quadrant. He loved my ass. He loved my toes. He loved my legs. He loved my thighs. He would get in a fetal position in my lap. I used to think there was something wrong with him. But then I tried to talk myself into it. I'd think, well I guess everybody's got different ways.

So when we finally slept together, he was unsuccessful. And that's when it came out that he couldn't make love if he had a condom on. Now, that's a new thing for me in the '90s. Did I trust him? Well, he'd told me that he'd had two long-term relationships. So I didn't make him use condoms. That was the stupidest thing I've ever done.

As soon as he discovered he could do it without a condom, it was all he wanted to do. He fucked me on the beach, he fucked me on the deck, he fucked me on the staircase. All quick, but it was like a kid discovering chocolate.

We'd been together for six weeks, and he was acting incredibly jealous. I couldn't have a conversation with him about having seen other male friends. One time, I was having dinner with him, and his jealousy came up. He took my hand across the table and said, "I'm sorry. It's just that I can't believe that I have you. I don't feel like it's real."

So I later said to him, "I think you should stop being so jealous. I haven't seen you once in the last couple of weeks without the first 15 minutes being about whether or not you're jealous. So why don't we just say we're making a commitment. Nothing big. We'll reexamine it in a week. And I may say tomorrow I don't want it. But at least let's give it a try."

He said, "I'm with you a hundred percent."

The next day he called me and said he was going out to his parents' house on Long Island. I asked him if he wanted me to come. He said yes. Understand that the whole dating process until then had been on my territory. As soon as he got me on his territory, I got to see what he was.

When you first meet somebody, they are their own ideal. They're what they want to be. And that image can be maintained for at least two months. And then they end up becoming what they really are. Now we were on his territory. We were staying in this little fake garage behind his parents' house. This filthy garage. With futons on the floor. It was like the little high school kids had come home. He was 28, but he'd brought all his laundry. It disgusted me. It was a sobering experience.

I got to see how he behaved with his parents. He was so rude to his mother. He was so disgusted by her that every time she opened her mouth, he was like, "Shut up."

And he began to treat me the same way. I turned to him at one point and I said, "I'm not your mother. Everything I say is wrong. I touch my hair, you tell me not to touch my hair. I talk, you tell me I'm not talking loud enough, it's irritating you. I talk louder, you tell me I'm deafening you. You hold your ears. I say something, you correct my grammar. You are so critical. Why do you like me?"

The next weekend, he said he was going to Long Island and he would see me on Sunday. I said to myself, "Should I be upset about this? No, I shouldn't. Yes, I should. Here's this guy, he wanted me to be committed to him. And he's going to Long Island, which is where he'd really rather be."

He didn't end up going because it was pouring rain. On Friday night, I went out with someone else. And Paul called me five times on Saturday morning and asked me where I'd been. I said, "I had a date. And by the way I don't think we should have a commitment anymore. It's fine if you go to Long Island every weekend, but then you shouldn't be the only person I see. My feelings are really hurt."

He said, "Okay, I'll make more of an effort. I don't want to lose you. This means so much to me. I'm really fucked up. I'm with my shrink, and I'm trying my best."

I said, "Okay, I really want to see you tonight."

He said, "I don't think so. If I saw you tonight I'd be acting. I feel this pressure. I really want to be myself. Maybe we should meet at Bloomingdale's tomorrow."

I stayed home and cried. He went out and partied with his friends. Sunday night we went out to dinner, and he didn't speak to me. Then we went to my apartment, and he went outside for 20 minutes to have a cigarette. I said, "Are you sure you want to stay over?"

He said yes. He got into bed and he didn't touch me. He rolled away from me. I was up all night. I was reaching out and touching him, and I felt like he'd disappeared. At the same time, I was so mad at myself because I was being this sycophantish pathetic creature. I was touching him, and he wouldn't touch me, and I asked if he wanted to make love, and he said no. The next day, he went home and I thought, that's it.

He told me he was going to stay in the city on Friday night to see me. I said, "I think we had a hard time on Sunday night."

And he was like, "That's the real me. Sometimes I'm moody. So accept it."

We went out on Friday night. He was quiet and uncomfortable, he looked hurt. I'd had a framed picture of us from Nantucket blown up for him. And I gave him a sterling silver fish from Tiffany's. He seemed uncomfortable taking my gifts.

And I felt like I was trying to buy his love back. I felt like I'd lost him, but I didn't even know if I wanted him. So finally we went back to my apartment and I sat down on the couch with him and said, "Honey, I've done a lot of thinking, and I think that we should take a breather. You don't want to stay over. You were uncomfortable all night the last time you did. We're not happy. I'm not happy."

All of a sudden he started being affectionate, stroking my hair, holding on to me. We made out until two in the morning, and he left. He called me in the morning, and said, "I had the best time and I can't wait to see you again."

And then I never saw him. He'd call me and say, "I'm so depressed. I haven't been out in days." And then he'd say something like, "I went to a party last night."

I was like, oh great, he can go to parties, but he can't see me. So finally he called me, and I said, "Paul, do me a favor, and don't call me unless you want to see me."

He said, "I'm afraid to see you."

A lot of time went by and then all of a sudden he showed up on my doorstep on a Sunday night. We went out and I sat with my arms crossed. He kept reaching out and touching my face. He said, "I want us to try again."

And I said, "I'm not available anymore. What makes you think I'm sitting around for a month?"

And I said, "You wanted to be a couple. You forced me into it, crying about jealousy, begging to know who else I was seeing.

Meeting my parents, me meeting yours. All that you did entrenched me in a relationship. And then you're telling me that as long as people hold off and don't let you cross the threshold, you're okay. The threshold is commitment. And when you get what you want, you turn on a dime and walk away. It's outrageous and misleading and I don't trust you."

He walked me home and leaned up to kiss me, and then he said, "It's really cold out here."

And I said, "You're right. It is." And I walked in and closed the door in his face. And that was the end.

Except that I found out through a mutual friend that an ex-girlfriend of Paul's had been a stripper. He picked her up at a strip joint and had slept with her for a month and a half without condoms. I called up Paul, who was by now seeing someone else I know from high school, and I said, "How dare you? You lied to me."

He said, "You never asked me about her."

I said, "You gave me a selective history. You never told me you slept with a stripper. How could you not use a condom with me?"

I got an AIDS test. I was lucky. It was negative.

✳ **Molly & Josh**
Molly Nelson, a Manhattan-based writer, was in her mid-twenties when she met Josh Harrison.

I met Josh at a party. It was my birthday, and I had gone out to dinner, and by the time I got to the party, I was already three sheets to the wind. He called me two or three weeks later. At this point, I had only very vague recollections of meeting this guy. But I wasn't dating anyone, so I agreed to go out with him.

We were meeting at the bar of a local restaurant. He totally played on the fact that I didn't remember him. He sat at the bar, just waiting for me to recognize him. I looked at him and tried to catch his eye. Finally, he was like, "You don't even know who I am, do you?"

Already, he had this one-up thing on me. Later, when I knew him, I realized that there were all sorts of clues I should have picked up on, but I didn't. He was incredibly charming, but he always had to be in control. That night, we were talking about what we did. He found out all sorts of things about me, but gave really evasive answers about himself. He made up goofy stories. He was a dancer with the Joffrey ballet. He was the cousin of the man who owned the company I worked for. I never got a straight story from him. It wasn't until about our third date that I started feeling like I was getting a sense of a real person. And I liked him when I got to know him. He was never boring.

We started dating. I remember meeting him one night after he'd been celebrating his birthday with his friends. They had a tradition of coming up with elaborate schemes for each other's birthdays. Torture really. They'd given him some sort of ridiculous product, and he'd had to try to convince people on the street to buy it. There was always stuff like that going on in his life. He was very into adventure.

Things seemed pretty good between us. Except at one point we had an argument about something. The way he dealt with it was that I didn't hear from him for three days. That's the kind of thing that really sends me over the edge. I got very upset, but afterwards we agreed that he wouldn't disengage for three days again.

That summer, we went on a couple vacations together. Around that time, Josh started to push for us to live together. I didn't know why all the urgency. At the time, I was flattered. Now I think he wanted the security. He wanted to have a firm grasp on me.

We really talked about it a lot before making the decision. I actually made him sit down and write out his expectations. I did this too. I really didn't want it to be a "wouldn't it be fun to play house?" kind of thing. I wanted to understand where our expectations might differ. We had had such a wonderful time on vacation that I thought, why not? This is a person I really do enjoy spending time with.

So we moved in together, and I would say that was when the problems really started. On a practical level, he was very difficult. He was working freelance, and he would work around the clock. I would come home from work, and he'd be sleeping, and I'd have to be quiet. I'd felt like I'd moved in with him with the expectation that we would really try to make things special. And not only was he not making any effort, he was making things hard for me.

For his thirtieth birthday, I made reservations at an inn. I told him to save the weekend. I had presumed that he understood he needed to be on a regular schedule. By the time the weekend came around, his hours were completely inverted. He stayed up all night Friday, and slept all day Saturday. We ended up coming back early.

There were still great things about it. On my birthday, my present was a series of hats. Each hat had tickets to various events. A chef's hat was cooking classes. A sports hat was a hockey game.

But then he started to think about going to medical school. And then he thought it made sense to move back into his old apartment, because it was near where he might go to school. He was talking about a completely different life. I knew how obsessive he was about work, and that medical school would mean studying constantly, and that I would never see him. So I made up my mind to move out. Much sooner than he expected, I came up with a plan, found an apartment.

Then it became another story. He started talking about how he'd wanted me to move with him. I stuck to my guns. At this point, he went about trying to win me over again. He tried very hard to make things work, to make me happy and change my mind. I had entered his life at a very turbulent time, he told me, and he was sorry that he had let our relationship become a casualty.

I moved into my apartment, at which point he decided that he really didn't know *what* he wanted to do, and he was going to go to Europe for the summer. I was very hurt. But once he was in Europe, he started writing me these incredible letters. He realized that what he really wanted was me, and that was all that really mattered. When he got back, he wanted to try again. I went over and traveled with him for two weeks, and things went pretty well.

When he got back, he'd sublet his apartment again and he asked me if he could stay with me. I hadn't even had a chance to get settled into my new place, but I stupidly said, "Come here, and let's think of it as temporary."

He got a job at an investment bank, and that was better. It provided some stability and some structure, and he was making a good salary, so he felt like he was being paid what he was worth. There would be a month when things went well, then there'd be a hellish weekend when we'd have a fight. Josh's way of dealing was still to withdraw. I found that really painful. I could be crying and upset in the bedroom, and he'd be in the living room, not wanting to deal with it. Not wanting to talk. To me, that epitomized his inability to connect.

His way to deal with our troubles was to start to talk about marriage. That seemed ridiculous to me, because we hadn't worked out how to live together.

That's when I started to see a therapist. Josh always made me feel that part of the problem was that I had unrealistic expectations about our relationship. I wanted things to be perfect. But that wasn't the real world. Whereas I felt that he wouldn't look at ways in which we had very real problems. I needed an objective observer. I needed to know if the problems could be solved.

Every week, when I went to see the therapist, there was something new that had thrown me off. Josh was always throwing me wild cards. All this was really taking a toll on me. I'd gotten much less confident about myself. I felt like I was always working around him, without ever questioning the pretzel I was turning into. Even my friends could see that I wasn't the same. I'd become a mousier person, attuned to work around him and not upset him. But then I started to assert what I wanted, and then we started to really have problems.

What it finally came down to was the issue of my friends. One of my closest friends had sublet his apartment. And he started to develop a series of resentments against her. She paid the rent late once. She painted the walls a color he thought was horrible. He really started to dislike this person who was my closest friend. And he ended up making it an ultimatum: Spend time with her, or with me.

We went on a ski weekend that went really badly. All my friends were there. A friend of mine was really flirting with him, and he was sort of flirting back. I'm not usually the kind of person who cares about things like that. But this culminated in a series of dares in which she ended up running naked around the house. Which was totally inappropriate. He's not the kind of person who would normally push that kind of thing. I felt it was all designed to get at me. It was a painful weekend.

In his mind, all my friends were talking about him. Which, in a way, they were. Not because they disliked him, but because they were worried about me. For me, this was the last straw. I was not going to give up my friends as part of some superficial attempt to make things go better with him.

He moved out. And, probably thanks to my being in therapy, there was no going back on it. The emotional price that I had to pay for being in that relationship just wasn't worth it. Josh was challenging, in the sense that he brought something to the relationship. He had an interesting life. I'm interested in people who love their work. That made me vulnerable to someone who presented this smart, exciting, charismatic self, and had a huge ego at the expense of me. But there wasn't room for me in the relationship. It was all about him.

In the beginning, I was flattered by his attention. But when it became a day-to-day relationship, he was really difficult. It became about his ups and downs, his need to be reassured and to get ego gratification.

Every time I took a step back and compromised, Josh learned that he could take over that much more area. Now, I'm much more careful about not changing myself so much. And instead to take the risk and say, "That's not acceptable to me."

Maybe there are women who marry geniuses, who decide it's worth all that to be involved with this incredibly stimulating person. But I don't want to do that.

✳   **Maura & David**

*Maura Mason is an artist who lives in Brooklyn. Referred to
me by a friend of a friend, she showed up at my apartment late
one afternoon with an iced coffee in hand, sat at my dining
room table and poured out the details of her relationship with
David White.*

I do like being in a relationship, but I was in this stretch when I was on my own. I met this lawyer through a friend. I've always gone out with artists—creative, difficult people. David was not an artist, but he was still a serious person, a thinker. He worked hard. He'd gone to good schools. But he was also very funny.

We met in a bar. I hadn't really felt anything for anybody for a while, so I just decided I liked him. He asked me to go home with him that night. I said no. I thought he was pretty cavalier. That was kind of a turnoff, but I also liked the invitation because it was provocative. I gave him a little kiss on the cheek. But I told a friend to tell him that I'd like him to call me. After that, I ran into him a couple times. He said he'd like to call me, but he never called.

Then I ran into him at a party. There was this electricity in the air. I was into it. I wanted to get to know this guy. We sat next to each other on the couch, he grabbed my hand, he walked me home that night, and we made out for an hour and a half on my doorstep. It was great. And then he proceeded to tell me he had a girlfriend. Which was really a drag. I didn't invite him up.

I went to California for two weeks. When I got back there was a long message on my machine, and a letter as well, saying that he wanted to see me. I thought the fact that he liked to write letters was another plus. The pluses were adding up. He was tall and athletic and cute. It was just such a bother that he had this girlfriend, but I thought I could handle it.

So we made this rendezvous in Central Park. We met there, and we were very flirtatious and he started reading me things out of Anaïs Nin. It was almost too much. We walked around to the zoo and talked about our backgrounds, and spent the whole day in Central Park.

It was maybe an hour before dusk. He asked me if I would like to come back to his apartment. I'm very impulsive. I knew he had a girlfriend. But I didn't care, I was going to sleep with him. We walked to his apartment. Just as we were walking up the stairs, he grabbed me and started running down the stairs. His girlfriend was right in front of us. Walking up the stairs. But she hadn't seen us. We went to a bar, and we sat down and he was holding my hand. I was starting to feel sorry for him.

He told me about how he'd been with her off and on for the last three years and he really loved her, but she needed a lot of care and looking after. She was also looking after him. But he also said that he wasn't in love with her in the physical way. He didn't like sleeping with her anymore. My advice was to break up.

And then he started in on his philosophy of relationships: He really felt that he wanted to have more than one relationship at a time. That was healthy for him. He felt that people should start thinking about alternatives. Why should he give up his care for this woman to be with someone else? Why couldn't he have both?

I said, "Well, you have to work it out with her. I have to go. This has been a great day."

He was walking me to the subway, and then he goes, "Oh, let's just take another walk through the park." I was still wanting him. And so we walked through the park, and we just decided to do it in the park. We consummated things behind the Metropolitan Museum. It was just getting dark. And then he had to go home and deal with her. That was okay. I thought I could handle it. A little adventure.

But then he started calling me. This went on for six months. He'd call me, and we'd see each other, and have this thing, and he'd freak out afterwards and run. Leave my apartment and run back to Lucille. Or he'd have a big fight with her and call me. I'd call him. Sometimes she would be there, and he'd have to say that it wasn't a good time. It would make me so angry that I would just say I'd had enough.

He would write me letters trying to explain his problem. Once again, he would try to sell me on this whole idea of multiple relationships. Not polygamy in the sense of the Mormons, but he thought that a group of people could live together and share each other. I was saying, "I think it would be very difficult." I'd had art instructors who had open marriages, and bitterness always accumulated. It just ended up being this odd battle between the two people.

I asked him if his girlfriend was into this. No, she wasn't. She was totally against it, and it caused her a lot of pain. He did tell her about me.

I was really getting mad and frustrated. I was wondering why I wanted to keep seeing him. I was trying to break it off. Part of what kept me in it was that I felt he was vulnerable in a way, because he allowed himself to be pathetic. From being very strong and arrogant and wanting to be in control, he'd become vulnerable and I felt sorry for him. I wanted to understand. We met in May, and this went on through September.

Finally in September, I said, "If you're not going to break up with her, I don't want to see you anymore."

I had all this passion for him, but it was being destroyed. Everything was centered around his problems. His relationship. His wish to change society.

We broke up, but he kept calling. I was obsessed for a while, I

would talk about him all the time with my friends. But then I figured, I was driving myself, and them, crazy. I started getting over
it. I didn't hear from him for a month or so, and then he called me
up and told me his mother died.

Then I was really sorry for him all over again. I wrote him a letter. And then I called him and Lucille was there, and she just started screaming at me. I realized I couldn't even call him. That was it.
So when he started calling me around Christmas time, I was really
short with him. He'd call me and I'd hang up. I was just amazed at
his persistence. I was really losing a lot of respect for him.

But I was still very much sexually attracted to him. So one time I
was housesitting this very nice brownstone in the Village and I
invited him over. It was just so coy. We were trying to be really
seductive with one another. I was making dinner and we were
making small talk, but there was all this tension. The frustration
was building. It wasn't very satisfying. We had dinner. And then
he told me he had to leave because he had to go back to his girlfriend. He'd been calling me, he could obviously tell that I wanted
to be with him, but he had to go back to his girlfriend.

I ended up seducing him. And then he just freaked out and said,
"I have got to go."

I noticed his datebook had slipped underneath a chair. And I
said, "Go ahead and go," and I grabbed his socks, ran down the
stairs naked, and I threw his socks out in the garden. I said, "Go
out and get them. But if you do, I'm going to lock the door." He
had to leave without his socks. I also knew that his datebook was
underneath the chair.

He left and I was upset but kind of laughing. I was a major
snoop, and I looked through his datebook and saw all these different women's names. Dates. I was so jealous, and so pissed, and
pissed at myself for sitting on this bed, looking at his notebook.
He called me the next day, saying he had left his notebook there,
and I said that I had thrown it away. And I did. He was mad at
me, and I didn't care. I went into the garden and got his socks,
and threw those away too. That was it. I was through. I was completely finished.

And then a week later he called me up again. It was ridiculous. I
was mean to him again. I think I was dating other people a little
bit. Come spring, he wrote me a couple letters talking about his

mother, and his girlfriend, and how he wanted to get out of the relationship. The reasons why he was in the relationship. His therapy and his therapist. It was like he was trying to communicate with me. So then I start the ball going again. I was sick in bed, and I called him.

He said that he would come over and bring me some soup. He also told me that he had broken up with his girlfriend. All of her stuff was out of the apartment. I was happy about that. I guess I still wasn't over him. I still liked him. We started going out pretty regularly after that.

He was very interested in group relationships and "poly-fidelity." He started getting all this stuff from California—all these books on polyfidelity from these old hippies. That was another part of our discourse. He was getting off on it. He loved it. I was playing with it a little bit. I think that's why he liked me, because I played with it. Argued about it. The books were ridiculous. They really were tiresome. David liked to be the center of attention, have the other women. But where did other men fit in his theory?

Now we were a couple. But he was telling me these fantasies he was having about other women. He wasn't acting on them. But I was getting pissed. Because I felt like we were at the beginning of our own thing.

He was also interested in sex clubs. He didn't necessarily have any fetishes of his own, but he loved to go to the fetish clubs. Places like the Fetish Factory that had light S & M things. He told me different stories about these clubs he had gone to. That piqued my curiosity. I think that's another reason why I stuck around. I just wanted to explore some things. I did end up going to some of those clubs. We never participated. We dressed up once. My friends started calling me the Margaret Mead of the sex club scene.

I'd really want to analyze it, talk about it afterwards. David took it very seriously. He needed so much attention. I did like exploring, but I didn't like that he took it too seriously. It's one thing to be curious. I'm a very curious person. But it wasn't like he and I would go home afterwards and what we'd just seen would be the biggest turn-on between the two of us.

He also liked sex toys. I learned about sex toys with him. We did have some fun. But just when things seemed to be calming down, and we were getting to know each other more intimately, there was a barrier. He never said he loved me. That was something that was really missing.

There was always a crisis. He was depressed about his mother. Worried about Lucille. So it was always like: David, David, David. What's wrong with David today? I was slowly distancing myself.

Everything was settling down, it was getting into the fall. And then we're in bed one day, and he said, "I hope you don't get mad, but I have something to tell you. I answered an ad in the paper for a couple."

He'd sent a picture of us to this couple that had advertised in the *Village Voice*. "Couple looking for other couple, for a serious thing."

He said, "I hope you don't mind. I sent the photograph and they responded. And I'd like to show you what they sent me."

They had sent Xeroxes of two photographs. One was a close up of their faces; in the other one she had her chest bare, and he was holding her and kissing her neck. Andy and Marie. He goes, "I hope you don't mind, but I did call them."

I said, "I don't like how they look, number one. No way. I just want you to know that I'm not into it."

Then he wanted to go to the Phoenix Club, this swinging couples place. He heard about it through Andy and Marie. They went all the time. I guess Andy had liked our photograph and he kept calling. Those places are expensive. I said, "You pay for it, I'll go." We went. I didn't get dressed up. I wore a black turtleneck and a coat that didn't reveal anything. We went to this club where all these middle-aged swinging couples were. It was like this big disco. People were dancing. There were a lot of women in lingerie. It was funny because people were very direct. We went in and this kind of ugly guy walked up to us and started talking: "What are you into?"

I said, "Well, we're meeting a couple here." I just thought I'd play with it. The guy's wife joined us. And he said, "We're into having people watch us."

David came over and he was fairly quiet. I did a lot of the talking. I think he was taking it too seriously. We said, "Well, we'll let you know later."

Suddenly, I'm like, "David, that's Andy and Marie over there." They were much older than their photograph. We went over and sat with them. She was totally taciturn. He was very gregarious. They thought we were great already. They really wanted to have dinner next week. I'm jawing it up with Andy. And David's just sitting there, trying to think of something to say to Marie, but she's not saying anything. Then this other young couple that Andy had invited showed up. They were kind of cute in a way. Everyone was just making small talk.

David wanted to go watch the older couple do it. He wanted to run off with this young couple that just joined us. It was four hours into the evening, and I was like, "I have to go home now."

He was a little upset. But we left and went home. I was laughing. I thought it was hysterical. David was upset. He said, "They liked you better than me. You got all the attention and I didn't."

Suddenly something just clicked. I realized that I couldn't even believe how immature he was.

Around Christmas, I just broke up with him. He was so upset and so hurt. Like I had just used him and manipulated him. He had broken up with the other girlfriend for me. I cited very specific things. I said, "You really have to grow up. You have to learn to get some self-confidence. You have to stop using all these other avenues to figure out sex and intimacy."

He was so afraid to express love. It would have taken forever to really make our relationship seem like it was a natural rich thing. I wanted—and want—someone who understands it already. We were close, too, but it just wasn't good enough. I didn't want to be the teacher.

I said to him, "I just think you have to see your analyst for a long time. You probably won't be ready to connect to one person for a while."

Of course, he's still convinced about the poly-fidelity stuff. I respected the questions, but I felt like he was going about his search in a destructive way. It really hurt our relationship.

We went out as friends recently, and he asked me to marry him. But he had also asked his current girlfriend and his other ex-girlfriend too. He was serious. He was going to buy a house. We would each have our own room. I would have a studio. He was still taking this whole thing so seriously. He wouldn't give it up. I said, "David, you haven't changed. Do you think you're thinking of something new? This is the most typical male fantasy. We live with you. Do each of us also have three husbands?"

With the exception of David, who concocted an entire lifestyle philosophy to accommodate his wishes, the immature man's principle relationship tool is the admission of inadequacy. When Amy and Jerry had their confrontation in France, he was quick to say, "It's my fault." Paul told Stephanie, "I'm a bad person."

In the initial phases of the man's self-revelation, his "honesty" can be appealing. Maura described the way that her anger and frustration over David's inability to act was tempered by pity: "Part of what kept me in it was I felt he was vulnerable in a way," she recalled. "From being very strong and arrogant and wanting to be in control, he'd become vulnerable."

While this might sound refreshing to a woman involved with someone who will never admit to weakness or fault, the admissions ultimately ring hollow. The immature man seems to feel that being true to himself involves indulging his failings, rather than taking responsibility for behaving in a clear, decisive manner. As Paul said to Stephanie, "Sometimes I'm moody. So accept me."

Before the woman reaches the conclusion that her relationship is seriously flawed, she goes through a stage of self-doubt. Amy, a woman whose friends describe her as vital, attractive and intelligent, recalled a moment in which she began to feel "completely unattractive. Not funny enough. Not anything enough."

The trauma of a relationship with an immature man comes not in the form of a painful breakup, but rather in the woman's realization that the relationship has turned her into someone that she doesn't want to be. Both Amy and Molly talked about having become "pretzels." Molly referred to having become "a mousier person." Stephanie put it in harsher terms: "I was so mad at myself because I was being this sycophantish pathetic creature."

The woman sees herself as reaching out, extending herself emotionally and taking responsibility for the relationship. And while she's groping for ways to improve things, she slowly recognizes that, despite all her laudable efforts, she has been denying her own needs. Although her decision to break up—always against the wishes of the man, who panics at the prospect of loss—represents a reassertion of those needs, her sense of herself has been temporarily compromised.

Hot/Cold Men

This is perhaps the most frustrating kind of man a woman can fall for: He wants to be involved ... and he doesn't. His behavior moves from ardent to elusive (and sometimes back to ardent again) without discernible reason. The woman's best instincts tell her that his interest is genuine, but, at certain crucial moments, it evaporates. The selectively silent man radiates eagerness until certain issues come up that he just can't talk about. Often, those issues center around his ambivalence; rather than facing them, he exits. The man who rushes into relationships comes on strong and earnest, wielding his seriousness of intention like a badge of honor. When the woman he desires finally gives in to his lobbying, then his disappearing act begins. The man who flees from intensity backs off at precisely those moments when he feels closest to the woman he's involved with.

In the preceding two sections, the nature of the men's "badness" is clear. They either committed an action or actions that hurt the women, or were immersed in an impenetrable self-involvement that left the women out in the cold. In this section, it's often practically impossible to label *what* the men did or didn't do.

Some readers will judge the stories that follow to be nothing more than relationships that never got off the ground. They will label them as cases in which the man saw a fundamental incompatibility. But to quibble over whether or not the men in question acted irresponsibly is to miss the point. These guys are "bad" in the sense that the women involved with them suffered huge amounts of frustration and pain.

Without sufficient distance to see his heated coming and going as a pattern, a woman often infers that the man pulled back *because* of some essential quality about her. Often the man's elusive behavior makes the woman angry; in retrospect, she judges herself harshly for expressing this anger, and traces the relationship's demise to her lack of "control." Perhaps she pursued him—again *because* he was so hard to pin down—and she blames herself for having been unattractively aggressive. Perhaps she spoke up about her needs, or pressed him to talk about what was going on. As she tries to make sense of why such a promising relationship ended, she keeps coming back to the ways that she was assertive rather than accommodating.

Some might say that the reason these relationships are so confusing is that the woman has left behind the self-martyring shores of old-fashioned "femininity," in which she would have tried to hang on to the man by suffering in silence and, perhaps, by playing hard to get. Instead, she acted strong and pursued what she wanted. And it was that assertiveness that seemed to drive the man away. This causes the woman to torment herself with the questions: Are the consciously rejected old ways in fact more effective? If I had just put up with him, would he have "come around" of his own accord?

And in focusing on those questions, the woman at least momentarily forgets that this probably was a man who could never have made her happy. Even if he had tried harder to preserve the relationship with her, his ambivalence about intimacy would still have been an essential part of who he was.

With some distance, a woman can intellectually understand the man's role in what happened. The part of her that labels him a "bad guy" in the first place recognizes that the mysterious back-and-forths of the relationship resulted from his problems, not her own inadequacy. She can reach into the grab bag of the last decade's self-help literature and read about men who are passive-aggressive, men who are ambivalent, men who can't commit.

But the inner recesses of her brain may well harbor self-doubt. The cultural perception that women's anger is unattractive is lodged in there somewhere, and she may partially succumb to self-judgements like "I was hysterical" or "I became a monster." She may review her insecurities, and may carry decreased confidence to her next relationship.

Complicating her ability to make sense of the relationship is the fact that the man is so clearly not evil. In fact, he actually has good intentions. He honestly *thinks* that he wants to be in a relationship. The men who retreat from intensity, who were perhaps the most self-searching of the men in this section, were often quite forthright in claiming relationship problems as their own. (In several of these stories, the men warned the women that they had difficulties with relationships, and the women made the mistake of misreading these confessions as promises of change.)

In sum, it is precisely what's missing from the following stories—a clear sense of the man, his intentions and motives—that makes the relationships they describe the most damaging in this book. A man who takes a woman's money, or who verbally humiliates her, or even a man who drinks on the sly leaves a woman angry or sad. A man who punctuates his highly visible pursuit of a woman with periodic retreats into the shadows will leave her blinking in confusion, and, ultimately, doubting her own eyes.

The Silent Man

In Pam Houston's short story "Cowboys Are My Weakness," the narrator describes a conversation with her frustrating boyfriend: "I worked up to saying that maybe it was a good idea for me to start seeing other people. That maybe we'd had two different ideas all along and we needed to find two other people who would better meet our needs. I told him that if he had any opinions I wished he'd express them to me, and he thought for a few minutes and then he said,

'Well, I guess we have Jimmy Carter to thank for all the trouble in Panama.'"

Articulate in other realms of his life, the selectively silent man reacts to women's efforts to talk about issues in a relationship by changing the subject, clamming up, or pretending not to hear what the woman has said. He might, in fact, be called selectively deaf.

Accusing a subset of men of being unable to talk about emotions is a staple of male-bashing, one that's been lodged so often that it's easy to forget that there is true pain behind the tired words. But the women quoted below were among the most frustrated I interviewed.

Part of the reason these men's silence resonates so painfully is the way in which it rewarms memories of undemonstrative fathers—the original silent men in many women's lives. One woman told me, apropos of something unrelated, "My whole childhood, I can remember going up to my father dozens of times and asking him if he loved me. He'd say things like, 'You're my favorite six-year-old daughter.'" Right honey, he might just as well have said, and we have LBJ to blame for that mess in Vietnam.

But a lover's frustrating silences do more than just tap into a woman's latent anger at her father. They may also lead her to distrust her own instincts. The man's behavior suggests that he badly wants a relationship, and that he genuinely cares for the woman in question. On the other hand, his verbal absence at crucial moments comes off as an abnegation of responsibility, a sign that he doesn't care enough to go the distance. And since he won't talk about it, how can she figure out what's really going on?

The woman may initially choose optimism. She may project her own hopes onto the blank slate he's presenting her with. These projections may include her empathic theories about why he's as tied up as he is, and about how he really wants to "get through it" and open up.

Unfortunately, as was the case with the men with sexual problems, the challenge of "helping" him can shift her focus away from the question of whether or not she's getting what she wants. And if she does happen to have unresolved issues with a silent father, breaking through to the lover may take on even greater urgency. She may stick around longer than she otherwise would have, because the task of cracking him open feels so compelling.

And, in fact, her optimism may be misplaced. All the struggle to get him to talk misses what's often the real point: That his inability to communicate is a symptom, not the disease. He's not just unforthcoming: He's unavailable. And all the discussion in the world can't change that.

✳ **Caroline & Daniel**
Caroline Marone met Daniel Walker, a lawyer who'd gone to the same college as she, at the gym.

I'd been working out at the same gym for two years, and no one had ever looked at me. It was mostly old men, and this little clique of absolutely gorgeous gay guys. So one day, I looked up, and Daniel caught my eye. He was doing sit-ups and I was on a weight machine. He had the nicest smile. Like a baby, almost. These little eyes that rolled up. He was looking straight at me with wonder. It wasn't cool. It wasn't a game. He was looking at me, and I fell for

it. We had some superficial conversation, but I remember him saying he'd be back on Wednesday. I went on Wednesday and he
wasn't there and I got all upset.

A week went by. Then one night we were working out at the
same time, and he took me out for a drink afterwards. And we had
the nicest conversation. He seemed totally in control. We didn't
necessarily have that much in common, except an understanding
and a sense of humor.

It was shortly before Christmas, and he came over to my apartment because I was sick. I don't know quite how it happened but
he came up behind me and touched the back of my neck. And I
just backed up and turned around and fell into the most wonderful kiss.

Everything that happened from that moment on was incredibly
in sync. I've never had this with anyone before. Our bodies were
perfectly poised. It was like finding myself. And that's what kept
me in it for so long after everything got bad. Whether it was hugging or backrubs, it was just magic. And it was so comforting and
special to me.

But things fell apart really fast. I went home for Christmas. He
was calling me five times a day. Sometime during this period, I
mentioned that an old boyfriend of mine had been a junkie. He
wanted to know the whole story, and I got all emotional telling it.
He called me back the next morning. He'd worked himself into a
total panic, thinking about IV drugs and AIDS. He was convinced
that I had AIDS, that's why I was sick. He was convinced that I
had given it to him the one time we'd slept together. That was the
beginning of the trouble.

He wanted me to go get tested. I got tested. The two weeks
while we were waiting for the results, he was absolutely no help.
He was so wrapped up in his own fear. When I tried to confront
him about not being there for me, he just clammed up. We never
had any dialogue about anything difficult. He would just shut
down. I would tell him what wasn't working for me. And he
would clam up, and I would lose my nerve, and finally I would be
in a steaming rage. Because nothing I said was being addressed.
He would say that he needed time to think about things. But he
would never really get back to me.

Once I found out I was negative, we went back to having this passionate relationship, but the lack of trust got planted there on his part, so he had something to hold against me.

On Valentine's Day, he showed up with a ring. And a huge card. I was so touched. But after he gave all this stuff to me, he told me he was going off to Thailand for two weeks. He was leaving in three days.

When he got back, he'd come over maybe once or twice a week. It was always very impulsive. He'd call me at 10:30 and say, "Can I come over?" He'd have been drinking with some friends in the neighborhood, and he'd just show up on my doorstep.

At the same time, he would do this thing where he wasn't reachable by phone. I would try to call him. I would show up at his house. I'd get angry that I couldn't reach him, and he'd get upset. It turned out there was all this baggage about his old girlfriend trying to reach him. He had a clear pattern of passive-aggressive stuff. By late spring it started dawning on me that I shouldn't be doing this, but I didn't have the courage to get out.

He would never make plans in advance. I wouldn't know whether to make plans or not. I'd been going out with him for six months, and I never had any idea where he was or what he was up to. For all I know, he could have been cheating on me. When someone is not reachable, you get suspicious.

The irony with Daniel is that, in the end, I was the one who was unfaithful. I'd asked him to do things with me—to come visit my family at the beach, to come with me to my college reunion. He always found some reason not to go. So I went on vacation, I went to my reunion, and I went to visit a friend at a resort where she had a summer house. And I met another man.

I was coming back on the train from visiting the new man, and I ran into Daniel. We spent three weeks trying to break up, and ended up sleeping together. I ended things with the new guy I'd met. Daniel had pretty much checked out at that point, but I hadn't. I kept clinging to the hope.

He came over one night. He said, "My life is a mess. You're the only person I can talk to." I gave him a backrub and things got physical, but he wouldn't have sex with me. That was an absolute first. The only thing we had in the end was sex.

That Sunday I was in the park. I hadn't heard from him all weekend and I was upset, but it was typical. I was walking along, and I ran into him walking hand-in-hand with this other woman. Something in me just took on composure. And he was composed. I don't think she knew who I was. It was a very calm conversation, but the amount of emotional energy going back and forth … it was like a huge force. So finally I just said, "I want to talk to you before you leave."

He was going to Germany. I got home and left a really shrill message on his machine saying, "I need explanations before you leave town."

His plane was at three. He called me at 1:30 and left me a message. I called him back and his line was busy so I had the operator cut in. But there wasn't really anything to say.

People who knew him said they couldn't figure out why we had been together. He liked to go to baseball games and play rock and roll; I liked to go to galleries. We had this very isolated relationship that had nothing to do with our day jobs. Or my friends or his friends. But once he pulled back, it became this huge challenge to scramble after him. It was like a drug, and I got hooked.

What I learned is when guys are silent, be really careful. There aren't that many guys I know who lie outright. They just go blind on things.

✳   **Suzy & George**
Suzy Sayre is a New Jersey-based writer, who met George
Newhouse after a long spell of being single.

I met a guy, his name was George, on September 30 of last year. It was the love affair of the century. He was divorced, 35. Anyone meeting him would just think he is the nicest guy in the world. We got along incredibly well. We did a lot of things together. He called me. He wasn't ambivalent. It was nice and easy.

He was from Cleveland. He went out there over Thanksgiving and we really missed each other. He was going to go back again for Christmas. He said, "We're going to miss each other so much. Is there any way you could come out to Cleveland after Christmas, and see me and meet my family?"

To me, it was great. This person wanted to be my boyfriend. We slept together for the first time the night before he left for

Christmas vacation; it was a Saturday night. And then I was going to my family in Virginia, he was going to Cleveland. And then I was flying out to meet him the day after Christmas. We were going to be apart for a week.

We slept together and that was fine. I totally trusted him. Then he didn't call me in Virginia. He'd said he was going to call me and he didn't. I went through hell. I was with my family, and I was thinking, did he die? I was totally overreacting, but we'd just slept together, and I just wanted him to call. He finally called the night before I was flying out, which was Christmas night. I kind of got mad at him. I felt ill at ease the whole time I was there. I wasn't really sure why.

We came back. He had plans for New Year's Eve that he'd had for a long time. I had suspected his ex-girlfriend, whom he had gone out with for three years after his marriage, was going to be there. What was I going to say?

So he goes off to this New Year's weekend out of town. And I went to a party where I met a guy who wanted to go out with me, and I said, "No, I'm totally in love with this other guy."

We were at my apartment one night, and I was planning to go to Virginia. It was my mom's birthday or something. I said to George, "Do you want to come with me? We could come back Saturday."

He said, "Well I can't really go, but couldn't you go down Saturday instead of Friday, and you and I could go out on Friday night?"

And I said, "Sure, but why?"

And all of a sudden his attention became riveted on Larry King. And I didn't say anything. I was totally paranoid. I thought, he's planning on doing something with his ex-girlfriend.

I went to Virginia. I got back. I called him. He didn't call me for a day, which was not like him. And he called and he asked how my weekend was. I said it was great, and asked him about his. He said, "It was great. Interestingly enough, I was in Washington too."

My parents live right outside Washington. I asked him what he was doing there. He said, "Someone invited me to go on a press junket thing."

I said, "Who the hell invited you?"

He said Amanda, who was his ex-girlfriend. I lost my lid. This guy had been telling me he loved me.

This was in mid-January. At this point all the details begin to blur. Because it's clear he's spending a lot of time with this woman. He said he wasn't sleeping with her. I didn't know what to do. We connected so well. I didn't want to just walk out. I spent a part of every day in tears. He wouldn't listen to me.

I'd ask him if he'd like to come have dinner with me and a friend, and he'd say he had plans. I'd be like, "What are you doing?"

He'd say, "Someone invited me to dinner."

In the meantime, George was telling me he loved me. I said, "Does Amanda know about me?"

He said, "No, not really."

I was yelling at him. He was getting mad. I went out and bought a book called *The Dance of Anger*. And I called the guy I'd met on New Year's Eve and started dating him too. At some point I told George about him. I didn't know what I was doing. I was trying to be fair to everyone. I hadn't really gone out with anyone in a long time. I didn't know what the rules were. I was trying to be honest. I stopped sleeping with George, because I found the whole thing morally difficult.

Right before Memorial Day weekend, George and I went out to have a drink. Things had been deteriorating. And he told me that he had been telling some friends how well he and I communicated. I just lost it. Because I knew he was going to go see Amanda on Memorial Day weekend.

I blew my lid in this restaurant. I started screaming at him, and we got the check, and we had this big scene where I stormed out and he followed me. I was screaming at him, and he was following me. He was crying. I was crying. I said, "We can't see each other anymore. I've had it. This is ridiculous."

So we stopped seeing each other, but then I started getting flowers and letters. The whole bit. He kept calling. I finally told him about two weeks later that we couldn't talk to each other anymore. Because I needed to sort out my head. I didn't know what I was feeling.

George and I met and we just really connected. It was one of those windswept affairs. It seemed like everything was right. Then he did this stuff to me, and it was just so hurtful, mainly because he wouldn't sit down and talk to me about this ex-girlfriend in a direct way.

Some months have gone by. Now George and I are talking again. We never had a real sense of closure before. Now we're talking without all the huge emotions. A lot of what he did came out of insecurity. He didn't want to talk because he didn't want to change the situation. He was scared to tell me that he couldn't change the situation. Because he was afraid that I would leave. It helps me a lot to know that.

✴   **Jill & Ed**

Jill Borden, a television producer, described Ed Sommers as "the guy who was probably my biggest heartbreak." They had been in a class together in college, but she'd never really noticed him until they started bumping into each other after college.

I ran into Ed two or three years after college, at some party for a theater group. He hung out with my friend and me. He's the kind of guy who can really listen and can talk to women and stuff. We were smoking a million cigarettes and dancing nonstop. The three of us spent the whole evening together. At the end of the night, I remember him saying, "We should get together some time and roller-skate."

And I said, "Oh, yeah, right." And I slammed the door and kept going. And I didn't think about him at all.

Then I saw him two or three years later at another party. He was just doing his thing, which was hanging out, laughing at things that I said. Hearing me. And not taking up so very much space. A lot of guys will do all the talking, and just spill out every little thing about themselves.

At the end of the evening, he asked if I wanted to go to another party. And I said no, and he took my phone number, and I really didn't think about him that much.

Two weeks later, he called me on a Saturday to go out that same night. I had just that day broken up with this guy I was seeing, so I said sure. My attitude was that I didn't like him that much anyway, so why not?

We went out. I remember thinking at the end of the evening that it was just a nice dinner. I had no idea that he was interested in me as a date, even. It wasn't 20 questions-ish, the way a lot of dates are. We were just kind of chatting, and I remember having a relaxed conversation.

We started seeing each other, and I got more and more attracted to him. He was a computer geek, who did neat interactive research. I work in television, and I've been extremely interested in interactive stuff.

I sort of thought I had him wrapped around my finger, and then this weird thing happened where gradually I was wrapped around his finger.

Three months into the relationship, I said on the phone, "Ed, I don't even know if you love me." This was my way of broaching the topic: Were we going to make that exchange?

There was this really, really, really long pause. And he said, "Are you finished?"

I was kind of traumatized, but I somehow made it through the conversation. I don't know how I forgave him at that moment for being so brutal about that.

I think I brought it up again two months after that. He couldn't talk about it. He couldn't say, "I'm not able to say that." Or "I can't deal with emotions." He couldn't even say, "It's just not my way." He would just sort of wait for me to be done babbling.

He was very similar to my father and obviously I chose him for that reason. I remember feeling like I really needed to deal with this. So I took him out to lunch in the middle of the day, so there'd be no "are we going to have sex now?" thing going on. We went to a restaurant and I said, "Because I'm such a freaky weirdo, it's just me and the way I was brought up, and it's the way my mind works, I just need some kind of verification of your feelings for me. I understand from your point of view that my asking you to tell me that you love me is asking you to speak French, and you can't do that. But I need you to find some way of doing something like that. I need you to search within yourself and find some way of giving me something that will supply that kooky need I have."

This is what I thought a shrink would have said. It was completely to no avail. He said, "Okay."

There are so many mysteries as to what happened in that relationship, because I really do believe that he loved me. It was a serious relationship.

He went to California for a three-month job. We'd only been going out at this point for eight or nine months. I thought I would go out there for one weekend, and he would come here for one weekend. He absolutely would not come to New York to visit. He couldn't say why. He couldn't discuss anything related to his beliefs or his emotions. He would just stare at me. When I asked why not, he said, "Because I don't want to."

When I asked why he didn't want to, he said, "Because it's not what I plan to do."

I think I said in my mind, I'm going to wait. He wants to get through this. He wants to not be like this, because he loves me.

The day before he was due to come back, I remember I tried to reach him, and I wasn't able to. I just cried all night the night before he came home, and I didn't know why. I picked him up at the airport and I brought him back to his apartment. He said, "Let's go out to dinner now, and not have sex." I just knew something was weird.

I asked him if he'd slept with someone else while he was out there. He said no. I said, "Did you fool around with anyone else?" And he said yes.

I didn't flare up right away. I said, "Oh and how many times?" I asked very methodically. I tried to get as much information from him as I could before I blew up.

He thought that I was going to just get past it and continue the relationship. Of course, I didn't. All I wanted from him was some sense of why. What could we do about it? If he'd said he was sorry I would have taken him back in a second. Nothing. I remember screaming and crying on the phone: "Why? I just want to know why. Talk about us. Anything."

And it was just a complete silence on the other end of the phone.

If I were a shrink, I'd be saying that he was exactly the way my father was. That was my mother's whole issue with my father. My father really doesn't say the L word.

But if you'd asked me at the time why I liked him, I would have said it was because he was just so original. I've been given to understand that I take up a lot of space. There are not that many guys who can deal with that. Or who like women who are like that. I think I felt that, with him, I was permitted to be who I was. More than any guy before, he really understood who I was. Liked the parts of me that I really liked.

He laughed when I was over the top or in a crazed mood. We had the same sense of humor. Our private silliness was very much on the same level. That's always a sign of a good thing.

He really was the one who made the axe fall. He did the real verbal "we are breaking up." It should have been me. I should have been saying, "You are completely not coming through for me."

We had had tremendous sex, so we continued sleeping with each other every second week, for a period of a month or three. I was very attracted to him physically. Each time we had sex after that initial blowout, I wasn't thinking that we were getting back together, but I guess I was sort of looking for him to get back together with me.

I started seeing a shrink for the first time. And I think it really took me two years to get over him. I still have friends who say, "If that relationship could have survived, you guys would have been the best kind of funster, professional team."

Up to a year and a half afterwards, almost any time he extended himself to me, if he called me, I would think: He wants to get back together. I was hoping for it. Even after he started seeing somebody else.

We had one incredibly kinky sexual escapade at least four months after he started seeing this woman very seriously. Probably a year after we broke up. He had a friend in from out of town. The three of us were making out intensely at one of the Democratic National Convention parties. This incredibly ridiculous threesome, we were rolling on the street at 82nd Street and Second Avenue at three in the morning, like a sandwich. Making out. The three of us went back to my apartment, and nobody had sex, but there was all sorts of weird stuff that happened.

Even after I thought that I was completely over him and understood where things were, I still yearned for him. I would call him periodically. I wanted to get back together with him, but I basically expected that we could be friends.

We had periodic lunches. We were out to lunch one time. I was very happy with how it was going. We were having this chatty, laughy conversation. We were just appreciating each other's sense of things. I thought this was great. At the end of the lunch, I was pretty proud of the fact that I hadn't made any sexual comments. Or flirted or anything. I started walking him to an appointment.

He was going to go into this building. I went to kiss him on the cheek, with quite a bit of control.

He turned his face a quarter of a degree so that his lips met mine. I could not believe what happened to me. In one twenty-fifth of a second, my head flew back, one of my heels came up, my arms went back. I opened my mouth. You know the way you see women on the covers of those romance novels? Draped back. With their back arching, and the leg up? It was the most pathetic, sick, desperate attempt at a full mouth kiss. It happened so quickly. He pulled himself away, and he said, "You're really bad."

I was walking three blocks in a stupor. Thinking: I can't believe I did that. I can't believe I'm still crazy about him. I can't believe I have no control over myself. I can't believe I'm still attracted to him. I can't believe how pathetic that was. I can't believe how embarrassed I am. I got to the corner, and this street guy came up to me and said, "What happened? Something obviously just happened to you. You might as well tell me."

The woman in one of these relationships tries to understand the man's behavior, using her own psychological lexicon. Not sharing his difficulty communicating, she interprets his inconvenient silences as limitations within his control, mutable blocks that, with sufficient effort, he will work through. As Jill put it, "I said in my mind, I'm going to wait. He wants to get through this. He wants not to be like this, because he loves me."

But these stories are not only about silence. Look at the ways the men in this chapter were unavailable that had nothing to do with face-to-face communication: Caroline's boyfriend Dan was impossible to reach on the phone. He wouldn't make plans in advance. He declined all her invitations. And, finally, he got involved with someone else while he was still marginally involved with her. George not only remained very much entwined with his old girlfriend; he also wasn't free on New Year's Eve or Memorial Day or numerous other occasions. And Ed wouldn't visit during the summer, and had an affair.

In short, the men were not all there: If they had been, there wouldn't have been such a need to talk. George's explanation— that he didn't want to talk because he "didn't want to change the situation"—is one that bears listening to. No news very well may be bad news. As Caroline summed up, "When guys are silent, be really careful."

A boyfriend's impenetrable silence can lead a woman to feel "paranoid," as Suzy did the night when George suddenly became hypnotized by Larry King. The fact that she labeled herself paranoid when her suspicions were in fact legitimate shows the extent to which the relationship was shaking her trust in herself.

The demise of one of these relationships is often extremely painful, because the man is incapable of talking about breaking up. The woman may just throw up her hands in frustration and walk away, as Suzy did. But if the man ends things, the woman is left wondering exactly what went wrong. As Jill put it, "There are so many mysteries as to what happened in that relationship."

Jill remembered that every time Ed would call after their breakup, she would hope that he wanted to get back together. These hopes are understandable, given that a strong sexual attraction persisted, and more importantly, that he had never really conveyed to her what about the relationship hadn't worked for him. The part of her that had intuitively believed in his love couldn't believe that he wasn't ambivalent about disengaging.

Jill turned that post-breakup lunch into a funny story, offering herself as the butt of the joke. She called herself "pathetic," "sick," and "desperate" in a single sentence. She berated herself for both her feelings, and her lack of control.

This is the greatest danger of the silent man. He elicits strong feelings, but a communication vacuum forms at the heart of the relationship. The woman has no sounding board for her hopes and frustrations. The result is that she often ends up feeling isolated and crazy for even having emotions at all.

The Man Who Rushes In

This man approaches the object of his desire bearing a gift: himself. He is, he tells her, practically before he learns her last name, open, available and ready. Unlike the womanizer, who comes on similarly strong, seriousness of intention oozes out of this guy's pores. The woman, initially skeptical of what she sees as too much pressure too soon, eventually capitulates, only to find that what she's been offered is, in fact, as ephemeral as she'd originally feared.

This behavior, like that of the silent man, invites a guessing game. Why the urgency? And why the retreat? The problem here may be that the man wants love, any love, and he's so eager to find it that he allows his imagination to anoint likely targets, without doing any of the judgmental probing that would allow him to see if his feelings have substance. *Or* this may be one permutation of ambivalence: He genuinely is attracted to the woman, but once she pronounces herself available, his fears of being trapped are triggered.

In all of the stories that follow, the man was the one to leave. In two of the stories, he moved on to someone else, in what seems to an outside observer to have been an equally impulsive fashion. In each case, the woman, who had meant to be cautious, but who had been lured out of her self-protective shell, was left wondering exactly what had just happened to her.

✳   **R o b e r t a   &   A a r o n**
Roberta Willard had just ended a difficult relationship when she met Aaron Wright through friends.

I was just beginning to come out of my cocoon after a really hard winter. I'd had surgery for cervical cancer and the difficult end of another relationship. One night, I was out for dinner with four wonderful women friends. In no way was I intending to meet men. I was leaving the restaurant at about 11:30, and I heard someone calling my name. It was Don, a friend from high school. He was sitting at a table up front with his girlfriend Ellie and this other man named Aaron.

I had noticed Aaron already, when he'd gotten up to go to the bathroom. He was a type that I like: tall, dark curly hair, glasses. He'd walked by and we'd all looked at him, and one of my friends said to me, "Roberta, he's your type."

I just snapped right back, "Oh, he's probably some nerdy lawyer."

So as we were leaving, this handsome man turned out to be sitting at the same table as my friends. I sat down to talk. He was very drunk, I found out later, although I couldn't tell at the time. He was rambling on and on. Somehow I happened to mention guitarists—Eric Clapton and Richard Thompson. He picked right up on that, and began talking about Richard Thompson. Who was, in fact, one of his obsessions.

I knew this man was crazy, clearly, but he was also very, very intelligent. We hit it off. He was the ex-boyfriend of Ellie, Don's current girlfriend. It was the first time the three of them had been out in a while. Because Aaron had just gotten divorced.

I was attracted to Aaron. I called Ellie's office the next day, and I asked for his number. She said that she thought he would be delighted to hear from me. So I called. I was nervous. We made a date.

We went out that Sunday night. We had a really nice time. He was really smart. An environmental lawyer, on the right side of

things. He drank a lot. Also chain-smoked. After dinner, he asked
me if I would like to go to my place to listen to some music. I said,
"I'm a little reticent about having you up to my apartment on a
first date."

He said, "I wouldn't take advantage of you. I just want to listen
to some Fairport Convention." It turned out he had about five
tapes in his knapsack.

We came to my apartment and listened to music and began
talking. He was very, very perceptive, and I found myself really
pouring my heart out to him. I told him what a hard time I'd
been through. He said, "You're so mysterious. There's a sadness
about you."

I started telling him about what had gone on with the cervical cancer. And then he said, "I want to give you a hug." I was so charmed.
We hugged, and then we kissed for a while, and it was lovely.

We were sitting on the floor after he had kissed me, and he said,
"I just want to say, I think we should see each other. I think we
should have a relationship."

And this just seemed way too fast. But I said, "Well, yeah, I
would like to see you again."

He began calling a lot. We made a date to go to the theater on
Thursday. He'd actually wanted to see me before then, but I felt
like I wasn't ready. He made it clear that he'd been obsessing
about me the whole week and he couldn't wait to see me. Thursday loomed large for him.

At the time, I thought: This is a man who's really not afraid of
his feelings. Finally, I meet someone who's smart and sensitive.
He's in therapy. He's lived with quite a few women before. I felt
like he wasn't afraid to jump in.

We went out to the theater on Thursday. That was really fun. We
had a bite to eat, ran into a colleague of his, began talking. He said,
"This is the first time I've run into someone from work who's seen
my private life. You hit it off with her well. We'll have to go out with
her and her boyfriend. This is great. I can really integrate my life."

I thought, this is exciting. Someone who's discovering himself.
We came back here, and he wanted to stay over, and I didn't want
to have sex for the first time on a weeknight. We ended up fooling
around for a while, and then he went home.

Saturday rolled around, and he said, "Let's go out to a really nice restaurant. Why don't you pick a place?" I had all these ideas. And then he kind of forgot that he'd mentioned this. He came over in sneakers and a T-shirt, and he sat down and said, "I was thinking, I think we should have sex the whole night."

I said, "Whoa. Wait a minute. If you let me come to you, I will. But you can't crowd me."

He said, "I'm really glad you said that." We went out to a neighborhood place for a bite and then came back here. I'd sort of been planning this whole seduction number. Getting into it. What was I going to wear. What candles was I going to have. The first time we made love was really tentative, nice and comforting but ... well, first times are always hard. But then the next morning, it was just wonderful.

He was saying things like, "We could rent a farmhouse in Brittany." "We could go to Mexico." "We could go to Puerto Rico for the weekend." "I really want to show you Cancun. I know a fair bit about Mexico." This was a fantasy.

I said, "I can't afford to do any of those things."

He was a lawyer who made tons of money. He said, "It can be done."

I was thinking, I finally met a man who says these things. But I was also thinking that things were going way too fast. I told him that he was scaring me.

He said, "I'm afraid you're going to think I'm a bad investment. I'm just divorced."

I said, "I want to open my heart, but I can't just do it on command."

He said, "I feel the same way. But give me time. I could fall in love with you."

He always wanted to spend both weekend nights together. I didn't. I needed my space. We started spending about one weekend night and one weeknight together.

In a few weeks, we got invited over to Don and Ellie's for dinner. Aaron and Ellie had some unfinished business as far as their relationship was concerned. Aaron told me that he'd left her after they'd lived together for three years because, even though he still loved her, he found himself not attracted to her anymore. I asked him how soon after meeting they had moved in together. It had only been two months. With another ex-girlfriend, it had been three weeks.

Aaron and Ellie went up to the bedroom and had a very heavy conversation. He came downstairs, and then we went home shortly afterwards. We were in a cab in a traffic jam, and he said, "You know, maybe I do need a six-foot-tall blond babe with big tits. Maybe this isn't going to work out at all. Maybe you just think I'm some semi-literate hunk. You guys were all talking about art and all these openings, and I didn't know what the hell you were saying."

We had talked earlier about insecurity, and I had expressed my fear that a lot of men wanted six-foot-tall blond babes with big tits. He threw this right back in my face. I think he was drunk, but I didn't realize it then. I should have just jumped out of the taxi. I should have known this was curtains. I should have known this was a toxic man. He should have come with a warning label.

My head started spinning. I felt like there was a vice gripping my temples. The cab dropped us off and I let him come upstairs. I told him how hurt I was. He said, "I know I've been ham-handed, but you just don't understand what I mean. I've been very confused about the male myths and what I'm attracted to."

I said, "You don't have to work that out on me. You don't have to say everything. Save it for therapy."

We went to sleep without making love. The next morning, we ended up having sex and sort of making up.

We had another talk about how this was his first relationship out of his divorce and it probably wasn't going anywhere. He was really not available. But he qualified it by saying, "Hang in there. It's going to take some time, but I'm not saying it won't happen."

We kept dating, but the intensity was kind of lost. He called me a lot though. He would just call to talk. He worked very hard, but he was given to having thirty-five-minute conversations in the middle of a very busy workday. About everything. Like everything he did was fascinating. Like: "So, I got my new shirts from J. Crew yesterday." Or "I'm going to buy a new Walkman today." There was something so lame about all this. But I, being the good listener that I was, felt that this person needed encouragement. He needed to feel like he could talk about what he was doing. He was clearly lonely.

I was disappointed. I had had a lot of high hopes for this relationship. He was smart, he had a steady job, he *seemed* emotionally available, he liked to talk about his feelings. He liked sex. He kept saying, "I've never had amazing sex like this before. This is the best sex I've ever had in my life. I can't believe how tuned-in we are physically. I can't believe how sensual you are. I love the way you touch me." All this great stuff. We were very physically compatible.

One night he told me that he was going to New Mexico for a weekend to see Louisa, a friend that he and his brother had met when they were traveling in France the previous summer. The three had traveled around for a week. It was purely platonic. But I had a feeling about it. He reassured me, "She's too flaky. She's too much like me. I'm not attracted to her."

But I was jealous that he was going out there. In the meantime, I was going to France, to visit someone there who wasn't a romance, but with whom there was a distinct possibility that something might develop. I asked if he was jealous that I was going to France, and he said no. And I was upset that he wasn't jealous.

I was over at his place one Thursday night. He was going away for the weekend with some friends. He'd invited me, but I knew that all they were going to do was smoke pot all weekend. So I'd said no.

I should say at this point that he'd get high a lot when we were together. He admitted to me that he had a problem. He also drank a lot of beer. He said he wasn't sure if he had a problem. His shrink really wanted him to look at that, but he couldn't. He said that life was just better intoxicated.

Anyway, he was packing to go away, and I started massaging his shoulders. He was going through his drawers, and he said, "This is going to be hard."

And I said, "Are you going to miss me?"

And he said, "No. It's just hard to pick out which turtlenecks to bring."

I was so embarrassed. I just curled up into myself.

He said, "I told you that I wasn't really available."

"I guess I'm just hoping. I'm trying to enjoy this for what it is," I said. "But when you tell a woman that you want to take her to Brittany and Mexico and Puerto Rico, and when you send her tulips at the office, and when you tell her to hang in there, and when you want to spend both weekend nights with her, to me that indicates a desire to be serious."

He said, "That's what you wanted to believe. The story you were telling yourself in your head."

I just started to cry and I said, "Don't bully me." We went to bed.

I couldn't sleep. I never slept well with him. It was three in the morning, and I just got up and left.

I left for France and he left for New Mexico at about the same time, and we said we'd see each other when we both got back. I wrote him a postcard. I actually missed him. I missed being in bed with him. When he got back, he said, "Let's get together."

He came over on Saturday, as usual ten minutes early. He was chronically early. He was not dressed for dinner. He was in sweaty workout clothes. He asked about my trip and I asked about his. He said, "It was very interesting. A lot of personal stuff happened. I had a spectacular weekend with Louisa, and she and I decided that we belong together."

I said, "Are you getting married?"

He said, "Yes, that's the goal." They'd decided not to make love, because waiting was the spiritually correct thing to do. She was going to pack up her belongings and move in with him.

We went out to get something to eat. We went to the same cafe where we'd met, and we sat at the same table where we'd met. The waiter came over. There had been a wedding there in the afternoon and the waiter recognized us, and he said, "So, when's yours going to be?"

I said, "Never. This is our last date."

✳   **Pam & Doug**

Pam Hitt met Doug Swenson shortly after she moved to New York City. She emphasized the way in which both she and Doug fell for manufactured images of each other. Her story illustrates the role that active and hopeful imaginations can play in the early stages of attraction.

Doug was different from all the people I had been meeting in New York. Everyone else was struggling. They weren't sure of the directions they were going in. They were beginning artists or writers or musicians. Having come from Minnesota, I was now living in an incredibly depressing little apartment. And then Doug came into a friend's studio. And it was like: Ah, someone different. Different from the weak ragamuffin guys I'd been seeing, guys I had to take care of. Doug had confidence. He had a car. He was going places.

I was singing with a country western band, and he came to see me perform. He caught me when I was really coming on strong. I had energy. I was fixed up. I was bleached blond. Really dolled. I played up that image, that role, for the singing thing. So he fell for that. He loved that he could take me home in the morning, and I'd be wearing a dress with sequins falling on the sidewalk and my hair all over the place. We both fell for an image of each other. Were we both wrong. Little did he know that I was a farm girl from the midwest. The glamorous was part of me, but such a small part. And I was buying into an image that I wanted. He was more upscale than I was. Than my friends were. We'd go to great restaurants. He had money. He was just out of law school, but I think he had been selling drugs before that. But he had to put that behind him if he was going to become a lawyer.

We were going out two, three times a week. But he was going through a real depression. He had finished law school and he was applying for jobs. And trying to get into that corporate law world, which was really a difficult thing for him. Going from living in California and doing drugs, and switching over into mainstream society. He was looking for work.

I wasn't in touch with myself. I was scared to death in New York, still. I'd pulled away from everything out in the midwest when I got here. I didn't know what I wanted to do. The singing was good but I was still looking for someone to define me. Instead of me defining myself. I wanted to just get involved in his life. His life looked pretty good.

I wasn't actually that ambitious as a singer. I wasn't that ambitious at my work. I didn't know what I was doing. These became glaring defects. He couldn't handle where I was at, because it was mirroring his own ambivalence.

He was very much a father figure to me. Very protective. When we'd go out, I'd be really uncomfortable going to a place if it was too fancy. But he would just make everything easy. I felt real special, real important when I was with him. My own self-esteem was quite low. He provided reassurance. Until he started to realize that I wasn't what he thought I was.

Initially I'd felt like I had to live up to his image of me, but then I stopped. That's my own self-preservation ... I can't live a lie. There were some things that we related about, and he definitely knew how I lived. He knew my friends. I was making my own mark. I think he always liked to live a little on the wild side. I think he thought that I was more on the wild side than I was. The cutting edge. I'm really kind of middle of the road.

He was an opportunist. He thought I was going to do something for him, and when he realized what my capacities were, what kind of person I was, he had bigger plans.

He was living his fantasies through me, because he was kind of vapid. He didn't think that much. He was not a true thinker. He was more like a locust or something. When I look back now, I don't consider him someone with an ethical outlook. He slid by. By playing the game and looking the part. By schmoozing, he got to where he wanted to be. But he's not anybody whom I would admire.

We had been seeing each other so much. We were really locked into each other. And then all of a sudden, bam, I went to this party and he was there with someone else—someone I'd introduced him to.

We all had the same friends. It was real obvious to him that I might have been at the party. And there were all these pictures of the two of them together. That was it. We never talked again.

This guy came from a male world. He had a real sense of power. He *took*—because he knew he could. And I was like, "How could you?" I wouldn't dare. You just don't do that. It's not right. For him, you do what you have to do to get where you want to go. In a way, I get attracted to that attitude, because it's so against my moral philosophy. It looks really strong.

Time was how I got over it. And realizing that the relationship was about trying to buy the myth of someone to watch over me. Someone to take care of me.

✳ **Suzy & Cliff**
This is the counterpart to the story Suzy Sayre told on page 205. Cliff Fox was the man she met at a New Year's Eve party when her other boyfriend, George, was off ringing in the new year with his ex-girlfriend.

My boyfriend had to be out of town for New Year's Eve, so I went to a party and I met Cliff. He wanted to go out with me, and I said, "I can't. I'm totally in love with this other guy."

But things were falling apart with my boyfriend so I proceeded to call Cliff and say, "Let's go out to lunch."

We went out to lunch, and we started dating. Cliff knew that the other guy, George, was still in the picture. But he'd just turned 40, and he told me, "I'm having a crisis, and I'm looking for love and I just want to get married."

He treated me very well. He took me to the opera. He saw me on weekends. He was really challenging me in a good way. I started to get really attached to him.

I wasn't sleeping with Cliff yet, because of George, and Cliff was a little pissed about that. But he was willing to see what happened. I finally split up with George. Cliff and I spent Memorial Day weekend together, and we slept together.

Not too long after Cliff and I started sleeping together, I had this conversation with him on the phone. Until then, he had always been very lovely and aboveboard. Then we had this weird phone conversation: I felt that he was distancing himself.

He said, "I'm just not ready to make any big decisions right now. I don't want anything to be too serious. I know we were talking about going to see *Jurassic Park* together, but I'm going to see it with another friend. Is that okay? You shouldn't be upset."

I'm like, "Fine, I could care less."

He said, "My brother and my niece are coming into town in a couple weeks. You know that play *She Loves Me*? Did you want to see that? The reason I ask is that I'm going to go see it with my brother and my niece."

I didn't care about the play, but I said, "You know, Cliff, I feel really pushed away."

He said, "Oh, no, honey. I'm not pushing you away."

I put down the phone, and then an hour later, I realized that he'd been really obnoxious. So I was up all night crying. The next day I picked up the phone and I let him have it. I said, "You can't do this to me. This is ridiculous. This is bullshit."

He said, "I think you're really great, and I would like to continue seeing you. I don't really know what to say. I feel kind of tongue-tied."

He handled it pretty well, because I really was kind of hysterical. So I said, "Okay, well, I feel upset, so I want to get off the phone."

That night I spilled scalding soup on my leg. Got second degree burns. I called Cliff the next day, and I said, "Well I've been punished for yelling at you."

He laughed. He'd gone to see his shrink. He said, "I feel a lot better. I find this intimacy stuff really scary."

We went out that night, and we had a perfectly fine time. Things went on okay for a couple of weeks. He had to go on a business trip for ten days, then he was gone for another ten days to visit his family. We talked on the phone about how much we missed each other. Then when he got back he called me and said he wanted to come over. He came storming into my apartment and threw his arms around me. His heart was pounding. I thought it was really weird. He pulled away, and he said, "I'm having troubles with the relationship."

He sat on my couch and there was just this outpouring. "I don't think I'm feeling the way I should be feeling. I keep asking myself, why don't I love her more? You're everything I ever thought I needed. You're sexy. But I'm not falling in love; I don't know why."

I was completely stunned because I hadn't even seen him in three weeks. I was trying not to cry. I said, "I don't know what to say. I don't even know if this is open to discussion."

We had had this thing where we were going to spend a day out in the country having a picnic, and we'd planned it for a long time. He said, "The really terrible thing is that we'll never be able to go on that picnic."

I just looked at him, and I said, "Get out."

I was upset. I spent a week lying in my bed crying. It was awful. It had been a pursuit-panic kind of thing. The minute I became available, he started panicking.

Then I got a letter from him, with some pictures he had taken of me, saying, "I just wanted to make sure you knew that you're everything I ever thought I needed." He proceeded to list seven good qualities of mine. "But I just wasn't falling in love, and I didn't know why." And it ended "sadly, Cliff."

It was typewritten. It had been ten days, and I had finally stopped crying every day. The letter started it all again. I called him up after I got the letter, and just reamed into him. I was screaming. I said, "I don't need your blessing to get on with my life."

He was like, "Okay, okay. It was just my way of saying goodbye to you. I feel like I shouldn't call you anymore."

And I said, "You shouldn't."

I haven't heard from him since.

This is *his* garbage that he did. Which is something that I have to tell myself about eighteen times a day. I liked him a lot. He used to tell me that he thought we were soulmates. He had a therapist, and he seemed fairly conscious of his problems, and he seemed to want to work on them. He articulated them. The fact that he started balking almost right after we slept together upset me a lot.

A friend told me about this book called *Men Who Can't Love*, which is a totally hysteria-producing book. At this point, my apartment was full of self-help books.

My feeling with the whole relationship was that I was willing to see what happened. I was not asking to get married tomorrow. We had been on the right track, I'd thought. You're supposed to maintain yourself and work slowly. I thought it was going to take time, but I thought we were doing the right thing.

He was the one who put a lot of pressure on the relationship. Cause he said from the beginning, "I want to get married, I want to have kids." So we couldn't just date. I had to be marriage material. I felt like I was being interviewed.

I still write mean letters to him and keep them in my notebook. The thing about the whole relationship was that I felt like I never had a chance to express myself.

I'm kind of naive. I come from the provinces. When he used to talk about this fear of intimacy that he was trying to overcome, I was afraid I wasn't up to that. I worked hard and slowly to trust him. And he gave me every indication that I should. It wasn't windswept, but he was always on time, and he always called me, and I was really getting very, very attached.

I have this letter I'm planning on sending him. It's fairly even-toned, but I do want to send it to him, because I feel like I have a right to express my point of view. And whether or not I'll talk to him I don't know. I've been waiting to send it because I want to make sure that I'm not wanting some kind of a response.

In the aftermath, I've been writing fiction and I got some of that published. So I feel like I'm developing myself regardless.

It seems appropriate to reiterate a point I made in the introduction: Not every relationship is meant to be. On one hand, each of these stories could be read as nothing more than a promising beginning that went nowhere. When Cliff told Suzy that he wasn't feeling "the way I should be feeling," no one would say that he should have just buckled down and forced himself to fall in love.

The "bad" behavior is not in the man's leaving, then, but in the bulldozing way that he entered the relationship. Aaron told Roberta on their first date that he thought they should have a relationship. And although Cliff was aware that he had issues with intimacy, he was so intent on marriage that Suzy felt like she was being "interviewed" for the role.

Of course, the man's eagerness may in fact be a powerful lure. Despite her insistence on caution, Roberta was drawn by the fact that Aaron "wasn't afraid to jump in." Women who have histories with men who've teetered endlessly on the brink of involvement may find a man this seemingly available hard to resist.

And the woman may well have brought her own desires—to have a relationship, or, in Pam's case, to be taken care of—to the table, causing her own better instincts to suspend themselves. It happened that Doug, with his trappings of suaveness and self-assurance, perfectly fit Pam's bill ("He was a father figure to me," she recalled, at a time when she was feeling "scared to death.") So she went for him despite the fact that she didn't really admire his character.

Aaron is the only one of these men whose relationship history is reported, but that alone should have been sufficient warning. He moved in with one ex-girlfriend after two months, another after only three weeks. And everything about his approach, especially his wish to spend so much time with Roberta, suggests that he lacked the ability to function normally as a single person. Getting into a relationship, it's tempting to infer, was a defensive ploy to avoid being alone.

And when Roberta tried to talk about her disappointment, Aaron was not available. He accused her of wishful thinking because she took his statements about the future at face value. This "it's not *my* fault" maneuvering leads the woman into the painful realm of self-doubt. She blames herself for not having heeded her initial impulses towards caution, for believing in the man's fervent courtship, for having hoped that this easy-come romance might in fact be real.

Perhaps one of the reasons that Pam's story sounds different (more analytical, less angry) from Suzy's and Roberta's is that it took place several years ago. (Both Suzy and Roberta spoke to me a couple months after their relationships ended.) Pam had had time to process the experience, and so she was able to see how both partners' imaginations and ideals went into their choice of each other: "We both fell for an image of each other."

When anyone—male or female—feels certain so fast, chances are his or her imagination is hard at work, making over a flesh-and-blood human being into a dream lover. It's almost inevitable that disappointment will follow.

Cliff told Suzy that they were "soulmates." His letter said that she was "everything I ever thought I needed." Yet he "just wasn't falling in love." This could mean that an essential chemistry never existed from his end and that his hopes of having finally found marriage material blinded him to that lack. It could also mean that he idealized love, and thought of it as a magical state that would soothe his internal turbulence and make him feel whole. Of course, no lover would really be able to do this, so any nascent romance would fall short.

Suzy theorized that Cliff's withdrawal was a permutation of the fear-of-intimacy issue. During the entire period she was involved with both Cliff and George, Cliff was ardent, responsible and eager. It was only after she'd dismissed the other guy and started sleeping with Cliff that he began pulling back: "The minute I became available, he started panicking."

But all this unilateral searching for an explanation is exactly the harm of a man like this. The woman, with her reasonable wish to understand what just happened to her, comes up with all sorts of theories, but has no basis for testing them. The man, unequipped for self-inventory, is no help at all.

Recovering from one of these men can be harrowing. Despite the intellectual knowledge that the man was acting out internal issues, there's an irrational and often subterranean tendency to internalize the rejection, to feel that it took place because the woman was somehow just not good enough. As Suzy put it, "This is *his* garbage that he did. Which is something that I have to tell myself about eighteen times a day."

The Man Who Retreats From Intensity

These relationships start with sparks. Lots of them. Before the couple actually gets together, the flirtation is electric with promise. The first kiss is, as one woman put it, "hallucinatorily amazing." But once things are consummated, the man backs off, disengages, disappears. Some time passes, and then he's back, eager all over again. The details vary, but the pattern is cyclical: Intense fusing leads to retreat, which is followed by renewed pursuit.

This "I need you/I need to get away from you" tango is perhaps the most concrete manifestation of intimacy fear. In one of the stories below, Tim described his feelings to Samantha (in a letter, appropriately enough): "There's something that panics in me when I'm near you ... I don't know what it is. The quality of your intimacy. It's what makes being with you so wonderful. It's also what makes being with you so scary. Something in me flies."

The urge to fly that the man experiences seems to be a reflex, rather than a choice. As described in Tim's letter, it's an overload phenomenon, beyond his conscious control. Once the intensity of the moment fades, the man is reminded of all the ways in which he truly desires the woman, and so he tries again.

Women who fall for a man who does this feel safe in the beginning: they are receiving unmistakable signals that their feelings are reciprocated. But safety is what these relationships lack, because feelings of closeness are precisely what compel these men to withdraw.

Before the woman gets a clear read on his pattern, what she

experiences is elation. When the guy's in pursuit mode, anything seems possible. Her hopes are raised by the sheer heat of his interest. Which makes the slow dawning of disappointment all the more painful. Once the pattern has played itself out a couple of times, the whole relationship begins to make the woman fearful: She is constantly, as Roberta Willard said below, "waiting for the other shoe to drop."

One woman, whose story I didn't use, but who was "the deepest I've ever been in love with anybody" with a man of this ilk, echoed this: "We had a high-octane rapport, but there would be so many times when I would want him and he wouldn't want me. Eventually, I grew to fear him. Even after I started to fear him, I still wanted him. I was truly powerless."

A woman involved with a man of this sort is powerless to change him, certainly. As the endless back-and-forths of Samantha's relationship show, these are not relationships that solidify when trust develops, or that experience major evolution once the man and the woman can talk things over honestly. The fluctuations seem to spring entirely from the fact that the man can tolerate a certain degree of closeness and no more.

✳   **Samantha & Tim**
Samantha Erickson is a professor at a large university in the northeast. She prefaced her story with a more general comment about male-female relations: "There are so many women who are powerful and beautiful and know how to use it, and that's very confusing to men. In some respects, in me there's a kind of underlying desire for cultural vengeance. Men have done this for years, now it's our turn. But I won't tell you those stories...." Then she told me about Tim Schuler.

I've always been attracted to men who are extremely articulate. There's this full line of philosophers. And occasional poets. They're always really poor. But more than anything, there is an element of combat. I love the intellectual combat. I love that struggle. Maybe there is a part of me that is threatening, because I like the fight. It feels like brain exercise. Which can be a good thing if it's directed in a healthy way. But the only men who attract me are those who frighten me a little bit because they're so smart.

I was chairing a panel at an academic conference. I was walking among the booksellers, and flirting with these millions of charming men. At the table of the press that's affiliated with my university, I noticed there was this beautiful, angelic-looking dreamy man. Naturally, I really just wanted to look at the books at his table. I started thumbing through them, and I think I asked him a random question about some book that I was looking for that I knew they had published.

He started to answer, and then this very young, naive-looking boy came up and started trying to pick me up. Somehow this provided an opportunity for an alliance between me and the angelic one whose name I didn't yet know. We started carrying on this dialogue that was sort of a subtext to this other guy who was trying to pick me up. It was really very charming.

Tim was incredibly articulate. Incredibly powerful. He was working for this press but he was also a poet. His book was about to be published. He was one of those people who is so lyrical and powerful and philosophically subtle, who understands the pleasures of language.

I had to go to a talk. He said, "Come back. Come back tomorrow. Promise me you'll come back."

I went off to this talk, and I couldn't think about it. This rarely happens to me, but when it happens, it really happens. I was in one of those agitated states. I went to a cocktail party later, and I brazenly tried to pick up about twelve men.

The next day, towards the end of the day, I casually swung by the table. He said, "I've been waiting for you all day."

We talked. When I said it was time for me to go, he nervously said, "Well, could we have lunch sometime?" I said that I would like that a lot.

I do keep a kind of distance. The next day he called. I was screening my calls and I didn't pick up the phone. It was in the evening. He said that he was in a pub near where I lived, and "it would be angelic of you if you were somehow to appear. I'll be here until about eleven. I'm just writing. Show up."

I didn't. I wanted to but I thought I'd let things cool down for a little while. But I was very excited. And tape-recorded the message so I could listen to his voice forever. He had this very beautiful, deep, wonderful voice.

I called him back the next day. I guess we ended up agreeing to get together for a drink. I was meeting someone else for dinner afterwards. It was incredibly intense—the connection between us. The energy. We both drank much too much whiskey. But in a way, there was a certain impersonalness in the intensity. There was no acknowledgement that this was a potential romance. Except in the level of feeling that was being exchanged. We talked about books. We talked about philosophy. We talked about poetry. His poems. He quoted some fragments. I thought they were extraordinarily beautiful. We ended up walking thirty blocks together. He didn't want to leave. I was really late to meet this person for dinner.

He kept calling. We kept meeting for drinks. The intensity kept building, with nothing having happened. I started to think ... I know he's interested. He's calling every day. Something's going to happen. I'd been fantasizing wildly about kissing him.

It was one of those really beautiful spring days. I said maybe we could get a bottle of wine and go out to this park near my apartment. So I brought champagne and grapes. We drank, and talked and talked, and finally we came back to my apartment. Sat on my couch. There were these long silences. He had this wild blond hair, all unkempt, and he was tall and lean and angular, with these intense blue eyes. He was beautiful. We're sitting there. Long silences. Our arms are almost touching, but not quite touching.

He said, "Say something." And I said, "You say something." And he said, "No, you say something." And I chickened out. Finally, there was another silence and I touched his arm. And then he leaned forward ... and so on.

It was hallucinatorily amazing. Kissing him. Finally, we started falling asleep. It had gotten pretty intense but we had stayed dressed. At one point, I remember telling him that I'd been fantasizing about kissing him for weeks. And he said, "I've been totally obsessed. I've thought of nothing else."

We fell asleep on the couch. It was four in the morning and he lived pretty far away. Finally I said, "I think you should go home."

And he said, "Please can I stay? We'll just sleep near each other."

And finally I said okay. So we intended to stay dressed, but we didn't really stay all that dressed. We woke up in the morning, and it was a beautiful day. We went out for brunch. It was all starry-eyed and wonderful. We went for this long, long walk in the park after brunch. I felt the intensity, but a difficulty in communicating about personal things. I guess I'd thought once we'd made the breakthrough, the barriers would fall. At one point I said, "My friend Roberto is coming down to see me next weekend, but I really don't want him to. I would rather see you."

Tim said, "Well, not that I care who you're sleeping with."

I said, "I want you to care." And then I just kind of let it go. Then later I said, "Well, I sort of care who you're sleeping with. Not that I want you necessarily not to be sleeping with anyone ... but are you sleeping with anyone?"

And he said, "No, I'm not."

I said, "There's nobody around who's important to you? I'm surprised, somehow."

And he said, "Well, there's this woman Jacqueline who's kind of there. But we're not really connected."

The next few weeks we saw each other. He came over lots of the time after work. He would walk into my apartment and we would start madly kissing. It was so intense and wonderful. We didn't sleep together immediately, but we did relatively soon.

The first time that I said "I'd like you to stay," he got up and said, "I think I have to go home and work."

I think the first time I said, "Okay." The second time it happened, I said, "Tim, I know there's no understanding between us of anything, but it just seems so strange. You desperately wanted to stay that first night, when I said that you shouldn't, and now you don't seem to want to, when I want you to."

And he said, "Well, it's my work. When I'm in the middle of writing something, I just have to be writing it." So I let it go again.

When he'd leave like that, I wouldn't call him, and a couple of days would go by. And then he'd call me really frantically. "When can I see you?"

I remember, at one point, asking him what he was doing that weekend. He said, "I'm trying to get some work done, but maybe we'll see each other."

And so I called him the next day. No answer. Left a message. He didn't call me back. It was this weird back-and-forth, where, on the one hand, there was all this intensity, and the next minute he'd be really distant.

Then the stories about Jacqueline started coming out: "Jacqueline's in visiting from Chicago. I really have to spend time with her."

I said, "Okay. I'm surprised you didn't say more about her before, when I asked you ... but fine."

I remember one time meeting him for a movie, and him being really paranoid, saying, "I really don't want Jacqueline to see me."

I said, "I thought you had this loose relationship with her. That's ridiculous."

And he said, "Well, she knows something. We kind of have this weird relationship where we have affairs, and we both know it, but it's never publicly acknowledged, so we don't humiliate each other."

I still kept letting this stuff go because I kept thinking, he's just slow. He's not emotionally developed. We'd talked a lot about our families. He had an alcoholic father who committed suicide when he was a teenager. He hated his mother. He clearly had all these emotional barriers. I was writing in my journal all these things about him. In frustration.

Finally I just stopped calling him back. I started getting desperate messages from him. So finally I called him back. And I said, "Look Tim, this is just too frustrating for me. I'm getting so many mixed messages from you. That first week, especially, I felt so much intensity. I never feel this way for people. I really felt that we understood each other. I care about you. I want you around me. But I can't do it if it's not mutual."

He said, "I guess you scare me."

I said, "Well, it's just too frustrating. I can't figure out what it is that you want. Let's just see each other and we'll talk about it."

So we met in a cafe, and he was saying that I seem to have all these men around all the time. I said, "It's obvious that I want to be with you."

He said, "Maybe I just can't be intimate in the way you want."

I used to have a box for student papers in my hallway and he put this really intense, beautiful letter in the box. He was really open. It was everything he isn't in person, besides being exquisitely written. He said, "There's something that panics in me when I'm near you, when I'm there at night sometimes. And I don't know what it is. The quality of your intimacy. It's what makes being with you so wonderful. It's also what makes being with you so scary. Something in me flies. I don't know why. I want so much to overcome that."

The letter was why I kept seeing him. After the letter I gave him my journal.

This happened to be at a time when an old lover of mine from Paris was coming to New York. I said to Tim, "I would have told Thierry not to come, if I had thought it was making any sense between us. I don't want to be with him."

The first day Thierry was there, I walked downstairs, and my student box was full of flowers. And another letter. This letter was just one more gorgeous outpouring. "What surprised me in your journal was not just how frustrated you were, but how angry you were with me. I need to see you. I want to be with you."

Every day that Thierry was there, there were messages: "Five minutes so we could just see each other." These unbelievable love letters like I've never gotten before. So open. So raw. They moved me so much: "The idea of being in a place where you've been is heartbreaking to me...."

I had plans to go to Germany. I told Tim, "I wouldn't have made these plans if I had felt that things were happening between us."

And he said, "I wish you hadn't. I want to be with you."

At this point, I'd sublet my apartment because I was going to go away. I was staying with a friend. Tim's birthday was coming, and I really wanted to be with him. And he said, "I can't see you because I'm seeing Jacqueline, but I can see you the night before." It was the night before his birthday. I bought a bottle of champagne; we went out to the park. I wanted to sleep with him. Badly. But I was staying with a friend, so I couldn't take him there. We couldn't go to his place because of Jacqueline. So I said, "Alright, let's go to a hotel."

He didn't have a penny. We went to this hotel. I'd bought him all these wonderful presents—books that connected us. So we made love. It was getting less wonderful each time, because I was feeling like it was just sex. More and more, the sex started feeling less connected to intensity of feeling, more and more connected to "let me fuck her." He was weird about it. He couldn't talk about it.

So we made love, and then he said, "Well, I really better make a phone call."

So he called Jacqueline from the hotel room. And then he got off the phone, and he was like, "I have to go."

I felt so humiliated, because I've written all these little cards, and I've paid for this hotel room. I was absolutely fuming. I said, "Alright, well, I'm leaving for Germany on such and such a day. Maybe we'll see each other before I leave."

So he started calling me. "I have to see you. I have to see you. I'll do anything."

I went to Germany. I was miserably lonely. I was looking for a letter from him every day. He didn't write. After having written me every day when we were in the same town. It was my birthday. My birthday came, my birthday went. He knew it was my birthday. Finally, he called. He said, "I can't wait till you come back. Call me the minute you get back."

So I called him once I'd gotten back. He was like, "Can I come over now? I want to come over right now."

I said alright, so he came over. Suddenly he was really distant. We talked for 15 minutes, and he was like, "Well, I have to go."

I said, "Tim, that's it."

He called me for months after that. He still calls me. I just basically don't return his phone calls.

✳   **Stephanie & Scott**
Stephanie Horowitz first spotted Scott Lehman on the subway. Scott's comment—"I've never been able to be someone's friend and their boyfriend"—is one way that men explain this chapter's phenomenon.

Before I met Scott, I was in a phase in which I'd stopped dating completely. I didn't know how to meet guys. I mentioned it to my therapist, and she told me that she'd met her husband through the personal ads. So I took out a personal in *New York* magazine. I got about 75 responses. It was so much fun—it brought me right out of my rut. I'd set up five dates in a row. Each one of the guys asked me out again. So I had my confidence up.

At the end of that week, I said to my mother, "Maybe when I stop looking, I'll find. Who knows how I'll meet him. Maybe I'll meet him on the subway."

The very next day, I was on the subway going to work and I saw this guy. He was leaning forward, and he was reading the sports page. I thought, "Why doesn't anyone like that ever ask me out ... someone who's tall, thin, good-looking, sort of a guy's guy, hunched over in a way that makes me know he likes watching a football game on Sunday?"

I was having this fantasy about him, and he looked up and looked right at me. I looked back at him, and I put my sunglasses on and felt mortified. I got off the subway and he followed me all the way to work. He turned around right in front of my building and asked me if I wanted to have lunch. I said, "You shouldn't pick up people on the subway. I could be Ted Bundy."

So then he thought I had a sense of humor. I gave him my card and said, "Think about it. If this is something you're sure that your mother would want you to do, call me."

We had lunch the next day. It lasted five and a half hours. It was incredible. We started out as great friends. Like *When Harry Met Sally*. But I also knew that I was attracted to him. We saw or talked to each other every night for a week, and I realized that I wasn't sure if he liked me as a lover or a friend.

He talked a lot about a woman he'd lived with for four years. I thought that if he could live with someone, then at least he was capable of having a relationship.

One night we went out to dinner after a movie, and he walked me to a cab, and turned and kissed me. It was the sort of kiss with hints of things to come. I was absolutely floating. All I could think was: I want him. I want him.

That weekend we went out and came back to my apartment and had an incredibly passionate night. He was an entirely different person in bed. He told me things about himself that he was uncomfortable with. He talked about his family, his work, his life. I remember thinking, now I'm really getting to know him.

He said to me, "I really have to take things slow."

I remember thinking to myself, "Oh my god, he's so sensitive. He really wants this to last."

We had this incredible night, and then he went off, and I didn't hear from him for four days. I was apoplectic. I called him up, and he said, "Did I hurt your feelings? You have to understand, I'm a jerk. I don't have good relationships with my family. I don't have friends. It takes me forever to open up. I didn't mean to hurt your feelings. It's just me."

This presented me with an unattainable goal. I was going to be the one he opened up to.

But slowly and surely I realized the closer we got in bed, the more distant he got on the street. We'd have dinner, and this guy whom I'd once had a five-hour lunch with would sit across the table from me in a restaurant, and look around and not speak to me. Then we'd come back from dinner and end up in bed, and he'd tell me about his work and his family. And I would dread the morning, because we'd walk down the street, and he wouldn't talk to me. He'd walk five paces ahead of me. He'd never take my hand in public. He'd never be affectionate.

After three months, I couldn't take it anymore. I was in pain, and I lived to be in bed with him. He'd never introduced me to any of his friends. I decided it just wasn't worth it to me. I'd rather be alone. So I took him out to lunch and I said, "I don't think we should see each other any more."

He said, "What are you talking about?"

I said, "I know you say you don't have relationships with anybody, and I know you say you don't communicate, but I don't understand why it is that we can't be close."

He said, "I have a problem. It's something I've known about for years. I've tried to sum it up for you before. I've never been able to be someone's friend and their boyfriend."

I said, "You should see a shrink because you deserve to be happier."

He said, "I will never see a shrink. That's for crazy people."

He hugged me on the street and I walked away. I cried.

Three months later the phone rings at work. "Hi, it's Scott. Want to take the subway home?"

He told me that he'd been seeing a shrink two times a week. He said, "You were right. You were more than right. I've gone out with other women, and all I can say is, they're not you."

So we started seeing each other again. And he couldn't get enough of me. He called night and day. But then the same pattern started again. We had a wonderful sex life. But he'd call me up and say, "Tonight I'm going to this party. I really don't want to go," but yet he still wouldn't change his plans to see me.

One Friday, he'd wanted to get together, but I'd had plans. So I asked, what about Saturday? He said he's going out on Saturday night. I'd become this person I can't stand. I said, "Well, why can't we ever spend the day together on Saturday?"

So we got together. He was mean and nasty all day. Eventually I burst into tears. I said, "All day, you're so distant. You tell me you have plans, but you won't tell me what they are. It makes me feel suspicious. You know what, Scott? You can see someone else."

He said, "I'm not seeing anyone else."

I end up sobbing in his lap. He hugged me and we started fooling around. And then he said, "We shouldn't sleep together. I don't want to leave you this way and go out."

So it was clear that he was going out with another woman. He left me nude in my bed at 7:30 at night.

He called me the next night, and said, "I just wanted you to know that it was Elizabeth [a girl from his office] that I went out with last night."

He called me to tell me that I was right in my suspicions? And that I should just deal with it? I decided to take him out to lunch and tell him that I didn't want to sleep with him anymore. He said, "I'm sorry, give me another chance."

I said, "You've made me cry twice. I can't sleep with you anymore. I don't want the weekend to come around, and to have no one to spend it with."

I sat across the table from him, and Scott was Scott. I found him completely uninteresting. Negative about everything. I had fallen into the trap of thinking he was negative about me. He was negative about life. He hated his job. He hated his apartment. He bitched about money. I never saw him again.

✳ **Angela & Neil**
Neil McGrath ended his affair with Angela Holmes because, like Scott, he couldn't handle being close friends with the woman he was sleeping with. His story differs from the others in this chapter in that, rather than coming back to her to resume the sexual relationship, he aggressively lobbied to stay in her life as a friend.

I met Neil and we had a flirtation. He was the first really nice guy I'd liked in a while. He was really All-American. I met him and immediately said to myself, I want to have a relationship. I acknowledge, I had an agenda.

At my birthday party, we'd only known each other for a few weeks, and we were having a great time together. At the end of the party, he said, "I think I'm going to go home."

And I said, "I think I'll come with you."

He looked like he had swallowed a rock, he was so flipped out that I'd said that. It was very funny, because I wasn't embarrassed at all. And he was like, "Oh my god, I can't deal with this."

And I was like, "I think it's the natural thing to do. I think it would be really great."

It just seemed natural. We were really attracted to each other. We were having such a nice time together. You know how you have a thing about this person's body, where you just feel drawn towards it? You want to be closer to it. That had been happening. That first month, we were best friends and lovers. It wasn't as if we had the most intense relationship in the world, but both of us were going through hard times. I liked sleeping with him. I wasn't madly in love with him, but it all felt really, really nice.

And then more and more and more, we would have a great evening together, and he would walk me home and say, "I'm going to go home now."

It started happening most of the time. I remember the last block just started to feel so weird. Waiting for it to happen. It was so painful when he would do it. The separation really hurt a lot. It was this physical pain, the pain of separation.

He also had this really weird thing: If we were at a party, and I showed any sign of affection for him, he would kind of flip out. It was so weird. He would always act much more friendly and flirtatious with all my friends. That was easier.

One night, I made him dinner, and then we decided to go to a party downtown. We took our bikes. It was really late at night. We owned the streets, rode around, went to the party for one minute, went and had a drink, came back and it was so much fun. It was so nice. And then he said, "I think I'm going to go home."

And I said, "We have to talk about this."

He basically said, "I can't deal."

He'd been saying to me all along that he wasn't used to being friends with the woman he was sleeping with. When we'd been at the party, he'd seen a couple of women that he'd had something with in the past. And he said, "So and so would never go on a bike ride with me."

As though it made it unattractive to him that we could go on a bike ride. To me, that kind of thing can be incredibly sexy. He said he wanted to be close to me in every way but the physical. I said, "Forget it. Let's take a break."

I was disappointed, but I saw it for what it was. I didn't want to see him. I was disappointed and I missed him because we'd had a nice time together, but I wasn't hung up about it at all.

He was quite hung up about it. He got really upset. He felt like I was rejecting him. I said, "I'm not rejecting you. We need some distance."

So one day he was really upset, and I went over to his place and we had a very good conversation. I acknowledged to him that it hadn't been all his fault. (This is what I thought at the time—now I'm sort of back to thinking it was all his fault). I realize that to some degree when I met Neil, I did have an agenda. I think I was feeling particularly like I wanted to be with *somebody*. I met Neil and he was going to be my boyfriend. In fact, I was pushing the relationship beyond where it naturally was. I wanted it to be more real and intense. He had a lot of problems. I had my own stresses. It doesn't make for a perfect relationship. I felt like he wasn't all wrong in backing off. I said that to him.

From that conversation, we began, little by little, to start hanging out again. First, it was once every week or so. Then it was more. We were having a really great time together. We liked to do all the same things. He's really bright. We're at very similar points in our careers. It was just nice to talk about that.

But then I started to naturally feel like I wanted to sleep with him. We were so close. And so my natural inclination was to go a little closer. But he had this wall of hesitation and fear and ambivalence that, no matter how normal and natural it might have seemed to keep going towards intimacy, he wasn't going to do it. He couldn't deal with it. I started to have the same shuddering feelings of pain and rejection.

But this time I had no agenda. I had no intention of getting back together with him.

He tried to be honest. He tried to do the right thing. But he unwittingly flirted with me. We kept getting drawn into this thing that was going to be aborted. It only ended up triggering all my horrible feelings about myself. It takes a guy to mirror all these things. I'm not desirable. I'm not this, I'm not that. In fact, I really realize, it was about him.

He was having a hard time in his life. He'd say, "I'm not feeling my best, my sexiest."

But you don't always meet a person at the greatest time. To me, that's not really a reason to run away. "And you're not either," he'd say, "and that's not attractive."

He implied, if I were only stronger....

But the crucial thing is that he didn't let go. If he really was going to be a good guy, he would have let me go. He called me every day.

All of this made me feel so ugly. Ugly is a weird fairy princess type idea, but it was the only kind of answer I could come up with. Two bodies getting together is supposed to be the most natural thing in the world. For some reason, for me, at that point it was the most difficult thing. Why was this thing that's so natural and a wonderful counterbalance to our incredibly intense intellectual lives just impossible? Even when it doesn't seem like it should be.

These ambivalent guys are a lot more subtle than the pathological bad guys. They do share your values. But they're the product of the '50s and early '60s, when there was a very patriarchal system in place. Mothers were basically subservient to fathers. I do think there's a weird little crisis going on now for some men, probably to some degree because of feminism. Women accept that it's okay to project their strengths, and guys can't deal. They don't want to rise to that challenge. And that's really bad.

These things do play themselves out to a great degree over sex. I'm so shocked to say this and believe it, but sex is such a symbol of power. It's almost like some men are seeing that they don't have it anymore, so all they can do is withhold. It's this weird power play.

✳   **Roberta & Larry**
*Roberta Willard had heard about Larry Samuels for years
before she actually met him, but when she finally did, she was
immediately intrigued.*

My first memory of Larry was of being told about him in 1978. The sister of my college roommate said to me, "You must meet Larry.

He's just your type." I either saw a picture of him or just ascertained that he had a beard and glasses, and was very bookish and was a writer and well-traveled.

I never got to meet him. I went to Europe after graduating from college in 1981, and I actually tried to get in touch with him, because I'd heard that he was traveling too. I wrote him a letter, and got a letter back, much later, from his father, saying that he was in Scotland. I guess I should have known something from the fact that his father was answering his mail. I would never want one of my parents to open my mail.

So I never met Larry. Through the years, I'd hear things like: Larry's interviewing for a job in L.A. Larry's moved here. Larry's moved there. Larry's living in Berlin.

The years passed. In the fall of '91, I was ending this rocky relationship. A friend mentioned that Larry, who now lived in Kansas City, was in town for a job interview. She called me up and said, "Why don't you come meet my friend Larry and me at the Metropolitan Museum of Art to see the Seurat show?"

I'd actually seen the show, just the previous day. So I met them afterwards. I saw Larry and I fell in love with him at first sight. It was partly the advance press. Until that day, I'd never had the experience of seeing someone and feeling like they had an aura around them. I felt like he was reaching me by the temples of my head.

We talked. He was pretty much as I thought he'd be. Very reserved. Somewhat inaccessible. Sardonic. Witty. Handsome, charming and eccentric.

He finally mentioned the word girlfriend, and I was despondent, but he then began to describe how his relationship with her was on the rocks. She was incredibly narcissistic and imperious. Very demanding. He was crazy about her, and she just wouldn't give him the time of day. Now I see that that said a lot about him.

At the time, I was getting interested. His relationship seemed to be on the way out. I only spent about an hour and a half with him. Afterwards, I said to my woman friend, "If he lived in New York, he'd be a big distraction."

I spent the whole day thinking about him. And the whole evening. I went to see the man I was trying to patch things up with, and I still had Larry in the back of my head.

Then the next day, my friend called me, and she said that Larry had called her to ask what my story was. I was just jubilant about this.

Then I got a message on my machine saying: "Hey, this is Larry. I enjoyed meeting you very much."

Then I left a message for him, and I heard from him again. He wasn't in New York anymore; he was calling me from Hartford, where he'd gone to see his parents and this woman, who he was marginally involved with. He left me another message and said, "I'll call you again."

So we started talking and writing. This was in October, and around Thanksgiving, I decided I was going to go see him in Kansas City. He met me at the airport. I was so nervous. I'd lost about ten pounds—I hadn't been able to eat. I carried the image of him around with me like a bird on my shoulder. I was obsessed by him.

So he met me and the first thing I thought was that he'd gotten a bad haircut. He had this leather jacket, and I could tell he was trying to look like a Berlin punk. We drove around Kansas City and had a really fun dinner at one of those tacky steak houses. We drove around and went back to his house and we built a fire and we made out and it was so incredibly romantic.

He was very stilted about things. We went upstairs and he was like, "I don't know what you'd like the sleeping arrangements to be. I have many places to sleep, but I think it would be very nice if we had relations this weekend."

My heart sank when he said "relations." It just sounded so clinical. But I said, "Let's just sleep together in our pajamas."

So we spent the night together in our flannel pajamas. It was so nice. We lolled around the bed the next morning, talking and making out. And then we went to a museum and drove around, went out for dinner. We went to a big blues hall, and then we went home and went to bed. It had been a nice lead-up: dinner, and then listening to these really sexy blues. For a first time, it was actually pretty nice. But it was next to impossible for him to have an orgasm.

Sunday we drove out to the heartland of Missouri and went to antique stores and walked around these tiny towns. We went to a concert that night. Monday, we stayed in bed the whole day, and then I left.

He dropped me off at the airport and then left really fast. And I cried my eyes out afterwards. During the weekend, he'd said he wanted to see me again. He invited me to a party he was going to have for Sadie Hawkins Day, and I just didn't want to go. I really wanted to see him, but I didn't want to be doing his party planning and have no time with him.

After the weekend, he didn't call me for ten days. I was really flipped out. I had our mutual friend call him because I was such a mess. She mentioned my name in another context and he said, "Roberta. Yes, Roberta. I really should call Roberta."

She asked, "How was your weekend?"

He said, "Oh, please. I'm sure you've heard every sordid detail."

She said, "No, not really."

He said, "It was well near perfect."

And she said, "Sounds like love."

And he said: "Perhaps. I'm not sure."

She said something like, "You know, Larry, love doesn't come along every day. You have to make things happen."

So he finally called. I knew it was going to be painful. And it was. The whole relationship was like that. He would call about every ten days. When I told him that I'd decided not to come for Sadie Hawkins Day, I said, "I just think we have so little time with each other we've got to make it as good as possible. And that doesn't sound like the optimal weekend."

He wrote me a letter telling me I was putting him up on a pedestal. I may have been doing that to a certain extent, but I think I was just seeing the good in him. Seeing the beauty that was there. He was articulate. Very smart. There was something very naive and sensitive about him; he hadn't found himself. Very vulnerable but he'd just closed himself off from all the disappointment.

But he was very witty. He had very good taste. Well-read, well-spoken, interested in the arts. Interested in everything, really. And if he didn't know about something, he would listen to find out about it.

In the same letter, he said, "My life hasn't been that great so far and you're a total anomaly to me. To be involved with someone who is stylish and beautiful and sensual ... I feel like if I shake my head it's all going to break apart."

The next time we saw each other was the beginning of March.

He was very concerned about the cost of plane fare and so was I. But it was worth it. We had another incredible weekend, this time in New York. I knew that I was in love with him. I told him. We were walking down the street. He was talking about Lenore, an old girlfriend, and I said, "Maybe she's madly in love with you still, because I am."

It just slipped out of my mouth. He gave me a big kiss, and said, "I'm getting there. I'm working on it." That gave me hope.

Then I saw him in April, because I had to be in Chicago. When I was leaving, I said, "I love you. I know you can't say that yet. But I need to tell you."

And he didn't say anything. And that was really the last time the subject came up. He signed a book that he gave me: love. He never said the word.

That weekend he asked me to go to Spain with him. That was mid-April. We went to Spain in mid-May. We had our difficult moments and our good moments. He didn't touch me for the first 48 hours we were there. He didn't want to sleep together. He walked half a block ahead of me, going at a much faster pace than I wanted to. Then he began to relax. We had some nice lovemaking during that time. I was very attracted to him, and he had a really nice body, but he was always kind of mechanical during sex. He just never really let go. That's an area I've never really had problems letting go in.

After Spain, I asked him, "So can we see each other again soon?"

And he said, "I don't think so. I feel like I have a lot going on."

I was pretty upset. I didn't see him again until the Fourth of July. All the time I'd be waiting for him to call. I'd call sometimes, but it never felt like he was that attentive to me. He was always glad to hear from me, but he would always say how busy he'd been. A million excuses. I'd hear a litany for 20 minutes: "Oh, this happened. Then you'll never believe what happened after that."

He'd become such a cynical person, looking at life like bad shit happened to him, and that's what life's about. And the good periods in his life were but chance.

We had a nice weekend together July 4th. He was going to be coming east over Labor Day. So we were going to see his sister, and he wanted to meet my parents, which I took as a good sign. We went to his sister's perfect little house in suburbia with two beautiful little children. Perfect husband with a very well-paying job. It was strange. It was not the kind of life that I wanted, but I was so jealous of the comfort. Of her calmness.

That weekend, I said, "Larry, I think we need to talk."

And he said, "We'll take stock in January."

And I just took it. I needed to talk but, okay.

After Labor Day, we'd had another weekend in Kansas City. I'd suggested that I come. The plane fares were low. So I did. It was very nice but we'd had an upsetting talk in a restaurant. I'd said, "Larry, I need you to call more. I need you more."

And he just said, "I don't think I'm what you want. I don't think I'm what you need. I can't give this to you. I tried so hard, but I can't give this to you."

I was crying in the restaurant. I don't think I was willing to face the fact that he was right.

He came to New York in November. I was on jury duty. I was kind of dreading his visit. Looking forward to it, but knowing that something was not right. I wasn't sleeping well. I felt like Larry was an intruder in my home. What was he doing there? What was he doing, throwing my schedule off and being demanding? I think I knew things weren't working, but I wanted them to be better.

There were so many things that were good about Larry. I was really attracted to him, he had so many interests, we could just talk and talk and talk. I used to joke about our sex and culture week- ends. We'd have classical music, we'd go to a play, we'd eat really good food. It just seemed like the makings of a good relationship. But I found myself waiting for the other shoe to drop. We'd had not great sex and then the night before he left we had amazing sex, the most amazing sex we'd ever had. It just opened me right up again. I had been beginning to think that I could take the relation- ship for what it was. This great sex blew my doors right open.

The first week in January, I called him and I said we had to talk. And he said, "Well, I was thinking that I was going to write you, because all the thoughts get jumbled and lost when I talk."

And I said, "No, Larry. You say you're going to write me and you never do. We have to talk now. I'm getting sick of caring for you so intensely, and not having you give it back."

And he said, "I care for you in my way. And I did the best I could, but I can't love you. I've never loved you. I've never opened up to anybody as much as I have with you. No one has ever understood me as well as you have. I've certainly never had as amazing, satisfying sex. And I can't love you. I can't love anyone who's good for me."

I was very sad. We talked for an hour and a half. I cried. I kept thinking of that girlfriend in Hartford, the one he chased and she never had any time for him. I think he can only love people who are bad for him.

He talked about how he used to want to be with someone very much and he just stopped wanting. Because women never found him attractive. So he just did what any cynic does—he closed himself off. I got sad about it.

He called me once or twice after that, and I just couldn't really talk to him. I was mad at him. He just wants to be domesticated in his little house with his baby grand piano, all by himself. All he needs is a baby grand piano. He plays Schubert impromptus by himself.

A lot of what I was seeing that day in the lobby of the Metropolitan was potential. I kept saying: If only. And then I realized that he wasn't going to change.

He really wants children. He really needs to find a very undemanding corporate woman, who's very high-powered, works a lot. She'll earn the bread, and he can be the house daddy. He wants children far more than a relationship.

I think he might find someone, possibly someone who's older than he is, and not so demanding, and I will be afraid to hear about that person, because it will still feel like an imperfection in me. What couldn't I do? What couldn't I be? What does she have?

When the women in this chapter articulated their frustrations, the men did not dispute the facts or try to change the subject. In general, intensity avoiders are not averse to communication. In fact, they often seem to try pretty hard to do the right thing.

But when the men above were confronted, their responses had the effect of stopping the conversation, because they took the form of self-blame. In his self-revelatory (and seemingly honest) letter, Tim spoke about how he wished he could overcome his unconsciously triggered urge to run. When Stephanie confronted

Scott, he replied: "I'm a jerk. I don't have good relationships with my family. I don't have friends. I didn't mean to hurt your feelings. It's just me."

In an early letter to Roberta, Larry revealed some of the insecurity and fear that was numbing his response to her. He wrote: "To be involved with someone who is stylish and beautiful and sensual.... I feel like if I shake my head it's all going to break apart."

Candor often has the effect of temporarily disarming the women. A man's acknowledgement of his problems may give her hope. But she may also hear more intention—more promise of effort—in his self-criticism than is actually there.

The men's statements are often admissions of failure. The true subtext may be something like: I fear these are the qualities that will eventually cause you to leave me. They've ruined my relationships before. I do like you, but I'm not at all convinced that I'm capable of change.

Angela and Neil's story is different, obviously, in that he didn't want to resume sex after the initial rupture (I should say that I did hear similar stories from other women). But like the other men in this chapter, Neil was clearly getting something he valued from Angela. Something he didn't want to give up. He just couldn't equate sex with those feelings of emotional attachment.

And so the hot/cold pattern continues. Samantha and Stephanie simply couldn't take it anymore. So they broke up. Angela also cooled things down with Neil, although they remained friends. In Roberta's case, the pattern was harder to see, because Larry lived halfway across the country, building some inevitable distance into the relationship. She finally forced the issue. And his reply, like the passage from Tim's letter, demonstrates the helplessness that these men feel. They wish they could love, but something in their psyche prevents it. Larry said: "I've never opened up to anybody as much as I have with you. No one has ever understood me as well as you have. I've certainly never had as amazing satisfying sex. And I can't love you. I can't love anyone who's good for me."

The danger, of course, is that the woman takes this personally. Angela reported that Neil made her feel ugly. And Roberta felt as though she'd wanted too much, as though the relationship hadn't worked because of something she'd done. When, sometime off in the future, she hears that Larry's hooked up with someone new, someone "not so demanding," Roberta fears, "It will still feel like an imperfection in me. What couldn't I do? What couldn't I be? What does she have?"

What she couldn't do, it's easy for an outside observer to see, is be satisfied with a relationship predicated on insecurity. She couldn't stand to love someone who was constantly reminding her, through his absence, of the ways he didn't love back.

But women, especially those who have a tiny corner of themselves that suspects that they are unlovable, will naturally find confirmation of their fears in one of these men.

Epilogue

Where Do We Go From Here?

What's a woman who has just read this book to do? Get on with her life, basically. I don't want her to finish these stories and, having seen glimpses of herself in several of them, now determine that she's got a "bad guy problem."

Bad guys are not a malady of women's making. I don't want women who've fallen for them to think that they have to enroll in some Women Who Love All Wrong program. *Or* to think that if they *do* succeed in fixing themselves (More Stairmaster! More Shakespeare! More therapy!) that somehow their next relationship will come with a fail-safe guarantee.

This chapter, I hope, carves out a middle road between the misguided urge to cure ourselves of bad things that other people have done *to* us, and the equally misguided urge to throw up our hands in helplessness and accept whatever shoddy treatment is thrown our way. The road I'm suggesting presumes that we are pretty healthy to begin with, but that we can benefit from thinking about some of our needs and behaviors that we may take for granted. It's the old "knowledge is power" argument, really, but I'm not suggesting that we use the insights gained in the preceding chapters to better manipulate men. The knowledge we're seeking is of ourselves, and the power is to pursue what *we* want, not what someone else wants for us.

With that goal in mind, I'm turning my attention from the men to the women who loved (or liked or lusted after) them. I reread the transcripts of all the interviews I did (including those I didn't end up using in the preceding chapters) to see what, if anything, surprised me. I tried to figure out why women fell for these guys, why they stayed with them, and why they were so hard on themselves in retrospect.

Unlike the rest of the book, I should warn readers that the pages that follow have a slightly exhortatory tone. (Those allergic to authorial pontificating may want to close the book now.) I didn't mean to let this sneak in, but having lived with these stories for the past year, I have some strong opinions.

Why are we drawn to bad guys?

Some bad guys seem to be good guys when women meet and fall for them. They appear to offer the standard laundry list of desirable male qualities: they're smart, they're funny, they're handsome, they're sexy, they're nice. When they do their bad thing, it comes as a total surprise.

But other men flash danger signs from the start, the way a male bird flashes his gaudy plumage. The womanizer is clearly a womanizer. The hustler clearly wants something. The possessive man throws his macho weight around. The addict has a checkered history. Some of the hot/cold men are just plain complicated individuals. The woman sees the bright feathers, and she responds eagerly.

In my interviews, two reasons for this are mentioned prominently: These men seem to offer a way for women to introduce some manageable danger into their lives, and they offer women a particularly seductive form of attention.

Many women I interviewed expressed the desire to live more dangerously than they do, to be motivated by challenge, not obligation. Often the bad guys who cross their paths seem to offer a readily available way to do this. These men provide easy access to the adrenaline rush that goes with danger: Colors shine more brightly, and a woman's mind clicks more efficiently when she's calculating her next move in a romantic battle of wits.

"I was once interested in this guy who was a James Dean type, really dark," said Molly Nelson. "What I've since decided is that I have that aspect—a dark aspect—to my personality, but it gets expressed in the choice of another person, because it doesn't get expressed in me. The problem with existing on a middle plain and not allowing my whole life to be more highly charged is that my need for excitement gets concentrated in this one area—romantic relationships."

"He had a bad reputation and I think that's partly what made me like him.... I'd heard that he would get into fights," recalled Casey Anton, of the boyfriend who went on to be both violent and controlling.

"I love the intellectual combat," said Samantha Erickson of her interest in men in general. "I love that struggle.... The only men who attract me are those who frighten me a little bit because they're so smart."

"The bad boy image appealed to me," said Kate Howe. "I liked the fact that he had this checkered past. He'd been arrested for heroin. I love these addictive personalities. Because I don't have one."

"The first thing he did when he was courting me was he sent me his rap sheet," one woman recalled of a short-lived romance. "With his mug shot. He'd been arrested a number of times. He was very romantic."

Many women who were raised to be obedient and accommodating long to break free, to explode into the noisy adolescent rebellion that they never had. Involved with a dangerous man, a woman can convince herself that *she* possesses some of *his* untamed spirit.

Although dangerous men will always be romantic figures for recovering good girls (and I count myself among their number), I recommend looking at the root of the problem: Why are we so damn fixated on making others happy and on keeping our life, as Molly put it, "on a middle plain"?

Women have much to gain by acknowledging that they'd like to *be* more adventurous, rather than accepting the contact high of loving an adventurous man. (And then coming down fast when adventurous proves to be a synonym for undependable and selfish.)

Something in my transcripts startled me: the sheer number of women who explained their attraction to a given man by saying that he paid attention to her, that he appreciated who she was. "I think I was just starved," recalled Angela Holmes, "When he paid attention to me, I was just completely rapt."

Roberta Willard said: "I was ... responding to the fact that he was giving me a lot of attention. He liked my mind. He appreciated my wit."

Women seem to draw energy from a man's approval, to blossom under the heat of his gaze. Really. Sometimes his *gaze* alone is enough. "His whole face lit up when he saw me. He was a very seductive guy," said Amelia Chase. Caroline Marone recalled: "He was looking straight at me with wonder ... and I fell for it."

It's not that any man's attention would necessarily have been good enough, or that all any man who wants to attract a woman needs to do is go out and stare appreciatively into her eyes (although, as much as I hate to say it, it would probably be a pretty good start). Often there are unique qualities of the particular man—perhaps his slightly aloof, withholding manner or perhaps his subtly signalled judgmentalism—that cause the woman to respond to him. What's significant is that she is being lured, not by his assets, but by the fact she has given him the power to make her feel desirable and good about herself.

This yearning—to be paid attention to, to be understood—is, of course, fundamentally human, and a legitimate component of "good" relationships as well. We can pinpoint any number of sources for it—in early family experience, certainly, but also in the many sexist backwaters of society where we as women may truly have been ignored. But when the need is particularly urgent, the man's role as designated validator can keep a woman in a relationship that is deeply unsatisfying in other regards.

Even if the relationship degenerates to a point at which the man has stopped providing the approval and attention she craves, the woman can then become fixated on winning it back. As Nora Frost, who for years invested her energy in the college classmate who didn't want to sleep with her, put it, "I remember realizing that there were people out there who thought I was attractive. But Hunt was the only person I cared about. Hunt was the only person who could validate me. And if he wasn't providing that validation, a million other people saying 'you're smart' or 'you're beautiful' didn't mean a thing."

I've found, in my own life, that it's useful to be alert—from the very beginning—to the role that a man's attention or admiration is playing in my response to him. Do I genuinely admire his character, or am I flattered because he makes me feel perceptive or smart? I'm all in favor of the way in which a loving man's attention encourages me to let my own best qualities show, but not of loving a man because he momentarily nullifies my insecurities. If I cede him that power, it will be very hard to be objective about what else I'm getting or not getting from the relationship.

And it seems obvious, but it's worth noting that the more positive reinforcement we are receiving elsewhere—at work, through our friends, through an internal sense that we're doing our work well or living our life fully—the less at risk we are of being blinded by that seductive look of appreciation in a lover's eyes.

What makes a bad guy hard to give up?

Not *all* are. In many of these stories, the relationship ended instantly when the woman discovered a betrayal.

But often women stay with these guys longer than an objective party would say that they should. Why? Some reasons are very straightforward. She feels deep affection for him. The sex is the best she's ever had. Or maybe she's committed to the life they've tried to build together. As Lucinda Swift, who was married to a nonfunctional man for 17 years, put it, "I was really into the concept of marriage and family."

All of these reasons are related to actual strengths of the relationship. But there are other reasons for a refusal to surrender that have more to do with the woman's own issues. Women get sucked into the challenge that some bad guys seem to offer—especially if the men pull back but don't leave altogether. And some women buy the romantic myth that there is one and only one man out there, and that to lose him is to lose the chance for love.

In his autobiography *Life Work*, poet Donald Hall recalls something the sculptor Henry Moore once told him: "The secret to life is to ... have something you devote your entire life to, something you bring everything to, every minute of the day for your whole life. And the most important thing is—it must be something you cannot possibly do."

These lines describe the lure of artistic endeavor, but also go a long way towards explaining why women get so hooked by the challenge of trying to win back a lover whose attention is fading. As Caroline Marone recalled of a time when her previously devoted boyfriend pulled back, the project of re-winning him was "like a drug."

Often, the draw of the challenge reflects the extent to which the present-tense struggle (to rekindle a dwindling affair, say) *seems* to offer the opportunity to relive the dramas of childhood. A woman wants to believe that if only she tries hard enough, she can rewin the attention and love she so eminently deserves. In that sense, Moore's quote fits perfectly: The task is infinitely engrossing, and the goals are impossible to achieve.

For instance, it's no accident that Jill Borden, the woman who aggressively lobbied her boyfriend to tell her he loved her also had a father who "really doesn't say the L word." She was clear on the connection: "He was very similar to my father and obviously I chose him for that reason."

Of course, romantic challenge can also be more narrowly focused on the conquering of a specific fear or sense of inadequacy. When Angela Holmes and Sam Logan were in Europe and he told her he didn't want to have sex, she recalled, "I'd had enough feelings of failure in that arena.... I was going to fight back.... I didn't say: 'Fuck you. I'm going to find a man who desires me and shows me he desires me.' Instead, I was like: 'I'm going to win you.'"

The cost, as Angela clearly recognized, is that she consigned herself to a less than desirable situation in order to focus on an issue relating to her own sense of identity, rather than replacing the man who mirrored her fears about herself, and reflected them back in her face every day.

Sometimes a woman wants to rewrite the script so badly that she temporarily surrenders responsibility for her life, lapsing into a kind of magical thinking: If only I try hard enough, I'll get what I want. As Nora Frost recalled, "I remember thinking that if I just kept doing all these wonderful things for him, he'd realize how indispensable I was, and our relationship could go back to the way it was.... It was my pathology that I kept thinking: if only. If only."

There is no arguing with the fact that these urges are compelling. The trick is to try, as Angela later did, to strip them down to their bare bones. What is the challenge really about? What better challenges are we missing by choosing to tilt at these flesh-and-blood windmills?

"I went to see the movie version of *Romeo and Juliet* when I was fourteen," Sarah Powell remembered. "Afterwards, I was so distraught and devastated that I was banging my head against the car window. Here is this perfectly nice, rather repressed WASP family, and the youngest daughter is banging her head against the car window. At home, I continued to sob until my father came into my room. He was beyond exasperation. He forbade me to see the movie again. Of course, I went back and saw it again, and the same thing happened, except that I just started crying earlier."

Especially for women from repressed families, life can become a search for outlets through which to express emotion. One avenue that's acceptable even to the stiff-upper-lip crowd is true love. Sarah described herself as constantly in the thrall of the romantic myth—hyping every promising romance to herself, and taking that thinking one step further: truly believing each to be the only one for her. If she were to lose it, this thinking goes, she almost certainly wouldn't find a comparably intense love again.

A woman who thinks like this has a powerful incentive to hang on to a relationship and to turn a blind eye to any and all signals that suggest doing otherwise. She has made her love irreplaceable.

This fervent belief that the man in question should be a mate for life can have the unfortunate effect of preventing us from asking whether or not this future is something we really want. As Amy Brown summarized, "When I look back, I see that all the seeds of trouble were there, but I was blinded by the desire to have it work.... This was going to be the guy.... I had planned it in my head.... And when you do that, you have more reason to make it work."

Why is anger so difficult?

Many of the women I interviewed, despite having labeled a man a "bad guy," still had ambivalent feelings about anger.

The women involved with the possessive men didn't tend to express much anger in recounting their stories, despite the fact that those relationships were among the most suffocating and frightening of any in this book. The women in the hustler chapter were also surprisingly muted. Many of the women in love with the various sorts of wounded men were sad rather than furious.

Certainly their restraint is in tune with our culture, which does not celebrate, or even really condone, women's anger. In the wake of the success of *Thelma & Louise*, angry women have enjoyed a certain superficial moment in the pop cultural sun. (For instance, a movie like *Fried Green Tomatoes* may present anger as a healthy means of growth, but its caricature depiction of the metamorphosis experienced by Kathy Bates' character went down as easily as a spoonful of saccharine.) The visceral, unprettified stuff—the real stuff—is still confined to the fringes. I remember pitching a story on female musicians who sang about anger to an ex-editor of *Mademoiselle*. "Oh no, I'm not interested in female anger," she replied without a moment's reflection. That's her right, certainly, but attitudes like hers perpetuate the sense that we as individuals feel that anger is something that should be swept underneath the rug.

I grew up believing that anger would drive people away from me, that raised voices were unsexy and unpalatable. I've heard liberal friends counsel other women to avoid alienating boyfriends with anger. I know women in 1994 who still subscribe to the suffer-in-silence school, or who complain to third parties rather than risk raging at the source. All this by way of saying that a woman feeling angry has seven or eight voices in her head telling her that she's more likely to get what she wants if she just shuts up and gets over it.

And fear of anger goes deeper than that. Remember the boyfriend who broke up with me two days after I found out that my father was desperately ill? He had spent months actively convincing me of his dependability; now suddenly he wasn't there for me when I needed him most. In the first few weeks after we broke up, I really let him have it on a couple of occasions. But afterwards, some strange corner of my psyche would panic: If I show him this monstrous part of myself, he'll never come back. The day after an angry fight, I would feel panicky until I'd called him and apologized.

It wasn't that I wanted him back, really. My reflexive reaction was less about him, and more about my fears about anger in general. If it were left to rage unchecked, I felt on some unexamined level, it would destroy my support system and leave me all alone. I was frightened by its power, and so I couldn't give in to its full expression.

So dealing with anger is not an easy thing: It's not as though we always control the "on/off" switch. But being mad at bad guys is an affirmation of our own worth. While I don't necessarily believe that anyone can rationally choose anger, it's worth making an effort. This might involve consciously putting empathy and pity on hold, and quantifying the tolls the relationship has taken.

Wendy Lewis told me the story of a man she had dated who, one day, just stopped returning her calls. After about three months, he called her casually, as though nothing had happened, as though he expected that she would play along and be friendly and not mention his disappearing act. Instead, she told him off. "I said, 'Excuse me. You have just been the biggest jerk, and I'm not going to let you off the hook.' Calling him a jerk was empowering. I felt stronger for the experience."

Why do women judge themselves so harshly?

When an acquaintance asked me what the most surprising thing I had found in my research was, I answered without hesitation: the depth and bitterness of women's self-blame. Here were men that women labeled "bad guys"—but what was ringing in my ears was the *women's* collective self-condemnation.

In part, this tendency may be connected to the fear of anger I've just talked about. Women who are unable to release their anger may turn it inward onto themselves. It also may be connected with a wish not to be completely powerless: A woman who was somehow at fault can prevent more bad things from happening by fixing herself. And many of us simply retain self-blaming tendencies from childhood.

The self-blame in the preceding stories essentially took one of three forms. Some women condemned themselves for lingering too long in a bad situation. Some women condemned themselves for parts of their personalities that emerged under the duress of trying to prevent the relationship from falling apart. And some blamed themselves for the relationship's demise.

"Apparently, I am a glutton for punishment," said Joan Silver, describing her willingness to take Joey Santanello back after he'd thrown one of his tantrums.

Lucinda Swift, who stayed with her depressed husband for 17 years, realized 13 years into the relationship that she didn't love him anymore. "The crime I committed," she said, "is that I stayed married to him for another four years."

Polly Logan condemned herself for having stayed with Henry Preston for two and a half years after catching him in the act of his first infidelity. This self-recrimination reflected the views of friends and family. Polly's mother had threatened to disown her if she went back to him. And when she finally did summon up the strength to leave, no friends of the couple would condemn him. As one of them said to her: "You put up with it all this time."

The knowledge (real or imagined) that other people are judging can have the effect of driving a woman and her sense of shame underground. Nora Frost recalled, "I made excuses—for him and about the relationship—to all of my friends. I never talked about some of the really horrible stuff. It was like being in a battered relationship—I didn't want anybody to know."

Much of the self-condemnation, then, is simply the internalization of what the woman imagines that others are saying. When in fact what is keeping her involved are her own genuine needs. Listen to Kelly Kiernan's explanation of why she stayed with the mean-tempered alcoholic for as long as she did: "I knew it wasn't a good relationship ... but I was so afraid to be alone."

In many of these cases, the women quite simply needed the man. They weren't proud of it. They bought the standards I discussed in the introduction: that they "should" be involved with someone, but that if they didn't leave a "bad" man, then they were clearly masochistic or overly dependent.

Despite the fact that many women grew up witnessing their mother's dependency first hand, they felt deeply ashamed of those urges in themselves. This, I believe, is the source of the first category of self-blame.

While women may see qualities in themselves that they don't like, I would argue that they are at the same time ignoring or downplaying the significance of a quality that they *should* like: the existence of strong, instinctive self-protective impulses. These are the "clicks," the "enough already ... I deserve better" mechanisms that prompted the vast majority of these women to look their fears of being alone in the eye.

Joan Silver knew the instant Joey shoved her that the relationship was over. Lucinda Swift summoned up the strength to enroll in a college class despite her husband's active discouragement. Polly Logan had that vision of her fiancé's infidelity on her wedding day, and knew without a doubt that she could not live that way. And when Kelly Kiernan's alcoholic lit into her verbally, she was out the door.

The second source of harsh self-judgement arises when a woman finds she's become someone she doesn't want to be in her fervent effort to keep the relationship going. Stephanie Horowitz said, "I was so mad at myself because I was being this sycophantish, pathetic creature."

Kristin Kane sounded mortified when she described agreeing to Carter's request that she give him a blowjob in a parked car on a populated street: "I can't believe how I debased myself with this guy. I really wanted him to like me."

Betsy Sawyer described how she was towards the end of her relationship with Tito, the illegal immigrant whom she had married: "I became this ugly rotten person who wanted to spend more time with him than he wanted to spend with me.... I desperately wanted to play out this fantasy. I was getting really clammy about it." She went on to describe herself as both a "monster" and a "control freak" and to say: "A lot of what was awful was that I lost it. I didn't get myself in control."

Even after the relationship is over, the woman's behavior is still grounds for ruthless self-criticism. Remember Jill Borden, the woman who threw back her head and opened her mouth when she mistakenly thought that her ex-boyfriend wanted to really kiss? She called her attempt to kiss him back "pathetic, sick, desperate." And afterwards she berated herself for lack of self-control.

What strikes me is that these women do not cut themselves a break by acknowledging that their men had, in effect, driven them crazy. Stephanie Horowitz's boyfriend charmed her socks off, then became both infantile and rejecting. Kristin Kane's boyfriend was cruel and seemed to take particular delight in pushing the limits of her eagerness to please. Betsy Sawyer's husband was literally tormenting her—avoiding her, calling her "Potato Girl," flagrantly sleeping with another woman. And Ed, Jill's boyfriend, had been unable to provide a single sentence of explanation about why he'd ended the relationship and had continued to have sex with her for months after their breakup. Given all that, it certainly seems sensible that Ed would have wanted to kiss her, and—given her quasi-acknowledged hope that they would get back together—not unreasonable that she would want to kiss him back.

Again, these women seem to be measuring themselves against some external standard of behavior: Not only should they quickly reject anyone who treated them badly, they should also be fully in control of themselves and their desires. This emphasis on control may be reasonable when life is going smoothly but hardly applies when a relationship that had high hopes invested in it is falling apart.

The third avenue of self-recrimination had to do with women's fears that, by expressing their needs or by being themselves, they somehow detonated the relationship. Amelia Chase recalled the relationship in which her boyfriend became unable to ejaculate: "I don't know if it was because he started to get to know me better, and he started to realize that I wasn't who I seemed. I'd started to show him that I was possessive."

This *despite* the fact that he had told her that this was a recurring problem that he had, and that it tended to arise over issues of intimacy. Still, she connected his dysfunction with the things she liked least about herself.

A woman may know intellectually that a man's issues were what doomed the relationship, but she may still have lurking self-doubts. In trying to understand why her relationship with Cliff fell apart, Suzy Sayre said: "This is *his* garbage that he did, which is something I have to tell myself about eighteen times a day."

Roberta Willard's fear of hearing that her Kansas City boyfriend has hooked up with someone else expresses the same irrational fear: "It will still feel like an imperfection in me."

Most women (most humans, I should really say) have insecurities. It doesn't do much good for me to stand on the sidelines and say that I wish it weren't so. All I can say is that if a woman's intellect is telling her one thing, and an irrational self-doubting part of her brain is telling her another, the best she can do is follow Suzy Sayre's example. She can repeat her intellectual knowledge to herself often, with the conscious intention of drowning her irrational (but persistent) insecurity out.

If I could make one bad-guy-related wish for women, I would not waste my wish guaranteeing that we would all have bad-guy-free lives. What I *would* do is wish the self-blame away.

This self-recrimination is as counterproductive as a thought process that I sometimes indulge in: I regret that it has taken me so long to get to the point in life at which I feel as powerful as I now do. If only I'd been born knowing what I know now, this line of thinking goes, what advantages I would have leapt on, what challenges I would have sought out, what different choices I would have made.

But in real life I know that the only true source of knowledge is experience. I feel powerful *because* I've survived lots of mistakes. My relationships with bad guys forced me, sometimes against my innate safety-seeking will, to define what I find unacceptable, and to explore the ways I can stand up for myself and seek better things out.

I don't mean to boil the preceding two hundred-plus pages of frustration and anguish down to a pat silver-lining message: Bad guys, like root vegetables, are good for us and help us grow. What I would say is that, like other challenges that we don't necessarily choose but that we grow as a result of, we tend to emerge from a bad guy's thrall a little stronger, a little smarter, a little clearer on what sacrifices we *can't* make to preserve a relationship.

My wish, then, is that we not focus on the things we did "wrong": the red flags we ignored, the wishful thinking we engaged in, the untidy anger we expressed. Instead, I would encourage women to concentrate on listening to the impulse that inspired those hopes and prompted that anger. This is the impulse that believes—that truly *knows*—that we deserve better than what bad guys have to give.